GIGONOMICS

A FIELD GUIDE FOR FREELANCERS

in the gig economy

by Julian Haber

DEDICATION

....

For
freelancers
everywhere
bravely
taking
charge of
their future
one gig at
a time

ACKNOWLEDGMENTS

THIS BOOK COULD not have been written without the support of a number of people who took the time to read, comment on and review the work as it progressed.

First, I would like to thank my wife, Anne von Finckenstein, for patiently reading draft after draft and editing early versions of the book. I would also like to thank my loving daughter, Tessa, for giving me a reason to learn how to gig in the first place.

I would like to thank my editor, Julie Barlow, whose painstaking work and attention substantially improved the text and helped make this book a reality.

Thanks go as well to many other friends and family members who have helped with the ideation, creation and review, including Otch von Finckenstein, the quintessential optimist, from whom I have learned to think of the best-case scenario first. Otch's early enthusiasm for the project and helpful comments helped shaped the early drafts of this book. Patrick Noble, for his patient reading and thoughtful comments on the early versions of the work, as well as for his companionship on our many Odyssey Walks, on which several of the notions that eventually percolated into this book were first born. Nanci Murdock, my co-host on Slashpodcast, gave me the idea for the title; our discussions of some of the ideas in this book helped me to elaborate on the theme. My designer, Meredith Lindsay of Media Mercantile who brilliantly conceived of my book cover, design, website and more and without whom this book would still be nothing more than a poorly formatted word document. I would also be remiss if I failed to mention several other people who supported the creation and development of this book in some way: my parents, Richard and Patricia Ann Haber, my sister Alex Haber as well as Arthur Ramsay Holden, Claire Holden Rothman, Jon Mitchell and others who endured my repeated requests for feedback on various drafts of the book.

In many ways the most important people in this book are my clients, past, present and future, without whom I would never have learned how to gig in the first place. A special mention to my many friends at iMedia for giving me the inspiration, letting me be a fly on the wall during sessions where I earned an unofficial degree in digital marketing, and for the late-night drinks in hotel bars and fireside chats with participants, many of whom have since become friends.

A special mention goes also to Roy Spence Jr., whose message about living a purposeful life inspired key parts of this book.

TABLE OF CONTENTS

....

INTRODUCTION 9

part one
WELCOME TO THE GIG ECONOMY 23

part two
GETTING STARTED 43

part three
THINKING LIKE A FREELANCER 75

part four
GIGGING..151

part five
HOW TO KEEP ON KEEPING ON 365

epilogue
SORE OR SOFT? 391

INTRODUCTION
....

If you want to build a ship, don't drum up the
men to gather wood, divide the work, and give
orders. Instead, teach them to yearn for the
vast and endless sea."

—Antoine de Saint-Exupéry

DO YOU WANT a job, or do you want to work? This may seem
like two ways of asking the same question, but the distinction between the two lies at the very heart of what this book is about. The
choice is yours to make. The challenge is in recognizing it, and having the courage to make the choice.

If you want a job to show up at and do what you already know how
to do or are told to do, in an organization that is already built, for
which, in exchange for your mind, labour and precious time, you are
paid a salary, receive benefits and get the perhaps false but still present

assurance of future gainful employment, then this book is not for you.

But if you want work — real, honest work that begins and ends, pays off if you do it well, can be hard, even exhausting, at times; work that you can always see the sense and purpose of, that builds something, creates something, makes the world different because of you: then read on, because this book was written with you in mind.

Freelancing is a real job

The first time I handed over USD$4,000 in cash to a complete stranger on the streets of Cusco, in exchange for local Peruvian soles, I was a little nervous. It was 1995. I was 21 and working my first freelance job — adventure tour leader in Peru (and later Mexico, Honduras, Guatemala and Belize). After one whirlwind "training" tour, where I hitched along with another more experienced leader, I'd supposedly learned all there was to know about my three-week itinerary through Peru. Changing money on the streets was one of the first lessons I'd been taught. I would have to pay most of the fares, entrance fees, local guide and hotel stays for 12 passengers in cash, so I needed a lot of it. Since the rates offered on the black market were much higher than the official rates given in money-changing houses or banks, that's where we did it. When I received a large wad of several thousand soles and stuffed them into my leather jacket to walk back to my hotel on the Plaza de Armas, I felt like every pair of eyes on the street was following me. I thought I'd get a brick in the back of the head any second and have the jacket ripped off my pale, weak, gringo body, which was still not accustomed to the altitude.

But it never happened. The money traders, mostly Peruvian women, were scrupulously honest, as were nearly all the other Peruvians I worked with in the six months I led tours there. This was just how things were done when most people worked in the informal economy — what we'd call the gig economy today — which was the main economy for most Peruvians in 1995.

My year as a tour leader turned out to be extremely useful training for learning how to live and think like a freelancer. Looking back, I think of it as a kind of freelance boot camp, though I wasn't really aware of it at the time.

It was a thrilling way to spend a year, visiting the ancient ruins of Machu Picchu and hiking along the Inca Trail with a group of 12 passengers in tow, ending the days in some local Andean bar filled with other travellers from around the world. I very quickly realized that changing money on the streets was just one of the many things I'd have to learn how to do differently to get things done in Latin America. I had to learn how to think on my feet and how to find a way when the regular rules, signs or indicators I expected to be there just weren't, or they didn't apply. In Brazil there's even a phrase for this: "*o jeitinho brasileiro,*" which translates literally as "the little Brazilian way." It actually means thinking opportunistically and finding creative and inventive ways to get things done when there doesn't seem to be any other way.

For example, you might have to figure out, as I did on my first solo excursion with my first tour group, how to take a bus into town. Our goal was to have dinner in a hip neighbourhood called Barranco. Unfortunately, I had no idea where the bus stop was, or even which bus to take, let alone how to hail one or where to get off if I did manage to find one. In 1995, most people got around Lima using a (seemingly) chaotic system of privately run minivans called "*combis,*" which were all in competition with each other. People stood on corners and waved and drivers would swerve across three lanes of traffic and come screeching to a halt to scoop up the riders. To disembark, you shouted for a stop and hoped your driver — who looked like he'd been up all night drinking — heard you and cared enough to stop where you wanted him to.

The system worked well for the millions of *Limeños* who used it daily to get to wherever they wanted to go. It seemed chaotic to me because it didn't fit my expectations of how I thought taking a city bus should work. It was only when I adjusted my expectations to this new reality that I learned how the system worked. Getting around was a breeze after that.

That first three-week trip through Peru was a string of mini excursions visiting local sites and staying in backpacker-type hotels. We traversed the country, touring ancient and colonial cities like Cusco, the former capital of the Incan empire, and Arequipa. We crossed mountains, drank coca leaf tea (mate de coca) in cafés high on the altiplano, flew over the Nazca lines, large ancient geoglyphs in the Nazca Desert in southern Peru, visited the floating islands of Uros in Lake Titicaca, and took a riverboat deep into the Amazon jungle, where we stayed at the Tambopata Lodge.

All along the journey, as I negotiated prices for transportation, hotel stays, restaurant meals and guided tours, I learned how to hustle. Whenever I ran into trouble or couldn't understand why things weren't working out the way I had expected, I realized it was because I was expecting things to be the way things are back home. I should have been observing and learning how things worked where I was travelling. Once I stopped expecting and started paying attention to how to get things done in Peru, everything went more smoothly.

If a segment of the trip looked impossible due to a train derailment or a road getting washed out, I found other ways to travel to make sure we got to our destination in time to stay on schedule. When passengers wanted to try ayahuasca (a hallucinogenic made from jungle vines), in the jungle, I found and hired a local shaman to come along with us and guide us through the hallucinogenic journey. When our reservations got lost or restaurant bills appeared with a slew of drinks we never ordered, a passenger got robbed or got altitude sickness or was laid up with turista, I managed to wrangle a solution with the help of local contacts I made along the way. I learned who to trust and how to make deals working with local suppliers, small outfits and individual guides and tour operators. In other words, I learned how to work differently. I grew to enjoy the challenges and the different ways of solving problems that came along. With no one to turn to for help and people looking to me to provide solutions to their needs, I learned how to be self-reliant and resourceful and find creative ways to deal with any situation that arose.

Although I loved being a tour guide, I wasn't ready at that time to fully embrace it. I started to worry about my future. I worried that I needed to do something more serious, try to get a "real job" and start a "real career," and the longer I was booting around the altiplano, hiking around the Andes or experimenting with ayauasca in the jungle, the farther I was getting from what I thought a real adult life was supposed to be about.

It's a typical reaction many people have when they are facing the possibility of working independently. My reaction? I quit and went home.

It would take me years to finally recognize that had I continued working as an adventure tour leader, everything would have been just fine. The company I was working for went on to become one of the best adventure travel companies in the world, though it was still kind of a ragtag army of adventurers at the time. If I had stayed on, who knows what could have happened? Maybe I would have risen to become a director in the company. Or I could have started my own operation or led other tours in Asia or Europe and travelled the world....Woulda, coulda, shoulda.

What I did was give up because I erroneously believed that doing something that I really enjoyed and was good at for a living was incompatible with having a real career. I mean, if I was having as much fun as I was having, how could it possibly be serious?

Boy, was I wrong. Dead wrong. I didn't know it then. But I do now. Because today I'm back doing something I love that's a lot of fun and is completely, uniquely a career I've crafted for myself, one gig at a time. It took me longer than it would have had I believed then what I know now to be true: that freelancing is a real career. It's a real job. And just because it feels like an escapist fantasy, that doesn't mean you can't live it too.

It's a freelancer's world

I've been a freelance photographer for 15 years now. In that time, I've gone from being a completely unknown amateur with one mid-range (film) camera and a very crappy website to being flown around the world to cover conferences at five-star resorts. Today, I regularly book enough gigs in my areas of specialization to warrant building a small team of other freelancers I often outsource work to.

Freelancing has transformed my life. It has given me a sense of identity and allowed me to grow slowly but steadily at my own pace, while still having lots of time to start a family, travel and work on creative side projects. It has brought me into contact with hundreds of different companies in industries as varied as aviation and digital marketing, and enabled me to meet thousands of interesting people while providing me with a good, reliable living. I have a career that gives me a chance to learn continuously and improve on my craft. I feel incredibly lucky and grateful for what I believe is one of the best jobs in the world.

And you know what? You can do the same thing. Which is probably why you've picked up this book in the first place. I hope that by reading it, you'll be able to avoid some of the mistakes I've made and waste less time getting to where you want to be in life.

You just have to believe that you can. And my hope is that this book will help you along the way.

Wherever you look now, people are setting up shop for themselves, working out of co-working spaces and running newly launched independent businesses. How people define themselves has changed, too. Being self-employed or working from home no longer carries the stigma that it did just a few years ago. Because the world has changed. Work, especially, has changed, and the survival skills a freelancer develops — being adaptable and open to change, being open to learning and using new technologies, knowing how to work independently and collaboratively, being comfortable with ambiguity, willing to take some risks, ready to spot and react quickly to opportunities, and generally being determined to take responsibility for your own career development, growth and financial future – are now prerequisites for success, no matter what you do for a living.

Having successfully built a thriving business (not without some failures along the way), I decided to write this book to break down the entire process of becoming a freelancer and help people become better freelancers sooner, stay at it longer and make more money while freelancing. This book contains everything I've learned about how to take the most advantage of freelancing to maximize its rewards —and how to mitigate (if not eliminate) the risks (financial, emotional and professional) of a freelance career.

I believe you can learn to freelance, just as you can learn how to play poker or become a better cook or a better investor. Like any skill, it can be improved upon and, with practice, mastered. The art of living and thriving in the gig economy – a world of fragmented and myriad work opportunities made ever more accessible by technology – demands it. And those who learn how to do it well will be able to make the most of the rapidly changing economic landscape we are living in.

The work of freelancers touches us every day, whether we're aware of it or not. We use software written by freelancers and visit websites designed by them. We stay in apartments hosted by freelancers using Airbnb to make extra income, and take Uber cabs to travel around in. We order products online from freelancers, take courses they develop and hire freelancers to help with projects we are working on. We listen to freelancers on podcasts, watch freelancers perform in movies and television shows we love, read books they've written or edited (like this one) and listen to their music while we're relaxing at home. Freelancers are everywhere today, building up their personal brands one gig at a time. And soon you can be one, too.

And this book will help because...

I sat down to write this book for one reason: to help people who are new to the gig economy to launch and become better freelancers quickly and effectively, save money, land their first clients, grow faster and become known for doing work they love doing. Starting out as a freelancer can be scary, and though there are a lot of resources available on the technical aspects of freelancing (with new ones popping up every day), there are still very few that ever address the most important and challenging aspect of choosing a life as a freelancer: how to think like one.

This is the book I wish I'd read when I was starting out as a freelancer. It would have especially helped during the early years, which were fraught with anxiety and self-doubt, when I questioned whether freelancing could ever be a reliable way to make a living. Most importantly, I'd like to help budding freelancers believe in themselves and recognize that they can lead a thriving, successful career doing whatever they want to do.

Everything I've ever learned about gigging – from getting and keeping gigs to getting more and better gigs —is here. Although each individual freelancer's journey is unique, there are commonalities and key moments that every freelancer experiences. This book will serve as your guide every step of the way.

Who this book is for

This book is for freelancers of any age and at any stage in their freelancing careers, but especially for those who are just starting out. There has never been a better moment than right now to strike out on your own and do the work you are meant to do. I hope this book serves as a call to arms to anyone thinking of becoming a freelancer, or for those of you living through your early days of actually trying to become one. You have made the right choice.

When I decided to write this book, I had a few very specific people in mind. They are people I know who are going through the transition that every aspiring freelancer is bound to experience. Though they come from all walks of life and each is unique, the people I wrote this book for share some common characteristics, both professionally and personally.

The people I wrote this book for are:

- First-time freelancers. Whether you're 15 or 50, going out into the world on your own is frightening. I hope to take a bit of the sting out of that fear by demystifying the experience while providing a realistic view of what you can expect, based on my own and other successful freelancers' experiences.

- Recovering corporate warriors. You may have just been let go from the company you dedicated the past 30 years of your life to, or you may just have decided, after the third layoff in a decade from a job you sort of liked (but not really), that it's time for you to take the leap and do something on your own.

- Rebooters/mid-career freelancers in need of a refresh. Let's face it: even if everything is going well in your freelance business, you may still occasionally suffer from night terrors about what might happen if that major contract falls through. Or you may just be feeling in a rut and in need of some fresh thinking and inspiration.

- Slashers. A slasher is someone who does more than one thing to make a living: for example, an artist who also blogs and runs a catering business is an artist/blogger/caterer. The slash designates a separation between different careers or revenue streams that are distinct though often mutually reinforcing. In the gig economy, many more people will have more than one way of making a living.

Although these are the main groups I had in mind writing this book, there are also valuable lessons for anyone interested in learning how they might grow their side hustle into a business one day, or simply be more effective and productive at their current job by adopting some of the habits of a freelancer.

Who this book is not for

If you are terribly afraid of failure, unwilling to embrace change, lacking courage and/or looking for a shortcut to success, this book is probably not for you. This book isn't about tweaking a business plan, adopting a few new tools and getting rich quick. If you're looking for a formula you can copy and apply, then move on down the aisle to Tim Ferriss' 4-Hour Work Week. (Spoiler: Don't expect to really work only four hours a week.)

How to use this book

This book is about learning how to work in the gig economy and how to make it work for you. That means learning new habits and unlearning some old ones that are no longer helpful. And it means looking at the world of work differently than you may have been doing in the past, or how you expected it to be when you were in school or working at your last job. The good news is, freelancing is something you will get better at the more you do it. It can also be a lot of fun, rewarding both financially and emotionally. The possibilities are truly limitless.

This book provides real, road-tested practical advice on how to structure your time, manage your finances, optimize your productivity and find opportunities all around you. It dives deeply into parts of running an independent business that many solopreneurs struggle with: choosing where to work, leveraging technology, marketing yourself/ your work, business development and networking, selling, pricing, and managing clients. It also covers the important stuff that sometimes gets left out of how-to manuals: the psychological aspects of working alone and dealing with isolation, the challenge of staying fresh and committed through the hard parts, and how to constantly replenish and renew your energy and maintain and develop the skills you need to succeed. Using the book you are holding in your hands (or reading on your phone) as a kind of field manual, you will learn everything you need to know about how to launch and succeed as a freelancer.

The book is divided into five parts, beginning in Part I with a brief overview of what the gig economy is, and the answer to the question, "Why freelance?"

Part II is about getting started. We'll take a closer look at what it really means to choose freelancing as a career. We'll also learn some valuable advice from Roy Spence Jr., co-founder of the Purpose Institute, and learn how to turn passion into profits by identifying your gig-able skills, turning problems into opportunities and getting some guidance on what to watch out for. Part II ends with an uplifting story involving Coach Harris (and me) about the power of believing in yourself.

Part III explores the three major themes of freelancing life — time, money and work — and offers tips, advice and insight into how best to think about these three influential forces in constructive ways.

Part IV is a deep dive into the nuts and bolts of living and working as a freelancer. The meatiest content of the book is found here, and each section is filled with useful information as well as examples and personal anecdotes illustrating core concepts.

Part V focuses on the importance of pushing through the hard parts and offers ideas on how to stay fresh and inspired through ongoing training and learning and taking time off on a regular basis to re-charge.

Throughout the book, I try to deliver a consistent message of not just hope and encouragement, but relentless optimism. The new world of work can be a joyful place, primarily because there has never been a better time than now for people to discover their true purpose and design their work around the kind of purposeful, meaningful lives everyone wants to live.

So let's start by taking a closer look at the gig economy and the drivers of change that are fundamentally altering the way most of us will work in the future.

THE FUTURE

OF

WORK

Welcome to the gig economy

part one

WELCOME TO THE GIG ECONOMY

·······························

WELCOME TO THE future of work. Working gigs, or "gigging," once considered the purview of travelling musicians, is becoming a familiar way of life for an increasingly vast and varied field of modern workers. A short list of people whose primary source of revenue is gigging includes:

- Artists (painters, photographers, writers, actors, musicians, composers, etc.)
- Professions supporting artists (recording engineers, stylists)
- Graphic designers
- Word workers (editors, translators, interpreters)
- Programmers
- Web designers
- Web workers of all kinds

- Home care workers
- Lawyers
- Accountants
- Marketers

Not everyone who gigs does it because they have to. Many people work on short, temporary assignments because it allows them the freedom to work from wherever they want (that's the digital nomad), work the hours they want, on projects they want, and as much (or as little) as they want.

But technology is turning what we used to count on as jobs into gigs. We imagine some jobs as being more secure than others, such as jobs with high human-to-human interactions (e.g. physicians or therapists) or those that require responses to unpredictable emergencies (e.g. paramedics or firefighters). But there is really no way to predict which jobs artificially intelligent machines will replace. Machines have the advantage of not needing to sleep, take vacations, breathe or drink water, qualities many employers would view as desirable.

The robots are coming

The combined forces of automation and artificial intelligence (AI) will almost certainly transform or even replace jobs that involve highly routinized, repetitive and systematic tasks. Many already are.* Telemarketing as a job (which still employs vast, often young, workforces in countries like the Philippines and India, and even more economically challenged regions in North America) is unlikely to survive the onslaught of chatbots.

These changes won't just hit jobs on the lower end of the economic spectrum. One of the most well-paid professions in the health-care

---

* https://www.theguardian.com/us-news/2017/jun/26/jobs-future-automation-ro-bots-skills-creative-health

sector today is radiology – a field ripe for transformation by AI-enabled medical imaging analysis.

While many jobs will continue to exist in some form, many companies are already using technology to trim their human workforce, either replacing their workers with robots and AI computing power or redeploying employees to different versions of their current jobs. These companies will inevitably convert the human jobs that are still necessary into contract positions. As a result, more and more employees will rely on a field of free agents, talent agents/brokers, freelancers and part-time workers rather than continue paying to maintain a permanent, salaried (and pensioned) workforce whose skills cannot keep pace with the rapid pace of change set by machines.

People have always had to adapt to technology that changes the way they work. The difference today is that technology is changing how work is structured and who gets to do it.

From a business perspective, it almost always makes sense to use new technology once it becomes affordable and readily available. What company today would return to a world without computers or email? What company of the future would train and retrain ageing personnel if they had the option of simply dipping into a pool of freelance talent who are already invested in maintaining their own skills and staying current?

When companies can get the same (or better) results with fewer employees, they will always choose productivity over people. This employee downscaling won't happen all at once or hit every industry equally. Change, like the future, is unevenly distributed. Some firms will keep "doing things the way we have always done things" for as long as they can make it work. Some will evolve by hiring out instead of maintaining in-house labour. Some firms will simply disappear.

To anyone already in the gig economy, that is good news. It means more work for you. To everyone else, it's time to start thinking about what's coming, because change at this level will affect everyone.

Gettin' giggy with it

That scenario could sound a bit terrifying, even apocalyptic. But it doesn't have to. Much ink has been spilled lamenting the loss of stable employment and the end of well-paid, comfortable, secure jobs. But there's another side to the story: becoming one of those free agents in that vast and growing pool of available talent can provide you with opportunities you could never had had as a full-time employee. A gig could become far more interesting and meaningful to you personally than any job you've ever had.

It looks like a lot will be left up to individuals in the future. The gig economy is here to stay. The sooner you learn how it works, and importantly, how to make it work for you, the better off you'll be. Happily, you may even find you start to like it and the freedom, growth potential and variety that comes with being a gig worker.

What is the gig economy?

Before we begin, let's get clear about what we mean when we use the word gig. Googling "origin: gig" turns up the following definition:

"Gig (n): ...a job, especially one that is temporary or that has an uncertain future."

Other definitions describe a gig as "a live performance by or engagement for a musician or group playing popular jazz music"; "a two-wheeled carriage pulled by one horse"; and "a light, fast, narrow boat adapted for rowing or sailing."

So a gig is primarily a job, characterized by being temporary and with an uncertain future, but it can also be thought of as a light, adaptable vehicle designed for speed.

That second part is interesting, because a career based on gigs is precisely that: an adaptable vehicle designed for speed. Being able to act quickly when you spot an opportunity is a valuable skill that greatly benefits you as a freelancer. Because speed matters — and is rewarded — in the gig economy.

The gig economy, therefore, is really just all kinds of gig grouped together under one big roof. In truth, it is segmented into good gigs (those that pay well, are interesting and lead to bigger and better contracts) and not-so-good gigs, like earning five bucks to stand in line for someone who is probably too busy making real money to do it themselves. But the sum total of all gigs, good and bad, is what people mean when they talk about the gig economy.

The gig economy is also called the sharing economy, the on-demand economy, the connected economy, the gift economy and the barter economy. Whatever name is used, the gig economy is still defined by temporary positions filled by autonomous, independent workers on short-term, even micro-term, contracts. The type of work is usually service-oriented, tech-driven and built around on-demand type services, but not always.

The future is already here

The underlying force behind all gigs is the technologically-driven change that is altering the way human societies are organized.

It's been happening since the Industrial Revolution, but nothing compares, or can prepare us for, the age we are living in now. Ours is an age characterized by rapid change, tectonic shifts in economic activity, and the end of jobs as we were taught to believe in them.

Whether we accept it or not, technology-driven trends are shaping our lives and transforming how we work, what we work on, who we work with, how we get compensated, where we do our work and why we do it in the first place.

These trends, the buzz words of our age, include data, big data, machine learning, automation on a massive scale, robotization, artificial intelligence (AI), virtual reality (VR), augmented reality (AR), sensors, the internet of things (IoT), social media and wearable technology, all of which are converging to transform the present into the future in real time.

As William Gibson, the American-Canadian writer widely credited with pioneering the science fiction sub-genre known as "cyberpunk,", famously put it: "The future is already here, it's just not very evenly distributed."

There is no question that "old-world" problems like poverty, hunger, disease, under-investment in education and all the attendant social ills that grow from these are still very much with us. Climate change, war, crime... all are real, all are here and all are contributing forces to the changing nature of work. But what has changed — dramatically, I would argue, and much more rapidly and thoroughly than many people have yet to realize — is the way these problems and others will be dealt with and (hopefully) solved. Humans are doing this by using their innate creativity to combine and deploy the technologies we've invented as a species.

We've all heard by now that Airbnb is the world's biggest hotel operator, even though the company doesn't own a single hotel. Uber is the largest taxi company, but doesn't own any cars. Facebook is the largest media company, but produces no content. And Alibaba is the largest retailer, but owns no inventory.

Change at this scale is hard to comprehend, but it's here and it's happening. Most of the educated people I know, who hail from middle- to upper-class backgrounds, are running their own businesses, working as freelancers in some capacity, or planning to do so soon. This anecdotal evidence is supported by real data from around the world. Gig economy workers — classified variously as independent contractors or people who earn some or all of their income from online platforms or apps — constitute one of the fastest-growing segments of the economy in the US* (though firm statistics are still difficult to come by). And although the largest segment within this group is still in "rides and rooms" (Uber and Airbnb), there are very few sectors that ultimately won't be affected by this trend.

The gig economy is frequently characterized by politicians and pundits as a negative trend that points to declining prospects for people looking for work. Choosing to gig for a living is often presented not as a choice at all, but rather a last resort. I don't believe that's true, and I'm living proof that it isn't. If a freelance photographer can make it in an age when everyone in the world has a camera in their pocket, think of what you can you achieve with your unique skills and talents if you have the will to make it happen.

While some may view the gig economy with fear and loathing, I'd argue that, on the contrary, it presents huge and growing opportunities for creative, independent people who want to take control of their lives, work on projects they care about and live on their own terms.

Of course it's worth wondering, why bother? But first, let's quickly clarify the difference between being a freelancer and being an entrepreneur. Though the terms are sometimes used interchangeably, there are some important distinctions worth considering.

Freelancer or entrepreneur?

Freelancing is entrepreneurial. Like an entrepreneur, a freelancer has enough faith in him or herself to start a business. Both freelancers and entrepreneurs would say they work for themselves. But their

---

* http://marketmadhouse.com/gig-economy-sustainable/

paths can lead to very different outcomes, so it's important to be clear about your intentions before you begin, because your choices will lead to different results.

While freelancers and entrepreneurs share certain characteristics, they are not the same thing.

A freelancer:
- sells his or her time by offering a service, delivered directly or through subcontracted freelancers;
- may also sell a related product or range of products;
- is doing work he or she cares about and wants to keep doing.

An entrepreneur:
- uses his or her time to build a company that sells a service or product (or both);
- may have co-founders, investors, employees and a plan to hire more;
- is building an entity that can be sold at some point.

You can't sell a freelancing business, but you can sell a business you start up as an entrepreneur.

If you're a writer, for example, you may develop a very successful freelancing business with more clients than you can handle, but what do you have to sell to a prospective buyer who may be interested in your client list? Your clients are choosing to work with you — not your buyer —and may not agree to be sold off.

As a freelancer, you may outsource parts of your business and broker sales or contracts for other freelancers as part of your success at winning big contracts, but that doesn't really count as a business you can sell.

The question to ask is, what do you have to sell once you remove yourself from the business? If the value creation part of what you do remains even without your active involvement, you have a business. If you are embedded in the activity and the value cannot be created without your involvement, you are a freelancer.

Freelancers tend to work alone or in small, loose networks, though they don't necessarily. Sometimes they work in virtual teams with other freelancers who band together when a contract is too big for one person to execute alone, or when one lead freelancer brings in more work than he or she can handle.

Entrepreneurs or founders tend to think differently. They usually care more about building a business and removing themselves from the process than a freelancer does. The work freelancers do is often an expression and extension of themselves and their personalities.

Business or gig-ness?

Another way of seeing the question is: having a business versus having a series of gigs.

If you're a photographer, writer, artist, graphic designer, web designer or blogger, or you derive the majority of your income from freelance work of any kind, you don't have a business. You have gigs.

A business is something you could conceivably build up into an operation that doesn't require your physical presence or hand in the operation at all. You could set it up, build it out, hire staff and then just let it hum along making money for you while you do something else. You could sell it when someone else becomes interested in buying it. You could be acquired by another business.

Gigging, on the other hand, just involves your time and your skills. You rent them out. Take the "you" out of the equation and you have no income. (Though there's no work more rewarding than the work you choose for yourself, and no wealth greater than having the freedom to make choices about how you spend your time, where, on which projects and for whom you work.)

Freelancers and entrepreneurs face many of the same challenges and will share many of the same behaviours and habits. Both must be constantly scanning the horizon, looking for opportunities. Both must dedicate time to thinking about their target markets, developing target client lists and understanding what their clients really need and are willing and able to pay for. Every successful freelancer or entrepreneur has built a business around solving a problem for people who know they have one and will pay to have it solved for them.

The distinction matters mainly in how you view yourself and the growth of your business. Freelancing can often be the precursor to developing a wider and bigger business that includes more than just your own labour in exchange for a fee. There's a lot of overlap between freelance and entrepreneur, and the two terms are often used interchangeably. You may start out as a freelancer and wind up spotting an opportunity to start a business and then becoming an entrepreneur. Or you may start out as an entrepreneur and discover you prefer the freelance lifestyle.

Although much of the content that follows was conceived specifically for freelancers, many of the insights and practices described also apply to entrepreneurs, particularly in the early stages of starting a business, when it can be hard to tell the difference between the two.

As we dive in, let's take a closer look at what that freelancing lifestyle can be, and why you might find yourself choosing it.

Why be a freelancer?

"Why would you choose to be a freelancer?" It's a question others might ask you, but more importantly, if you want to tap into your true potential, it's a question you need to answer for yourself.

Why go to the trouble of setting up a home office, designing a new work schedule, working for yourself and developing a life built around finding, maintaining and developing client relationships? What makes freelancing worth the sustained effort it takes to build up a client list, master self-discipline and your craft, and actually earn a decent living?

Freelancing is anything but free: you have to invest time and money and work hard to get started. In the beginning, you may find yourself working alone more than you are used to. You may miss the collegiality of workmates and the convenience of having an IT department to call when your computer crashes.

Why not just put your head down and keep grinding it out? You may not love your current job, but it still pays the bills. And if you're unemployed or underemployed, why not just put your efforts into finding a safe, stable, well-paying job. Isn't that what everyone wants?

Aside from the possibility that finding and holding onto a steady job may not be an option for you, there is a much more gratifying reason to choose freelancing. Through freelancing, you can focus your mind and your life's work on doing something you care about doing. This can lead you to what, in his famous hierarchy of needs, Abraham Maslow referred to as self-actualization (see illustration below). Maslow (1908-1970) was an American psychologist best known for formulating the theory of the hierarchy of needs. His view was that psychological health is based on fulfilling innate human needs that can be placed in ascending order, leading up to what he described as self-actualization.*

---

* https://en.wikipedia.org/wiki/Abraham_Maslow

SELF-FULFILLMENT
NEEDS

Self-
Actualization:

achieving one's full
potential, including creative
activities

Esteem needs:
presitige and feeling of accomplishment

PSYCHOLOGICAL
NEEDS

Belongingness and love needs:
intimate relationships, friends

Safety needs:
security, safety

BASIC
NEEDS

Physiological needs:
food, water, warmth, rest

MASLOW'S S HIERARCHY OF NEEDS

(+Wifi)

It may not be the only way to get there, but freelancing is a proven
path towards complete and total self-actualization and can lead to a
truly meaningful and purpose-driven life.

You may have seen the above diagram or some variant (there are
cheekier versions that put wifi at the bottom of the hierarchy, before
physiological needs) online or in a psychology textbook. It describes
the basic needs for a fulfilled human life, and up at the very top of
the pyramid is self-actualization. Once you've taken care of the bigger bottom layers, freelancing can help you move up the pyramid to

attain the peak of human development: the realization of your talent and full potential through exercising and developing your creativity, independence, free will and a real understanding of reality and your place in it.

It's a life of adventure, where you learn to push aside fear to focus on developing your skills.

It's a life of growth, where you embrace the unknown and the learning opportunities it brings.

Freelancing means having the freedom and flexibility to design the lifestyle you want instead of organizing your life around a schedule you don't control.

It means you can choose to stay home with your young children and actually spend time with them as they grow up, instead of scheduling blocks of "quality time" with them.

Freelancing is ultimately a synergy of skills you learn to deploy so that you can take the fullest advantage of what you — and life — have to offer. You can say yes to off-season travel, take as much vacation time as you need or can afford, or even extend your time away by working wherever you are.

Freelancing provides you with a truly amazing, fulfilling, dynamic, limitless way to live out your dreams and be a fully engaged, happy and productive person, contributing your best to the world.

But freelancing is not an easy path, and it's not without challenges and trials along the way. I wrote this book to explain the predictable challenges that are part and parcel of freelancing in any field, and provide ideas and techniques for overcoming them.

Choose yourself

Is it really any easier to look for a new job? Or work at one that makes you unhappy? Why not give freelancing a try?

Freelancing takes courage, and more importantly, resilience. It takes time. It takes patience. It takes faith — in yourself and the universe.

But then it becomes its own reward. If you stick at it (that is, stay true to yourself) and keep going through the inevitable hard times that will come, you will reach a point where you won't be able to imagine ever doing anything else.

You'll be doing work that you love doing, that you can't get fired from, that pays you more than enough money to live life on your own terms, in your own time, and for your own reasons.

In other words, you'll be free.

Even after hearing about all the potential advantages freelancing brings, you'll probably have some reservations about started a free-lance career. After all, it is a big lifestyle change. Thinking about making the leap can be a little nerve-wracking. What helped me was recognizing that freelancing is a choice, and accepting that choosing to become a freelancer is as valid and real as choosing to become a doctor, guitarist, marketer or computer engineer. No matter what your current situation is, it's critical to remember that you do have a choice. You shouldn't feel forced into freelancing, or feel that it's the default setting if you don't have a full-time job — even if that's how many of us (myself included) first find our way into it.

Choose freelancing

When I was alternating between freelancing and working regular jobs, and unsure about what path ultimately to follow, a friend of mine quipped, "You know, freelancing is a real job."

It's funny how sometimes just hearing someone else say something can shake you out of your circular thinking and make you realize what's staring you straight in the face.

Yes, you can jump straight to freelancing just by choosing it.

Rinse, wash and repeat

At the time, my strategy was to work a job as long as I could stand it while keeping my freelancing options open hoping something better would come along.

The problem with this strategy (if you can even call it a strategy) is that I was never fully committed to one path. When I was working as an employee, I was always looking out the window in case a better freelancing opportunity happened to come by, and vice versa.

I wish I had just seen freelancing as a valid choice from the beginning and gone to it right away. Making a deliberate choice about freelancing saves time and gets you where you want to be more quickly. Instead of half-heartedly committing to freelancing while keeping your options open, you can dive right in and do it right.

Trying to balance working as an employee with working as a freelancer isn't optimal for either scenario because it's hard to keep your thinking in sync with your actions.

When you're working inside a company, your goals are different from when you are working on your own. You need to be aware of internal politics, attend meetings and communicate on many levels within various structures, always paying attention to who holds power over you and who doesn't. It requires a special kind of thinking, but you spend a lot of energy on things that make sense for a worker trying to succeed inside an organization, but are completely counterproductive as a freelancer. If you are not committed to either your job or your freelancing career, you could wind up running yourself down and not ever getting the benefits that come from fully embracing either role.

To really take advantage of everything freelancing has to offer, you need to think like a freelancer all the time (a theme I will explore in depth in Part III).

When the going gets tough, the tough get going

But it isn't an easy choice, and there will certainly be times when you wonder if you made the right one. Use these times to remind yourself that you did make the choice.

The choice becomes your strength. It gives you confidence when the hard days come (and they will). It gives you a sense of pride in yourself and what you are doing. But most importantly, it's a sign that you are taking control of your own destiny.

There will be plenty of days when you experience doubt. You'll have setbacks. You'll compare yourself to others and you'll get tired, sore and sometimes you may feel like quitting. That's totally normal. Knowing what lies ahead means you can plan for it and be prepared. A lot of what's in this book was written with just this in mind and aimed at getting you through the hard bits faster and with less stress (and cost) than if you were doing it all on your own.

Deliberately choosing a career as a freelancer is both exhilarating and terrifying. You're literally embarking on a journey through the uncharted waters of your potential and entering a whole new world of possibilities. Freelancing is not just like any other job. You don't just punch in, punch out and live your life elsewhere. Freelancing is an all-in way of life.

When you choose freelancing, what you're really choosing is a life built around spotting and figuring out ways to creatively exploit opportunities. You are choosing to design a life that depends on your engagement, increases your awareness (both of yourself and what is going on around you) and dynamically generates new growth possibilities as you go along. It's a highly satisfying, energizing and fulfilling way to live.

When you approach freelancing as a deliberate choice, made with determination and commitment, you're already leaps and bounds ahead of someone who slides into freelancing because they didn't think they had any other options.

If you can do all that and have a clear sense of purpose from the outset, you'll be unstoppable. I know you may just want to cut to the quick and start gigging so you can get paid, but freelancing is about a lot more than just making money. In the next section, we'll look at how you can invest your freelancing career with purpose and use that to see problems as opportunities, generate ideas and launch.

So let's get started.

GETTING STARTED

part two

GETTING STARTED

....

Roy's Rules

WHEN I FIRST saw Roy Spence Jr., co-founder and chairman of GSD&M and co-founder and CEO of The Purpose Institute, step onto the stage at a digital marketing conference gig, I was covering in California, I knew he was different. Unlike most of the other presenters, he had no notes and no big slideshow behind him. He was wearing jeans and a black turtleneck.

Roy began his keynote speech with a story about putting purpose first in your life. He told us about his childhood and caring for his sister, who had spina bifida, throughout his life. He told us about how he couldn't spell and how, after studying for weeks he brought his C+ graded spelling test to his mother, a school teacher. She chastised him for wasting his time trying to be good at something he was bad at, rather than trying to be great at what he was naturally good at. He titillated us with stories of how he walked across the U.S. and how he and a couple of friends from Austin started one of the world's leading ad agencies and landed clients like Walmart and Southwest on nothing much more than Roy's own charm and storytelling skills. He showed us a video of him with not one but two U.S. presidents wishing his son a happy birthday, and then he got to the heart of his presentation.

"You need a purpose," he said.

Then he gave us what I'm now calling Roy's Rules. A shortened version of these, I believe, shows you the three most useful things you need to know to give your freelancing career the best chance for success.

Roy offers three core criteria for instilling a sense of purpose in what you do. All three are particularly useful and relevant for anyone trying to become a better freelancer and make it in the gig economy:

1. Love what you do.

2. Love the impact you have on the world.

3. Focus all of your attention on what you can be great at.

As I was snapping away taking pictures of Roy, trying to transmute some of the impact of his words into images, I was thinking about what he was saying. I'd never actually articulated to myself what it was I loved about my work as a photographer. His list somehow made it clear to me.

Even after I'd been freelancing for several years, I was still struggling to accept that I really was happy as an event photographer. Since it seemed like such a simple and unambitious thing to do, I tried not to think about it too deeply. No pun intended, making a living out of images of people attending events seems a little superficial. It just didn't jive with how I thought of myself. I had a classic case of cognitive dissonance. And in textbook fashion, since I couldn't reconcile what felt like two incompatible ideas, I avoided thinking about them altogether.

Listening to Roy made me realize why being an event photographer was actually meaningful and purposeful — and more importantly, entirely suited to me.

1. **Love what you do?** I do genuinely love the act of taking photos, scanning crowds looking for real human emotion and intimate moments. I love the technical aspects of photography and the emotional side of it equally.

2. **Love the impact you are having on the world?** I make an effort to make everyone I photograph look good, and maybe as a result of trying to see people in their best light, I do. People respond to my work. They tell me all the time they hate the way they look in photos, until I teach them a few tricks on posing and then show them the results. It makes me feel good to know that in a small way, I'm contributing to improving people's self-image and capturing important moments in their lives for them.

3. **Focus all of your attention on what you can be great at?** This line really hit home for me. I spent a lot of my early adult life trying to be good at too many things without focusing on what I had the potential to become great at. I did it out of lack of confidence, and I scattered my energy so that I was never fully engaged or committed to any one thing I was doing. When I finally accepted that I was a photographer and got serious about making it work for me, I not only became a better photographer, I also felt much more confident and secure with what I was doing.

I believe that by keeping these three simple criteria in mind as you conceive of your life as a freelancer, you will be able to build a fruitful and sustainable career. Why? Because they help you define your purpose. By loving what you do, you are automatically focusing on what you care about. Loving the impact you have means you will be committed to making a meaningful difference for someone other than yourself. And doing what you are great at to the exclusion of everything else means you will always be driving towards excellence.

Whether you are a graphic artist, software engineer, web designer, personal trainer or management consultant, a large part of your ultimate success in life, as in business, will be influenced by how meaningful you believe what you do is. Seeing your work as purposeful and acting accordingly brings meaning to your life. Recognizing that meaning can come from anything is a key insight that can benefit you as a freelancer. You can make an impact doing what you do. You simply need to know why you are doing it.

But let's begin at the beginning and walk through a brief guide to how you can build purpose into your freelancing practice right from the start.

Rule #1: Love what you do

If you build your freelancing business on something you are genuinely passionate about and interested in, you'll have a huge head start over competitors who are only doing it for the money.

Having a passion for what you do creates a sustainable competitive advantage that helps you to develop a long-term thriving practice. You will work harder, be more purposeful and achieve better results. No matter what you do, doing it with passion is always better, but it is particularly crucial for freelancing. There is no coasting in freelancing; you need passion to keep the wind in your sails.

What is a passion?

Anything you have a strong and abiding interest in doing is a passion. It could be fitness and healthy eating, design, massage therapy, cooking, coding, or discussing new ideas. If something excites and motivates you to learn more about it, it's probably something you have a passion for.

As a freelancer, of course, you'll need to be able to monetize that passion in some way, but it's not necessary to immediately think in terms of converting your passion into something you can sell. It's great if it does, but if it isn't obvious to you at this stage, don't worry about it. What really matters is identifying what you have — or could have — a passion for in the first place. (We'll get to how you can break your passion down into a gig-able skill, something you can sell, further on in this section.)

Some people already know exactly what they are passionate about, but for many others, particularly those for whom freelancing and joining the gig economy were surprise late additions to their life plans, it can be a little more complicated.

The biggest obstacle to discovering your passion is beliefs that limit you. Often we are aware of what we really like doing, but we don't believe that our passion can be converted into a job. We don't allow ourselves the freedom to creatively explore the idea of our passion in relation to what we want to do with our lives.

What your passion is (or what they are, because you may have more than one passion) may not be obvious to you. But just because your passions aren't clear to you immediately doesn't mean you don't have them. They are probably there. You might need to reach in, dust them off and give them a fresh new look.

Ask yourself these questions:

- What were you interested in as a child?
- What did you want to be when you grew up?
- Who were/are your role models?
- What do you like most about the work you've been doing till now?
- What do you like the least?

Now, if you already feel confident that you know what your passions are and are ready to begin, feel free to skip over this section. But if not, there's a proven shortcut to discovering where your passion lies, and it's something every one of us is born with. It's called curiosity.

Follow your curiosity

If you dig into anyone's passion, you'll find it started with an alchemy of interest, questioning, imagining and learning called curiosity. Think of curiosity as the nutrient that grows and sustains a passion.

Curiously, it was following my curiosity about sales that led me to become a full-time freelancer. And in my case, this curiosity for sales was something that bubbled up out of boredom and frustration.

When I was working in corporate strategic planning, a large part of my job was preparing presentation decks for the bid teams. The work was tedious and time-consuming. I spent my days digging deep into data, preparing spreadsheets, five-year plans, business cases and whatever else I was asked to produce.

The bid team consisted of a lead sales person, accompanied by sales engineers and other staff whose job it was to assemble and submit multi-million-dollar bids for the large infrastructure projects the company was bidding on all around the world. While they worked hard, from my perspective their job came with some really attractive perks. They spent a lot of time outside the office, working in temporary field offices set up in the cities where the bids were being tendered. When they came back, they regaled me with stories of dinners, late nights and travelling. From the sullen interior of my cubicle, that sounded like a lot more fun than what I was doing. So to say I was curious about sales would be an understatement of the highest order.

I had never actually done real direct sales before, but the work the sales team was doing seemed a lot more interesting than the slow-death-by-PowerPoint I was engaged in. So I asked questions, got to know the sales guys and hung out with them whenever I got the chance. Eventually, I managed to get myself transferred to another team and moved one step closer to sales. I even got to tag along on a few international trips, still mainly doing lackey work, but at least I was liberated from my cubicle!

My interest in sales stayed with me. I kept following that curiosity and it led me through some of my early (and rewarding) freelance gigs. I eventually became an independent sales lead, selling online ads directly to the world's biggest motorcycle manufacturers. Selling went from being something I was curious about to something I became quite good at and enjoyed doing.

Now what does selling have to do with becoming a freelance photographer, you may be wondering. More than most people think. I may have indulged my passion for photography and taken a lot of beautiful photos, but I doubt I would ever have worked regularly and consistently for clients who pay me to take photos for them had I not learned first how to sell. Sales skills are essential for doing any kind of independent work. Without clients, you don't have a business. (We'll take a deeper dive into selling in later sections of the book.) While a lot of people like photography and it looks like a relatively easy thing to do (especially with the ubiquity and quality of today's cameras/phones), taking pretty pictures and selling yourself as a photographer are two completely different skills. If I'd only tried to become a photographer without learning first how to sell, I doubt I would ever have been able to build up a strong enough client base to allow me to live and work and ultimately become a much better photographer.

The point is, whatever you are curious about right now is actually a foundation for beginning your life as a freelancer. Your curiosity will guide you right to what you are interested in and care about, and those are the components of passion. Using a little creativity, you'll be able to explore that passion and see possibilities and uncover hidden connections within it, one of which may turn out to be a way for you to do something with your passion.

Once you've zoned in what your underlying passions are, the next step is to see how they can be applied to finding a problem that someone needs fixing.

Can you turn a profit on your passion?

Yes, you can — though you may need to come up with more than one gig-able skill or service to do it.

Coming up with a list of things you can do as a freelancer is easier if you understand what lies at the core of your passion(s). Doing this can help you see connections to what you enjoy most about your passion. Then something about that passion can serve as the basis for your freelancing career.

For example, I am primarily an event photographer. I love many aspects of what I do, from the chance to be creative and play with new cameras and technology to the opportunity to meet lots of new people from a wide variety of backgrounds. But the core of my passion as a photographer is my desire to make and enable connections between people.

My photographs connect me with others, and they provide connection points for the people who are in them, who use and share them. I believe that a still image has a special kind of power that can reveal something about a time, a place or a gathering that holds meaning for us. We can easily miss that meaning while we are living through the moment. Whether I'm working or just living my life, I always have a camera with me, and I keep taking pictures when I'm travelling or just hanging out with friends. It's both a creative and meditative tool, and it helps me produce something that I feel is appreciated and valued by others.

My passion for connection, in other words, is activated and engaged through photography, but what I sell is my service as a photographer.

Identify your gig-able skills

To turn your passions into profits, you too need to define your passion in terms of a gig-able skill.

Start by defining clearly what it is you have to offer and figure out who needs or wants what you have enough to pay you for it.

Think of yourself like a business, and begin to unearth the passion-related skills you have that you can convert into a sellable service or product (or both).

The key here is identifying any and every area in which you have, or believe you have, the slightest bit more knowledge, experience or practice than the next person. With a potential market of millions through the Internet, having just 1% more knowledge than the average means you have a slight advantage over hundreds of thousands, possibly millions, of other people who could learn from you.

To have any kind of business, you need to meet all three of the following requirements:

1. Offer something (either a product or a service) that...

2. provides value to other people who...

3. will pay you for it.

The more you can identify in the intersection of those three circles, the more potential gigs you are going to get.

Try this by drawing a Venn diagram, filling in the circles below as indicated:

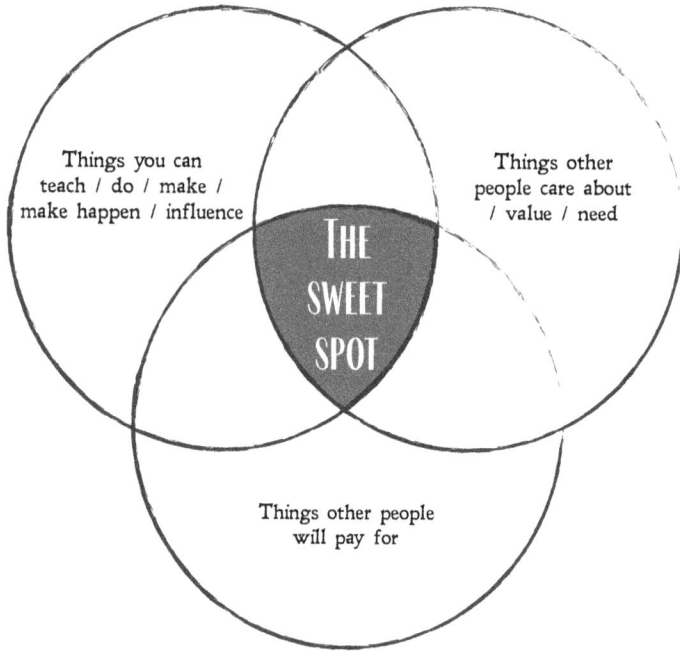

THE
SWEET
SPOT

Things you can
teach / do / make /
make happen / influence

Things other
people care about
/ value / need

Things other people
will pay for

In the first circle, put all the things you can identify that meets the first requirement. Make sure you only include things you actually care about and have a passion for. For example:

- What do you know even a little bit more about than the average person?

- Can you make / build / design / consult / sell / photograph / sing / write / draw better than the average person?
- Are you good at finding stuff online? Can you research and make it simpler for people to get the information they need?
- Can you curate or edit content into bite-sized chunks?
- Can you cook? Create recipes?

In the next circle, think of who (individuals, groups of people, communities, demographics, etc.) would value what you have to offer.

- Can you identify a group of people with a commonality, e.g. seniors living in a home or independently?

- For each group that you can identify, try to also include a few reasons why they would value your offer in particular. This will help later on when you start coming up with selling arguments.

Finally, in the last circle identify reasons why these people will pay you for the value you have to offer.

- Can they find it easily or is it difficult to access?
- How badly do they need it?
- How big is this group?
- How easily can you reach them? Influence them?
- Do you know who they are and how to talk to them?
- Do you have an "in" with them? All advantages are good.
- How much are they paying for similar value elsewhere?
- Are they growing or shrinking as a group?

By the end of this exercise, you should be able to list at least one main and two or three secondary skills that you can sell as a service or product to a group or type of person (buyer) that you can identify and describe, and for whom you can define the value you offer.

In other words, you've got enough of a business plan to get started. But how do you know if what you're passionate about and can sell is solving a real problem people are going to be willing to pay you to solve for them?

You won't really know until you try, but if you think of problems as opportunities, you should be able to come up with a lot more than just one problem you can solve. All you need is for one to stick.

Transform problems into opportunities

Find a problem that matters to someone else and that you can help with, and you're well on your way to freelance success. People pay other people to solve problems for them. Whether the problem is needing a new custom-built couch or wanting a new logo designed — when people hire a freelancer, they are usually buying a solution to a problem.

Have you ever noticed something you thought could be improved? A process you were involved in during which you gained some insight that could make the experience better? Or something going on around you that you thought could be done more efficiently? If so, you've already got one of the core skills a good freelancer needs. Now you simply need to see these observations as opportunities you can choose to focus on (or not) and grow into a freelancing business or an add-on to your main freelance practice.

For example, with the spread of social media, I realized that a lot of my event and conference photography clients were struggling with pumping out a steady stream of content during their events. They are often overwhelmed with onsite logistical details. Having to produce Facebook posts and live tweets is just one more task that usually falls on an already overburdened pair of shoulders. I realized that with my equipment, I could easily transfer a batch of images from my cameras and post to a client's social media accounts on their behalf, so I started offering the service of "Social Mediagraphy" as an add-on to my contracts. It turned into a nice little bonus on a number of contracts, and brought my clients added value.

Just making yourself aware of your surroundings and being open to possibilities will help you spot opportunities. If you notice a problem that interests you enough to try to solve it, go for it. Not everything you try or do will work out. That's immaterial. What really counts is to keep on looking for opportunities you can take advantage of.

The freelancer's fix

When you are still trying to figure out what to do and you are presented with someone else's problem, embrace it. The temptation may be strong to push it aside or pass it along to someone else if you can't immediately help, but by examining all problems that come your way, you generate opportunities for yourself. And by seeking to solve other people's problems, you may discover one or two that you are very good at and be able to turn that solution into a business.

Maybe you've already had a sideline early gig when you were younger that you never took seriously or treated like a hobby. Maybe you've noticed a few things going on around you right now that you think could be improved upon. Or maybe you're realizing for the first time that freelancing isn't the preserve of rare and uniquely talented individuals; it's for anyone who has the ability and awareness to recognize a nearby opportunity, and the chutzpah to try to do something about it.

I hope, as you progress through this book, that you will begin to recognize just how much potential and possibility you already have at your fingertips. Just having picked up this book and started to read it shows that you are thinking about your options and looking for ideas. That's what a freelancer does, just with consistent and deliberate application.

I also hope that you'll become conscious of the many latent skills and talents you already have or underutilized assets you own, which you may not have fully appreciated up to now. People are making money doing voice-overs for video scripts on demand (e.g. Voicebunny), waiting in line to get hockey tickets, or assembling Ikea furniture for new homebuyers (e.g. TaskRabbit), driving strangers around town (e.g. Lyft), and renting out their spare rooms (e.g. Airbnb). Just think of what you can do once you realize how many opportunities are hiding in plain sight, right in front of you.

Hardly a day goes by when I don't have an idea or spot a need for a new service. I may be using an app or visiting a website and see some tiny way to improve the experience or offer something related that augments what I'm doing. Opportunities grow out of ideas. Ideas proliferate like mushrooms as soon as you open yourself up to the possibility that whatever you are doing, seeing, eating, walking through, riding on, sleeping in or using in any way can be improved, changed, adapted to a different set of specific circumstances that maybe only you have the insight to see.

The world isn't finished yet. Enjoy the work in progress. This habit of seeing opportunities in your everyday life will be a constant source of inspiration on your journey to becoming a successful freelancer. You take the ordinary and see in it the possibility of something new.

What I've learned to do — and you will too, by reading this book — is to process everything I see, do, hear, buy, experience or learn about through the filter of being a freelancer. When I'm driving to and from the post office, picking up packages I had delivered to my home but missed the delivery for, I ask myself why there isn't a company offering a service to do just this. Maybe there is, or maybe I could start one.

When I'm on my hands and knees scrambling around, looking for a tiny screw that's rolled under the couch while I'm trying to put together an IKEA shelf, I ask myself why I didn't hire a freelancer to do this for me.

We're living in an age where virtually every single job, large and small and everything in between, can be broken down into bite-sized jobs being done by freelancing gig economy workers. New technologies bring new "problems," like needing someone to manage your social media accounts for you or send you a box of chopped vegetables and marinated meats for your "home-cooked" meal in under 10 minutes.

There are endless niches, large and small, being filled by gig economy workers, work being done by ordinary people like you and me. Just turn yourself on to the possibility and you'll soon begin to see more opportunities around you than you know what to do with. The trick, of course, is figuring out how to convert those ideas into a real functioning freelancing business. Coming up with ideas, you'll discover, is the easy part.

What to do with your great idea when you find out someone's already done it

When you're starting out as a freelancer, you may believe that coming up with a unique and brilliant idea is your biggest challenge. It's not.

I was, and still am, an idea addict. I keep a small notebook by my bed for thoughts that come to me as I am falling asleep or to record interesting ideas that pop up in my dreams. And I carry one around with me wherever I go, as I often get my best ideas after working out, while driving and travelling on the bus.

I even used to keep a spreadsheet tracking the life of my ideas. In one column, I'd describe the idea. In the next, I'd describe whom it was for or whom it could help. In a third column, I put the date when I first had the idea.

And the last column was for when I discovered someone else had turned my idea into a business.

I did this partly to make myself squirm about not being proactive enough to reap the benefits of my brilliant idea. But I also needed to remind myself of the most important thing about any idea: acting on it.

Ideas are cheap

"Mancamp," for example, was an idea I had decades ago while I was doing some demolition work with my older brother, who was running a construction business at the time. I had just spent a few years cooped up in a cubicle, working at a job that made me miserable. I felt a distinct pleasure every time I got to swing the sledgehammer against a cinder block wall that had to come down or get behind the controls of a Bobcat to push tonnes of gravel around. It made me think about all the frustrated office workers I'd known and how much they'd all enjoy a day doing exactly this kind of work. I envisioned starting an outdoor camp where anyone could go and learn how to use jackhammers and demolition bars and generally exhaust themselves taking things apart. I was pretty sure no one else had ever thought of this. But instead of doing anything with the idea, I just wrote it down and stashed it away in my "Ideas" file. I had that idea tucked away for years and had forgotten about it until one day, strolling through Hongdae, South Korea, where I was covering a conference in Songdo, I discovered someone else had acted on it. It's called Seoul Rage Room. I made an update in column four of my spreadsheet for June 2017.

The problem was not that someone had "stolen" my idea or that they had gotten around to turning it into something before I did. The problem was that I didn't do anything about it in the first place.

Ideas are the easy part.

Nothing is new anymore. No matter what your idea, someone somewhere has probably thought of it too. Maybe not exactly the same way you did, but more or less the same idea. If you, like me, are someone who regularly has ideas and gets inspired, this fact of life can be something that either demotivates you or spurs you onward. You get to choose how you react and what you will do.

It's doing something with ideas that counts

For that very reason, I'm never scared to talk about my ideas. I don't worry that someone is going to steal my idea or turn around and copy everything I've just dreamed up. Because no matter how original you think your idea is, the only ideas that ever matter are the ones that someone — anyone — cares enough about to act on. That's especially true for you and your freelancing business.

When you have a lot of people working on the same kinds of ideas in a market, that's called competition. And mostly that's a good thing. It's good for consumers and it's usually a sign that there's a lot of demand for the service or item those ideas are about. The winners in a competitive landscape are not always, or even usually, the ones with the best ideas. They are the ones who are paying the closest attention to what their customers really need and giving it to them, sometimes before they even realize they need it.

How do you feel when you read about someone else being successful with an idea you had, say 10, 15 or 20 years ago? (When I stumbled across the Seoul Rage Room, I just had to laugh. Halfway around the world and nearly 20 years after I'd thought it, there was my idea — an idea I'd let languish.)

If your idea has already been done, look to see if it was done exactly the way you would do it. If so, and you still believe you can execute the idea better — then go for it. Do it.

If you don't think you can do the idea better, can you add to it? Augment it? Offer something that makes sense as a result of it?

Does the execution of your idea by someone else give you another idea you can act on?

Do you still care about your idea the same way after seeing it done by someone else?

Here's a simple list (opposite page) you can work through to test any idea you have and find out if it's worth pursuing.

1. Have an idea.	• Write out your idea.
2. Write it down in detail.	• Describe it. What is it? A service? A product? Both? • Who is it for? • How will you make it? • Will you make it yourself or hire someone else to make it? • How will you fund its creation? • How will you sell it? • How will you promote it? • How long will you commit to it if you launch and nothing happens? • Does the idea help someone? • Does your idea solve a problem people know they have? • Does your idea solve a problem people don't know they have yet? • What is the problem it solves?
3. Enlist support.	• Will you partner with a developer or company to help you make it? • Do you know subject matter experts who can help bring your idea to fruition?

3. Enlist support (con't).	• Do you know people who can help you promote your project and get people to care about it? • Are you still committed? • Are you ready to work on your idea every day for six months to a year, making no money from it and not knowing if it will even work?
4. What will you do not to quit?	• Who will hold you accountable? • How much is too much?
5. How will you know if your idea is a success?	• How will you know if your idea matters to people? • Do you know who your customers are? • Or why they buy from you? (If they buy from you) • Do you care about the same things your customers care about? • Do you want to keep working on your idea because the more you work on it, the more it helps your customers? • Do you want to keep working on your idea even if you don't get paid?

If you know the answers to most of these questions and they are positive, then keep going and do it.

If not, chuck the idea and move on to another one that you actually care enough about to commit to. Having identified your core passion(s), you should have a list of several ideas to work from. Go back and run through this exercise as many times as it takes until you feel confident with the one you've chosen. It's much easier to start something over now, before you've invested any significant time or money in the project, than it is if you decide after launching it that you want to start again.

Things to watch out for

You're almost ready to go, but, like any journey it's often helpful to know what to expect before you start. While everyone's journey is in some ways unique, there are a few challenges that most freelancers encounter. Knowing what they are and preparing for them in advance can help you deal with them if and when they happen.

Freelancing doesn't come naturally to everyone. And many parts of freelancing are difficult. I know because I have personal experience with all of them. Working on your own can be uncomfortable, lonely and stressful. There's no one to gossip with, no one to bounce ideas off. Getting new work isn't always easy, rejection is common, and many times you just never hear back from a client and never know why. You're a permanent outsider. It's difficult to appreciate that a career based on a series of one-off gigs can provide for a sustainable, financially stable life. In fact, when you start, it feels like you are signing up for precisely the opposite of stability. And there are no benefits or savings plan to boot.

It's not easy "Bein' Green"

There's a famous song, sung by the inimitable Kermit the Frog (of Muppets fame), in which he muses lyrically about his feelings being green. With so many other colours to choose from, he worries that green is a pedestrian colour that blends in with ordinary things like grass. Then he realizes it's also the colour of big impressive things like mountains and rivers and tall trees, and in the end he realizes he's happy being green. It's what he wants to be.

Freelancers, especially those who have recently been employed, may follow a similar line of thinking. If you were once comfortable with the knowledge of your role inside the company where you worked and content with being a cog in the wheel, being on your own may make you feel very exposed and vulnerable. If you're a highly sociable person (as I am), you may find the sheer amount of time you spend alone to be daunting. The loneliness I initially experienced as a first-time freelancer was certainly one of the biggest challenges I had to learn to overcome.

There's also another challenge: learning to feel that the decision to freelance is a legitimate one. It took me a long time to really feel like I was choosing a freelance career. The problem wasn't just that it didn't always feel wonderful. The problem was that I was looking for proof it was working. At the time I measured my success only in dollars, so it was hard. I couldn't pretend (to myself) that I was doing well when I was booking a gig here and there, with long lags in between gigs. I thought only real tangible results would prove I could make it as a freelancer.

I think this need for tangible results has a positive side. For instance, it's motivating and it helps keep you focused on doing what you need to do to book new gigs. But it also has a downside. Being too focused on only one kind of result — money — prevents you from valuing the foundational work you have to do when you launch your free-lancing business (e.g. blogging, making connections, reaching out to potential new clients, clarifying your thinking), and accepting that you have to do it for your freelance career to take off. In the end, the work I was doing between gigs built the base for the majority of the work that followed. I didn't realize it at the time because I was being short-sighted and counting pennies. But the fact is, when you are starting out, you can't reduce everything you do to a win/loss measured in dollars. Understanding this will make your early days as a freelancer less stressful.

Of course, it's common to have moments of doubt and get scared off of freelancing, especially at the beginning. Early in my career, when I wasn't booking a lot of gigs, I felt like a loser. When I was working, I felt uneasy and worried that the good times wouldn't last and that soon I'd be back in the cold.

I wish I'd known then what I know now. I didn't appreciate everything that needed to be done to build up my freelancing business, and so I didn't use the time between gigs as effectively as I could have. Instead, whenever I felt freelancing wasn't working out, I looked for a job. Then I'd wind up working somewhere for three or six months and I'd want to leave. I felt I was on a kind of dystopian merry-go-round: now I'm a freelancer, now I'm a disgruntled employee. But I was never really feeling very fulfilled in either role.

The unvarnished truth is that when you are a freelancer, there is no perfect solution to feeling lonely or to balancing actual gigs with developing your freelance career. You'll have some lonely days as a freelancer. Getting through them will sometimes be hard. But it's much harder if you don't fully accept the role you've chosen for yourself.

On the outside looking in

To become a successful freelancer, you need to acknowledge that you're choosing to be a professional outsider. You'll be the one called inside for short-term contracts, but you'll never stay. You will be giving up any chance of being an insider for good.

Luckily, you get to choose how you think about yourself. Whether you initially approach freelancing with enthusiasm or caution, fear or even resignation, you should do your best to think about your choice as positively as possible. Think of yourself as a creative and positive external resource that can be brought in to situations whenever you are needed.

Very often, being on the outside of the organizations you work with is an advantage. When a company goes through restructuring or downsizing, employees worry about losing their jobs while freelancers may start getting more work. Being connected to more than one company means that even if one company starts spending less on outside suppliers and consultants, another company may decide they need more of you. In effect, you are building resilience into your career and building yourself an insurance policy that is in many ways more robust and reliable than working for a single employer can ever be.

I went through a period at the beginning of my freelance career when I struggled with my outsider status. In fact, I was pretty depressed. I didn't know how to think of myself. I wasn't following anyone's model and I just didn't see how I fit in. That made me feel like a failure and feel embarrassed, and I spent a lot of energy hiding, either by obfuscating what I was doing by calling myself a consultant without really specifying my field, or literally, by avoiding going out.

Fortunately, I realized I needed help before it was too late. I found a great therapist. My therapist told me a story about some of her other clients who almost magically experienced career success — which was the objective I was most consumed with — after practicing a combination of mindfulness, becoming aware of negative thought patterns and recognizing that how you define success for yourself is ultimately a personal choice. I wanted to be one of those people. Looking back, I can say that I did become one of them. After only a few months, meeting once every two weeks, I went from being unable to articulate what I wanted to be to calling myself a photographer. I never would have believed it at the time, but by first acknowledging that I had a problem and needed help, then learning how to change how I thought of myself and my ideas for what a successful career looked like, I was finally able to believe in myself as a freelance photographer.

There are many ways to combat loneliness and isolation (I address this topic again in Parts IV and V). You can work out of co-working spaces a day or two a week, hook up online with other freelancers and go to monthly meet-ups or simply set up "office" in a café or library. Just being around other people will alleviate some, if not all, of the tensions that being alone can give rise to.

When you do start booking more client work, you can make a point of visiting them or having calls now and then, just to maintain contact and develop the relationships. Some clients will even allow you (or prefer you) to work onsite, which can provide you with even more exposure to the business and solve the loneliness problem at the same time.

If you have already been dealing with social isolation and are finding it difficult, reach out to others and seek help. Again, this is a common problem, one that many other freelancers have faced. You don't need to suffer in silence. Over time, you will develop a regime that works for you. I combine client meetings with a regular workout schedule at my local YMCA, and proactively set up get-togethers and after-work drinks with friends and other freelancers as a deliberate strategy to offset the lonely times I experience as a freelancer.

Freelancing is a big lifestyle change, and as with any kind of transition, the more you know about what to expect the better prepared you will be to handle the fallout of those changes. I'm not suggesting you should wait to hit some kind of rock bottom before becoming a freelancer! You may be lucky and just knock it out of the park on day one. But if that's not the case, you should know that most other freelancers have periods of serious self-doubt and struggle through lonely days. Getting through them takes guts, and time to develop a regime that works for you. That, and a little bit of luck, will see you on your way to a successful freelance business.

Believe and you can achieve

Truly successful people — whether they are freelancers or not — have found where their passion and someone else's need intersect. And that's where they stay. They don't try to get better at what they are only ever going to be average at. They devote all their time, attention and focus to getting better at what they are already great at (Roy's Rule #3).

Coach Ralph is one of these people. "Coach" (his real name is Ralph Harris, but everyone knows him as "Coach") has been a volunteer at the YMCA for 47 years. He's a champion powerlifter and a constant presence in the weight room, where he gives pointers on how to lift weights correctly, the right position to put your body in, how to grip the bar, breathe and get stronger. He's encouraging, positive and honest with his feedback, all given in a strong Bajan accent. He tells you where you're weak and what you have to work on to fill out and get stronger. At the time of this writing, he's 81years old and he still works out every day.

Don't stop believing

One day, Coach Ralph was raising money for a charity he supports by selling T-shirts with this phrase printed on it: BELIEVE YOU CAN MAKE IT HAPPEN. The message isn't just right for people working out: it should be a freelancer's motto. Believe you can make it happen. And you will.

When I started believing that freelancing was a real career, I started getting more gigs. Because I believed in what I was doing, I talked about it more, and I was happy about it. This encouraged people to let me know when they heard of someone who might become a client for me. I started getting referrals from my friends and my personal network. I started to become known for my interests and the projects I'd worked on, which led to more gigs, which led to even more gigs.

When I finally admitted (to myself) that I was freelancing because I wanted to, not because I had to, I saw myself and my life in a whole new light. Instead of feeling anxious all the time and always looking over my shoulder, I felt confident and purposeful. I knew a change had taken place because I no longer felt envious when I heard about someone's cool new job or some success they were having. It was a feeling I experienced constantly back when I felt that being a free-lancer was something to be a little embarrassed about, like I was "in between" jobs and just filling in with a freelance contract to make ends meet. That feeling stopped when I finally and fully embraced freelancing as a purposeful choice.

Not surprisingly, that feeling inspired me to share more about who I was and what I was doing. I started blogging more seriously. I believe in the power of creating content and publishing on a regular basis. You don't have to take things as far as Seth Godin, who publishes every day and has done for the past several years, but it doesn't hurt to try. I manage a post a week, more or less, and even this small and very manageable publishing schedule has raised my profile and helped me to be found online by an increasingly wide and diverse pool of clients.

Do it on purpose, with purpose

When I finally realized why I was freelancing, and that I was choosing to do so, I stopped looking for anything other than ways to become a better freelancer. And as luck would have it, being a professional conference photographer has the advantage of putting me in many rooms with professional speakers from whom I can often learn a thing or two. My encounter with Roy Spence Jr., for example, offered just such an opportunity.

Many people can grind through hours and days and weeks and years doing things on purpose, but many still wind up feeling hollowed out and directionless because they don't have a purpose.

Knowing why you are going to do anything is far more useful than knowing what you are going to do. Doing something without knowing why or caring to ask is like being a wind-up doll instead of living as a fully engaged human being. Your why — your purpose — is where you need to start.

You can skip it if it seems too hard, but just working at whatever work you can get — aside from not being a very effective strategy for getting work in the first place — is not going to lead to anything but disappointment. You may make a few bucks and manage to stay afloat, but you will not thrive or really believe that the life you are living is the one you want to be living. You will not be engaged in your work, not invested in the outcome beyond getting paid. Put simply, you will not care enough to be successful.

So start by taking stock of where you are right now, using Roy's Rules to help clarify your thinking:

1. **Do you love what you do?** Every kind of work has parts that are unfulfilling and a bit tedious. I love being a photographer, but following up on unpaid invoices is not exactly the most meaningful or enjoyable part of my work. But on the whole, I can honestly say that I love my work. Examine your own relationship to your work and ask yourself if what you are doing is for love or money. Would you do it if you weren't getting paid? Which parts do you like most? Why?

2. **Are you making a difference?** Every single person on this planet needs to believe that what they do contributes towards

a better outcome. Everyone needs to feel their actions have an impact and their efforts are worth it. Do you?

3. **Are you doing what you are best at?** Where do you really have the potential to explode into greatness? Reserving all judgement on whether or not you believe at this stage that your talents are useful or worth investing in, simply ask yourself what you can uniquely do that for whatever reason is — or can become — extraordinary?

Having a purpose is not something you backfill into your life after working away at something you don't really feel connected to or passionate about. It's the central guiding reason for your life in the first place. It is the organizing principle around which you structure your work, and actually your life, without which you are simply toiling. Work that is not purpose-driven ultimately is not sustainable because it is devoid of meaning.

If we drill down into this list, the core starting point really has to come from where you can truly stand out. In order to build a strong, sustainable and successful practice as a freelancer, you need to become known as the best, go-to resource for what you have to offer. It sounds daunting, but there are really no limits on greatness. And there is plenty of room for all, once you realize how many potential avenues are open to someone genuinely looking for ways to solve other people's problems and do something they care about doing.

In the next section, we'll look at the three main aspects of freelance life. These three features —time, money and work — often seem like they are in too short supply. Learning how to think about them as a freelancer will change both your perception of their relative value and their importance in your life. I'll also give you the tools, tips and tricks you need to get the most you can from each.

Thinking Like
A Freelancer

part three

Thinking Like a Freelancer

How to think about time — your new boss

AS I WAS transitioning from working a job to working gigs, I remember finding myself constantly losing track of time. Even though I was never one to sleep in late or sit around on the couch all day long, I'd sometimes find myself in the middle of a week, not having booked any gigs for a while, forgetting what day it was or not getting my motor started till the afternoon. Aside from this being a depressing way to live, it was also highly inefficient. I realized that I needed to learn how to structure my time better. I no longer had the self-regulating life of someone who had to get up and be somewhere every day, surrounded by other working people, such that the notion of time was invisible. Working in an office environment or any kind of regular job requires you to be somewhere for a set period of time, and then the day kind of takes care of itself. When you are alone, forging your own path forward as a freelancer, you lose that structure. So you need to replace it with your own.

Time is a freelancer's most precious asset and in these next few brief chapters, we'll look at ways to view, use and measure your time to maximize your productivity and creativity.

Time matters because for many freelancers, it's what they sell. Even if you don't work at an hourly rate (a topic we delve into later on, in the pricing section) you need to impute a value for your time to ensure that you don't waste it and work yourself out of business by not properly accounting for it.

It would not be an overstatement to say that your greatest challenge at the beginning of your freelancing career is learning how to manage, structure and make the best use of your (seemingly abundant) time.

The meter's running

When I first began working photography gigs, I had no idea how much to charge for a gig. By asking around and doing some poking around online, I learned that photo gigs were either based on an hourly rate or priced as packages (e.g. in wedding photography). To me, any amount seemed arbitrary. I read about photographers who charged $1,000 a day or more and my eyes would bug out of my head. At the time, $35 an hour seemed like a good wage to me and I thought asking for more, since I didn't have much of a portfolio, would be greedy and would likely result in me not getting the gig.

This fear of "overbidding" on the value of your time (and risking losing the contract) is a huge limiting factor when you're starting out. Most first-time freelancers just can't imagine themselves earning big bucks for their time. They are petrified of bidding on jobs that they fear make them look expensive. As a result, most nascent freelancers grossly undervalue their time in at least one of three ways, if not all three at once:

1. They underestimate how long a specific portion of the work will take to complete for a delivered final submission.

2. They don't account for all the time required to do the work.

3. They think of their time in terms of cost to a client vs. value it creates.

All of these errors have a direct impact on the bottom line. If they persist, they will always limit growth.

On my first few photo gigs, I charged only for the time I was actually on site, ignoring the time I'd spend getting to and from a site. I only charged for what a client initially asked for, even if I'd wind up starting earlier or staying on longer on a job. I never charged for parking (even if I had to pay high downtown pricing for most gigs), and when I'd get home and edit the photos, all that time wasn't charged either ,as I thought I had to include it with my hourly rate. I didn't think I could charge clients for time I'd be spending working alone at home on their photos. I also had no idea how long editing would take. So I charged a little above what I really thought I was worth, but well below what I probably should have been charging. You can do the math: I worked far more hours on jobs than I ever got paid for.

Working for less than you're worth costs you money. Learning to accurately value and appreciate your own worth is a key skill for freelancer success. Look around: the freelancers you see doing well all charge appropriate fees for their work. They do so because they have learned just how valuable their time is. But how do you value what you don't measure accurately?

Manage your time

Time management tools — and there are many — are an essential part of any freelancer's kit. There's no shortage of cheap, easy-to-use time management tools and techniques out there. From simple timer apps to project management software, time denoted journals and workbooks and good old-fashioned paper and pen (the analog method I prefer), your very first working challenge is choosing one that will work for you.

Which one you choose should be determined by a deep and clear understanding of yourself and what helps you work best. Ask yourself: What gets in the way the least? There should be no psychic cost to using your time management system. It should be fluid and work seamlessly with how you work, where you work and what you work with.

Despite my love of technology, I mainly use a simple timer app on my computer and an open notebook with blank paper next to me on my desk. The timer creates isolated chunks of time in which I work on a single task (such as write for the next 45 minutes), while the paper and pen provide the structure for everything else I need to get done or respond to that happens in a regular working day. I can refer to the paper for my action items, note down any important tidbits of information that come in over the course of the day through my open ports (email, phone, other people, insights and ideas) and keep track of how I am doing. Having spent a bit of time initially experimenting and thinking about what works best for me, I now have a system that is almost totally automated. I create my "to-dos" for the day, assign an appropriate amount of time for each, hit the timer and go. It doesn't require any thinking. That should be the key element of whatever system you elect for yourself. It needs to be accessible by the automatic mind so your fresh, creative self can do what it needs to do.

Choosing and setting up that system up does require thinking and effort and is not a trivial task. You may need to try out a few different methods before you find the one that's right for you. And you may discover that yours is a hybrid of a few systems, blending digital and analog tools, as I do. But what you end up with should only matter to you. It has to work according to your specific working style so it's worth paying attention to in the beginning.

Once you start using your system, you'll quickly begin to learn how long specific tasks take you and how much effort you have to put into each one. A job you might have thought of as trivial (scrolling through your inbox) may wind up eating up a huge chunk of your day, while jobs you think of as very time-consuming (writing a good blog post) may take less time than you anticipated before you had your system in place.

The key benefit of finding and implementing a good time management system is that it gives you an accurate sense of how long your work actually takes. Knowing how much time you'll need to do a given task means you can give an accurate quote for a gig that requires one or more tasks.

Until you've started paying attention to how exactly you spend your time, you may, like most people, tend to underestimate how much of it you waste on non-productive things like social media, talking or chatting on the phone with friends, entertaining yourself with videos or articles online, or the sundry little tasks — like dusting around your computer or trimming your nails — that somehow creep in as you settle down to work on your computer.

Conversely, we also tend to overestimate how long it takes to achieve important goals or accomplish tasks that feel overwhelming at the outset because we haven't learned how long the component parts take. Writing a book, for example, is something many people would like to do but few ever do. And yet, if you commit to an hour or two or three a day of actual writing, you can easily write a book of respectable length in a few months. A mere 500 words a day results in a work of 30,000 words in just three months, with weekends off. Push the limit to 750 words a day and you've written 45,000 words in the same time frame. If you ask someone to estimate how long it would take them to write their first book, they will assume at least a year They will also assume they need to be alone in a cabin in the woods for much of that time to be able to concentrate solely on that one task. That kind of reserved space and rarefied focus is extremely scarce and out of reach for most would-be writers, so the fantasy conditions for success are never achieved. And the work is never begun, let alone finished.

The challenge for many first-time freelancers is often not properly attaching value to their time and mistakenly only valuing time they are billing to a client. The thinking is basically, either I'm working and getting paid, or I'm not working and not getting paid, therefore my time is worthless.

Of course, nothing could be further from the truth. The very first and most significant decision you should make as a freelancer is to view your time as extremely valuable and manage it as you would any other scarce and precious resource. While some of your time is paid for by clients, much, and likely most in the beginning, is not immediately paid for by anyone. That doesn't make it less valuable — in fact, it makes even more valuable. What you do with the time you have when you're not working directly on client work is what ultimately defines the scope of your life as a freelancer and takes you up the ladder far more quickly and efficiently than those freelancers who only consider their time as having value when someone else is paying for it.

This is akin to the "pay yourself first" advice you'll find in every book on financial planning you pick up. Your unpaid time is the time you can use to work on what matters to you. It is, quite literally, your life, and nothing can be more valuable.

So at the outset of your life as a freelancer, your time and what you choose to do with it are what will define your life and determine your success.

Choose wisely.

The present moment

An old adage in photography asks, "What's the best camera to use?"

The answer is: the one you have on you.

The same goes for a freelancer's time. What's the most important time in your life?

Answer: right now.

This moment that you have right now before you is the most important time in your life. It's all anyone ever has, but how often do we recognize it? How often are we fully present and focussed on the time and place we are in as opposed to thinking — or more likely worrying — about the future, or thinking about things we might have done differently in the past?

Brooding over what might have been or worrying about what could happen is like being one of those unfortunate dinosaurs who fell into a tar pit. It may be great for preserving a state of being, but it's not going to get you anywhere.

This moment now is what you have to work with. You cannot change the past, and the future is written by what you do with the present. By practicing on staying focussed on the present, you develop mental muscles that you can train on what you can control and change — and you spare yourself from wasting time and energy on things you have no control over and can't change.

Years after I quit leading adventure tours in South America, I lived with regret that clouded and discoloured my thinking. Whenever my present situation was tough, or I was feeling particularly stuck, I'd re-imagine how "great" things were when I was gallivanting around the jungles of Peru. That not only made me feel worse about the situation I was in, it made me regret the choices that got me there. But the worst part was that I became demotivated, wasted more time and usually exacerbated the conditions I was presently in. Just like the dinosaur going down into the tar pit, the more I brooded over a decision I regretted, the deeper I'd sink into a funk. The hidden costs to this kind of thinking are manifold, but perhaps the greatest danger is that thinking like this undermines your confidence and trust in your own decision-making. It can get to the point where you stop making any decisions for fear of making (another) wrong one. Before you know it, you're in a tar trap.

Take a deep breath

The more you have to pull yourself out of tar pits, the harder it gets. Dwelling on the past, or the inverse, fearing the future, are paralyzing behaviours. You need to address them before they become a problem. This is what mindfulness and learning to live in the present moment accomplish. They are the antidotes to the negative thought patterns that arise from looking backwards with regret or forward with fear. Being aware of the present helps you recognize when you are sliding backwards or slipping forward so you can catch yourself before you fall.

Learning to focus on where you are now helps you to see things more accurately, as they really are, and less as you imagine them. Discomfort is what usually drives us away from the present moment, because naturally we are trying to avoid feeling it. The danger here is that you are very likely to experience more feelings of discomfort at the beginning of your freelancing career than at any other time afterwards. If you allow yourself to fall into the habit of avoiding discomfort whenever it arises, you are only delaying the time it takes to move past this phase.

(Learning how to stay in the moment can be done using meditation and mindfulness techniques, physical exercise and practice. Accessing these skills is, I believe, a fundamental part of any successful life, but they are beyond the scope of this book. Take note, however, and look into ways you can learn and incorporate mindfulness into your daily life.)

When you train yourself to become aware of the value of the present moment, you also learn what you can actually get done with the time you have. It is very easy to stray off into wishful thinking if you think of your time as unlimited simply because you may not have a paying gig booked this week, or even this month. You may begin to trick yourself into believing that being a freelancer means you can work whenever, however, because you have all the time in the world. Or you may do the opposite, and feel so stressed out by having too much work that you think you have no time and can't get anything done.

Both kinds of thinking are illusions. Whether it's the illusion of time abundance or the illusion of time scarcity, both are deceptive. All you really have is this moment.

In this moment, you make a choice about doing something. And then you do it now. You don't wait, or put it off or wish you had more time to complete the task. You simply start the work and continue until you finish the work. Just like walking, you put one foot in front of the other until you get to where you are going. You don't have to rush and you don't have to slow down. You just need to give your attention to what you have to do now and do it.

Then move to the next thing, in the next present moment. And keep going.

Units of time

In the movie version of Nick Hornby's *About a Boy*, the protagonist, Will Freeman (expertly played by Hugh Grant), lives off the avails of royalties generated by a hit Christmas song his father wrote. Will is describing to his young protégé, Marcus Brewer, the idea of "units of time."

"I find the key is to think of a day as units of time, each unit consisting of no more than thirty minutes. Full hours can be a little bit intimidating and most activities take about half an hour. Taking a bath: one unit; watching "Countdown": one unit, web-based research: two units, exercising: three units, having my hair carefully dishevelled: four units. It's amazing how the day fills up, and I often wonder, to be absolutely honest, if I'd ever have time for a job; how do people cram them in?"

—Will Freeman

Will has the right idea, but the wrong focus. Because he is living an unfulfilling life, he is deliberately trying to kill time, rather than use it as productively as possible. As a freelancer, you'll apply the same concept but achieve the opposite of what Will is aiming for. Your units of time will help you increase your productivity and deepen your sense of fulfillment and accomplishment. Will lives a life where his material needs are cared for but his emotional life is empty. As you develop your own highly customized use of the concept of units of time you will be adding meaning and fulfillment, not taking it away.

When you work within a structured environment, there are lots of ways your time is managed for you. When you're on your own, it's all up to you. You will have to learn how to manage your time productively. Productivity systems abound (and I'll review a few of the ones I've found useful later on in the book), but the key skill they all bring out is learning how to focus on one thing at a time, for discrete periods of time.

This point was driven home to me when I finally established a regime I could stick to while writing this book. Like many would-be writers, I'd spent years of my life wanting to write, but somehow never finding (making) the time for it. I would periodically start a writing regime that would last a few weeks, then inevitably fall off when I got busy and distracted with other tasks. One big reason my writing plans never took off was that I overreached. Since I felt like I'd waited so long to start (and every time I started I felt that way), I'd set overly ambitious goals for myself, trying to emulate my literary heroes like Henry Miller or Dostoyevsky, who treated writing as a full-time job. I wanted to be a prolific, fluent writer and write every day. And most of the time I failed.

Just one thing at a time

Then one day I learned about the Pomodoro technique from an old friend who introduced me to the concept of GTD (Getting Things Done). The Pomodoro Method, invented by Francesco Cirillo, calls for breaking tasks into 25-minute units (the maximum amount of time on Francesco's Italian grandmother's kitchen timer, which was shaped like a tomato, hence the name).

That's how I would finally start writing, I thought to myself. Rather than pretend I would be able to stick to a schedule of writing for eight hours or more a day, a regime I never once managed to achieve, I set my targets much, much lower. I decided I'd try to write for just an hour a day, ideally first thing in the morning (after a kick-starter coffee). This simple habit enabled me to write much more often and consistently than any other technique I'd ever tried and largely failed at.

A unit of time is the time it takes to complete a task. It's important to do only that single task when you're working on it and not contaminate the time with distractions that only serve to fracture the unit of time into too-small bits.

Remember what life was like in high school? Your day was controlled by bells indicating the start and end of periods, between which you'd have three to five minutes to get to your next class. You probably started the day with Homeroom, then moved on to a 45-minute period of math or a 45-minute period for English, Phys. Ed., Geography, Computer Science and so on. Re-introducing units of time into your day is a bit like going back to high school, but without the acne, late notes and locker rooms.

By breaking your day into discrete chunks of time, you can get more done and stay fresh on the task you've assigned to the period of time you are using.

Some tasks will take more than one unit of time, which is to be expected. You can spend a whole day stringing together a series of units of time on a single task. What matters is to keep the concept of units of time going. Each unit gives you an opportunity to concentrate on a single task or a single aspect of a given task. Between each unit, plan for a brief break. This allows you to work for much longer stretches of time than you would otherwise be able to power through on a consistent basis.

What can you do with a unit of time? Pretty much anything that you need to get done, which includes your work as well as your play time:

- Reading a chapter of a book is a unit of time.
- Making dinner is a unit of time.

- Writing a blog post can be one unit of time or several strung together
- A phone interview is a unit of time.
- Cold calling leads is a unit of time.
- etc.

How long is a unit of time? That's entirely up to you. Start with something achievable but still useful enough to get something done, like 25 minutes. If you feel like that's too short, push it to 30, 45 or even 60 minutes, but don't try to go much beyond that or your units will start to get too unwieldy. Using a timer is important, especially as you are learning the habit, in order to give you the structure. Personally, I like working in 45-minute units, with five-minute breaks in between. You'll have to experiment with your own working style to hit upon the exact right amount of time, but whatever you settle on, it's important to stick with it.

The joy of implementing a units-of-time system is that it provides a key component of work life that first-time (and long-time) freelancers crave, which is some kind of structure to their day. Learning to use units of time helps build that structure.

Keeping (on) track

"You can't improve what you don't measure." These words are widely attributed to Peter Drucker, one of the big management thinkers of our time, though what he actually wrote was, "If you can't measure it, you can't manage it."

For a lot of freelancers, keeping track of time, projects, tasks and priorities can be challenging. Without the externally imposed structure that comes with a 9-to-5 schedule and having to provide progress reports to a boss, freelancers need to create a structure for themselves.

Working for yourself can be a lonely and isolating experience. You aren't part of any corporate measurement system and as a result, especially if that is what you were used to in your former life, you may feel rudderless and lost in a sea of unstructured time. Identifying what you want to measure and keep track of will help you develop a firm psychological framework for what you are doing with your life and form the walls of the structure you need for your career as a freelancer.

Your first job as a freelancer is to manage yourself, day in and day out, and to keep track of what's important to you.

You can use pen and paper, a program on your computer, or a combination of the two. For some, a simple spreadsheet stored on Google Drive is enough. Others prefer Omnifocus or some other task manager app. Go with what works for you, but make sure it is simple, accessible and something you can reach for without effort. Any friction between you and your tracking system will push you away from it, and that defeats the purpose.

So what do you need to keep track of?

I like to work on a number of projects at once and keep myself as busy as possible. While writing this book (which was one project I tracked), I also had to maintain my current business as a photographer, keep up my blog, make sales calls, book gigs and work them(!). All the while, I have to keep the other habits I'm inculcating or have built into my life, such as meditating, working out, reading and maintaining my personal network (both socially and professionally). Tracking also helps extinguish behaviours you are trying to control or minimize, like eating too many sugary snacks or drinking too much. I literally make a grid every week, marking off a little "x" for every day I manage (or don't) to stick to the habits I am trying to build (or kill) and the projects I'm working on.

There are different categories of things to keep track of. Being a free-lancer is a holistic practice that incorporates work/life balance within itself, so the categories you keep track of extend beyond your work. Everything — your mental and physical health, your family, your energy levels — plays a role in your success as a freelancer.

Things you should be tracking include the following:

Business-related: Your bookkeeping, estimates sent to clients, in-voices, profit/loss, expenses. I use Freshbooks, but you may find an Excel sheet or some other software works just as well for you.

Hit rate: How effective are your pitches? How many bids are you winning/losing? I used to keep a spreadsheet that included the name of the person who contacted me or I reached out directly to, their email address, company, role, date of first contact, request, my re-sponse, date of my follow-up and the final result, including both my submitted price and the final invoiced amount if it was a win. These days, I'm trying out Hubspot's free CRM tool. Over time, I have been able to identify trends in my bidding and I can now visualize my success in winning business and what adjustments, if any, I need to make to improve.

Your main priorities: I set these at the beginning of every year. Though it's an arbitrary start date, you can choose whichever time frame makes the most sense for you. When I set my priorities I don't just focus on my business. I look at my whole life and try to capture everything. I work from main categories like Family, Health, Mon-ey, Professional, Intellectual, Travel, Creative and Fun. Within each of these main priorities, I identify things I'm working on and set a realistic goal. For Money, it might be something like "set aside $5k in savings." For Professional, it might be "Write at least one blog post per week," "Make five cold calls a month," or something similar. Intellectual priorities include books I want to read, a learning goal like learning how to make videos online, or how to run a Facebook ad campaign. Travel goals are places I want to go to or experiences I want to have. Laying everything out like this helps me visualize not just the kind and amount of work I want to have, but how everything fits together holistically.

You should have these priorities written down and kept visible somewhere — an accessible file on Google Drive, for example, or a printed-out sheet of paper or white board in your office. Knowing what your priorities are and keeping them foremost in your mind helps you decide between what is important (what will move you forward towards achieving your goals) and what is only distraction (what will waste your time). Within this priorities list, I include work-related goals (e.g. launch new website, write book, double revenue), as well as physical goals (e.g. work out three times a week, eat more veggies, sleep a minimum of seven hours per night), and mental health goals (e.g. meditate for 10 minutes every day, practice optimism, keep a gratitude journal). Thinking about priorities is actually very difficult to do and takes a lot of mental energy. Getting them straight once and having them available when you need them keeps your mind free to actually work towards them rather than having to re-invest in thinking about what they are every time you need to plan out your time.

Habits: There are good habits and bad habits, and both should be tracked. Whether it's 21 days to inculcate a new habit or break a bad one, the trick to harnessing the incredible power of habits is daily practice and keeping track. I track everything from how many nights I drink vs. go alcohol-free to how often I work out, write a blog post, meditate and eat veggies.

Daily tasks: What do you need to get done today? The most effective to-do lists are short and actionable: three to five tasks, max. If it doesn't fit on an index card, it probably won't get done in one day. Make the list either the night before or the morning of and review it at the end of the day. Keep an adjacent list going of anything that crops up unexpectedly throughout the day. Over time, this technique teaches you to better understand the flow of your days and it allows you to see at a glance how much productive versus reactive work (i.e. responding to unplanned interventions) you get done in a day.

Short-term projects: What are the most important projects you working on? Again, these should be few and achievable within a short time frame: three months, max. Examples could include launching your website or refreshing an old one, outlining your book idea or writing the next three chapters in the one you're already writing, creating an online course or updating your video content, writing a guest post on Forbes or Huffington Post, creating a solid profile on LinkedIn or launching your Instagram account.

Long-term goals: What is the one (or two, tops) most important project(s) of the year for you? We almost always tend to avoid doing the important work that affects our most important projects in favour of the less important work that we can get done immediately. Rarely do we put our full effort into anything. To maximize your chances of success, limit yourself to fewer but more achievable long-term goals.

I used to set too many long-term goals and would often reproach myself for not achieving most of them. But I noticed that I usually did achieve, or at least make substantive progress on, goals I really cared about, which tended to be much fewer than the total number of goals I'd lay out for myself initially.

For example, I set a goal for myself to start a podcast last year, and managed to put out 16 episodes (you can listen to it here: slashpodcast.com). The book you're reading now was also a main goal for me in 2017 and (though it's taken a bit longer than I had expected to complete), by limiting myself to fewer long-term projects, I've been able to actually see it come to life.

Like any junkie, freelancers tend to prefer the quick productivity wins. But too much focus on these immediate checks on the to-do list can be counter-productive in the long run. While you have to do the paying client work and the daily tasks that aren't directly linked to any of your big ambitious goals, you must commit yourself to including some action towards them in every day. That's why writers who actually get stuff written do it every day. Allocate an hour or more if you can to working on something that is exclusively tied to your big long-term goal. Your future self will thank you for it.

Time spent doing tasks: What are you doing with all the hours available to you? How much are you using productively? How much is being frittered away on social media sites and falling into Internet rabbit holes? The most effective method I've found for keeping track of my time is to use a timer right on my computer. I set myself tasks in 45-minute chunks, and then either take a five-minute break or carry on for another 45-minute chunk if the work I'm doing is engaging enough and I feel energized enough to continue.

Ideas / loose thoughts: If it's in your head, it's occupying mental space and slowing you down. The human mind is both a wonderfully powerful tool and a hugely inefficient machine. Fill it up with too many stray thoughts or things you have to get done, and you quickly feel harried, anxious and unproductive. Scheduling periodic deliberate brain dumps (discussed in more detail in the section on GTD) greatly improves your productivity and frees up the psychic space occupied by incomplete tasks and that squeaky floorboard you need to fix. The brain dump is a powerful technique because it acknowledges the way your brain actually works. While you may think that you have distinct categories for work-related, personal and creative pursuits, for example, the truth is (as anyone trying to meditate for the first time immediately realizes) your mind is a jumble of thoughts swimming around in constant agitation. This "monkey mind" is going on constantly, just beneath the level of awareness. It feeds anxiety and generates stress, often without you being fully aware of it. Take time once a week to sit down with a pen and paper and simply spit out everything and anything that comes to mind. Date the page, but otherwise do not try to order the list or do anything other than completely void your brain of each and every thought you can lasso.

With practice, you will get very good at these mental cleanses (which is why the weekly repetition is important). I use the back pages of my current agenda or active binder to keep my brain dumps. Just writing them out often suffices to not only free your mind of their psychic weight, but also enable you to get them done. When I go back and review brain dumps from a month or two earlier, I'm often amazed at how many of the items I can tick off.

Keeping track is essentially about asserting control over your time and ultimately, your life. Whether it's a day planner, a weekly, monthly, quarterly or annual review, having a system in place that keeps track of what's important will make you a more effective freelancer — and very likely, a happier and more productive person.

But there's one thing freelancers tend to obsess about, particularly in the early days of their freelancing career: money. There never seems to be enough of it to go around, and the only things to track are bills and mounting expenses. It can sometimes feel overwhelming. So in the next chapter, we'll look at a few techniques I've discovered that can help you develop a more productive relationship with money and see how to view money through the lens of an emerging freelancer.

How to think about money: money management for first-time freelancers

The simplest way to give your freelancing business the best chance of success is to think lean. If you want to earn a profit, you need to take in more than you spend. If you don't (eventually) earn a profit, you can't sustain yourself, and your time and energy will be sucked into finding activities that do sustain you, forcing you off-course and making you set aside your freelancing ambitions.

Of course, that's much easier said than done, especially if bills are coming due and your first client is late to pay. It can take a while to calibrate your personal finances to adjust to unpredictable revenue streams, but doing so will stand you in good stead. You need to get clear about what money means to you and what it is really for.

I grew up with an almost pathologically panicked view of money, and the condition worsened when I started freelancing. Never having had a lot of money, I was driven from a young age to go out and get it. This had a positive impact on my entrepreneurial yearnings, but inculcated in me a genuine fear of winding up poor. Spending money was actually painful to me, and I hated the idea of wasting it on any-thing. Debt terrified me. Frugality came naturally to me.

But I soon realized that frugality had a cost when it came to free-lancing. I was so stressed and anxious about money that I tended to focus only on it, often at the expense of seeing the bigger picture. This shortsightedness was initially the biggest obstacle to my diving into freelancing. It kept me chasing after jobs because they offered the illusion of some financial security. It took me a long time (and many dead ends) to rid myself of this restrictive way of thinking and learn the true meaning of the adage "Penny wise, pound foolish." What finally did it for me? I realized I was thinking about money as the end goal rather than what it really is: not the final destination, but a means to an end.

Having money made me feel safe, but when I stopped to think about why feeling safe was so important to me, I realized that what I really wanted was to have the time and space to let my mind wander and discover what I was really interested in. That, of course, was living a creative life, which eventually led to photography and writing. I would have got to my freelance career in photography a lot faster had I skipped the fear stage altogether and realized that I didn't need nearly as much money as I thought I needed to make the space in my life for what I really enjoyed doing.

What is money for?

You too may find yourself thinking a lot about money as you begin your freelancing life. If you've come from having a "regular" job where phone and printing costs were covered by the company, life may suddenly seem more expensive than it used to be. When you're a freelancer, everything costs money, from parking onsite when you visit a client to getting your Internet package upgraded to handle all the online video courses you subscribe to. Spending and expense management can easily get out of control.

But sometimes you have to spend money to make money. You don't want to lose business because you didn't spend where you needed to. Penny wise, pound foolish. It takes practice and you will find your financial balance over time, but here are a few things I've learned that may help you get started.

It's important to note here that what matters most about how you spend your money is that you are doing it consciously. Just like losing weight: if you want to really get serious about your fitness, you need to become conscious of what you eat, how much and how often you eat. A lot of wastefulness in any habit is the direct result of not paying attention.

For example, I used to regularly buy one or two coffees a day in cafés, even though I could actually make a better one at home. When I took a closer look at this habit, I realized it was costing me at least $5 a day, usually more. I thought of what else I could do with that additional $150 a month ($5 x 30 days) and realized I didn't really need to buy a coffee every day. I still occasionally buy a coffee on the road or enjoy an afternoon in a café, but when I do, I am aware that it's a treat and not a necessary expense. Even allowing for five days a month of these coffees, I'm putting an extra $125 a month (or $1,500 a year) back into my pocket that I can use on something else that helps me reach my conscious goals. It may not seem like that much, but once I applied the same thinking to things like buying beer and wine, I realized how much money can sail out the door without any thought. You may even find ways to save money and have some fun, as I did when I started brewing my own beer at home. Not only did I drive down the cost of a pint of home-brew to just under about $0.86/pint vs. $8+ tip for a pint at a local pub, I also learned a new skill, drank fresher, better-tasting beer and had a fun new hobby to indulge in. Again, I didn't stop going to pubs (another favourite pastime), but giving myself the option to have a fresh craft beer at home certainly meant fewer nights out, not to mention hefty savings on the grocery bill.

1. **Think of money as fuel:** You need it to get you places, but in and of itself, it doesn't matter. Just as you wouldn't idle your motor for extended periods of time, take a look at any services you are currently subscribing to and not using regularly. Prune out any that you haven't thought about in the past 30 days and reconsider any you don't use more than a few times a year. if at all.

2. **Define your "needs" vs. "wants":** You need to eat food; you don't need to eat out every meal. Understanding the difference between needs and wants will put more money in your pocket than anything else you can do when you start out. Do you really need the premium version when the free one will do the trick? Do you have to pay to have your car washed regularly, or can you do it yourself? My definition of needs is things I either literally can't live without (e.g. food, shelter, workouts at my gym) and things I need to do my job well (which in my case includes reliable professional camera gear and reasonably current versions of photo editing software). If you're going to use it every day and it's a tool you need to deliver your service or product to a client, then it's a need. You need a domain name for your business, but you don't need 100 iterations of names.

3. **Organize your finances:** I use FreshBooks, but you can use a shoebox if that's more your style. The important thing is to

know where you are spending your money and whether it is on things or services that help you work smarter, faster or better. Are you spending to reinforce your need to feel safe and secure (comfort purchases), or are you buying things you would buy if you already felt that way (smart buys)?

4. **Try before you buy:** There is a plethora of available online services and tools that can do everything for you, but you won't really use 99% of them. Virtually every online service offers some lighter, free version. Try things out before you buy them, and only pay for what you love and want to incorporate into your work flow.

5. **Leverage credit card reward programs:** Credit card companies want your dollars and offer free travel points and other perks to get you to use them. I love credit card companies because they help me get stuff for free, which I am always eager to accept. The key is to cancel the card once you have fulfilled whatever obligation you accepted when signing up, but before the annual fee kicks in. (You can find the latest deals at greedyrates.ca.) Warning: never carry a balance. I treat cards like cash only if I have the cash to cover the expense, and go online almost daily to bring my balance to zero. If you don't, or aren't good at staying on top of your credit cards, then stay away from them.

6. **Share logins to paid materials with your collaborators and fellow freelancers:** While I'm not encouraging you to steal copyrighted content, I do think it's completely okay to share login credentials to sites you've paid for with people you are working with.

7. **Use libraries and free public resources:** You may be surprised that libraries still exist, but they do, and they are both fantastic places to work (when you need a change of scenery from working at home) and great resources for all kinds of information. Good ones carry new releases and even let you

take out books on your e-reader. They also offer free wifi and get books for you if they don't have them in their collections. Find out where your nearby libraries are and pay them a visit.

8. **Take public transit, use car-sharing, walk or bike:** Not having a car is a big money-saver. Depending on where you live, it may be a feasible option for you to consider. You'll save on monthly costs, insurance, gas, maintenance and parking (as well as avoiding aggravating parking tickets). If you can walk or bike, you save money and get some exercise as well (bonus!).

9. **Register yourself as a business and take advantage of any and all tax savings as a result:** If you work for yourself, you can write off as expenses anything you legitimately spend money on that helps you conduct your business. Check your local tax codes and speak with an accountant before going crazy writing off everything you spend money on, but in any case, legitimate business expenses include things like the costs of setting up an office, equipment you use and fees you spend on activities and associations you join to network and do business development.

Money matters. One of the reasons (though not the core reason, as I hope you've learned by now) that you're freelancing is to earn money. But you may be surprised how much you can save by simply reorienting how you think about money. Ultimately, your money is a tool, like any other, that will help you do what you need to do to stay in business and live the kind of lifestyle you want to live. Managing it wisely up front will help ensure you have more of it left over to reinvest, spend or save for the future. Take responsibility for your financial health — the sooner, the better. As a freelancer, you don't have a company pension, so be prudent with what you set aside to make sure you can take care of yourself when you retire.

Spend less money

If you intend to work as a freelancer, you need to have a basic understanding of finance. You don't need to be an accountant or a bookkeeper, but you do need to understand how to manage your cash flow, pay your debts down (and eventually off), invoice and get paid, keep track of your business expenses and pay your taxes. There are software applications that can help you with this, but you can't avoid the first, necessary step: taking responsibility for your financial health. You can't cut unnecessary costs until you know where all the money you currently spend is going, so you need to begin by tracking your spending, if only for a week or two.

And here are some things to think about:

Do you really need to own everything you use? In the sharing economy that is increasingly penetrating the real economy, there are more and more ways to get what you need without owning it. Transportation, work space and many specialized tools can be shared or accessed cheaply. This allows you to avoid taking on the full cost of ownership for assets that, if you buy then, may sit in your office (or your driveway) underutilized for most of their functional life. (The average car is underutilized for 95% of its life. A car-sharing program seeks to flip that utilization rate by increasing the number of users sharing the vehicle).

What can you do without? Here's a brief tale of two photographers. The first one decided he wanted to be a photographer and rented himself a beautiful loft studio. He kitted it out with a complete set of lights and gear, several cameras and a wide range of lenses. While his shooting style was still fairly undeveloped, he spared no expense when it came to his equipment.

The other photographer spent the first five years working as a professional with just one camera and two lenses, learning his craft. He rented everything else he needed, and no matter how much he would have enjoyed having his own studio, could never justify its cost as most of his clients preferred saving time by having him come to them.

A year and a half after starting out, the first photographer was out of business. He sold off his gear at discount rates and started to look for a job. Turns out clients actually cared more about the way they looked in the photos they paid for than the gear the photographer had "invested" in to shoot them with. Fifteen years later, the second photographer is still in business, and has just finished writing a book about freelancing...

While having the latest computer and the newest set of gadgets is a tempting way to kick-start your freelancing business, ask yourself if you can really afford the thousands of dollars it will cost to get them all and if you really need them to start. Can you work with what you have now instead, and acquire new pieces over time, when and where you absolutely need them?

Can you skip a meal? While this is not a diet manual, have you ever considered that how much and how often you eat is determined by a work schedule that has been arbitrarily imposed on you? Who says you have to have a breakfast, lunch and dinner at 8 a.m., noon and 6 p.m.? I work from home and simply graze on nuts, cheese and leftovers throughout the day, often skipping lunch or merging a late breakfast with lunch, effectively cutting a meal a day from my diet with no negative effects. At the very least, skipping out on any restaurant or store-bought meals will put more money on your pocket. Learn to cook, make extra so you have leftovers, work the freezer and waste less food. Everything you don't waste or throw out (for instance, because you ate out too often and let the leftovers rot in your fridge) will keep more money for your business. Conversely, every time you chuck a rotten container of yogurt or a loaf of bread that went stale, you're throwing money away.

Less is more. Frugality is a way of life. It goes hand in hand with viewing waste as anathema and will always stand you in good stead, whether it comes naturally to you or not. One of the greatest evils of our times, in my opinion, is excessive wealth and the obscenities that come from having far more than you need. By all means, you can accumulate wealth and get rich. This is not a diatribe against wealth accumulation. On the contrary, it is a manual for creating a kind of wealth that is more than just the contents of your bank account or a pile of cash under your bed. True wealth is having the time and the ability to do what you love to do and having enough people in the world willing to pay you enough to do what you love so you can stay alive and thrive. Failing to get that kind of wealth because you blow too much of your cash on things you don't need or could postpone buying is the worst kind of waste there is: it's the waste of your true potential.

Money is not a proxy for what you are worth

A lot of perceptions we hold about ourselves, especially relating to money, do not apply when you commit to becoming a freelancer.

For example, is a freelancer without any current booked gigs just unemployed? Or is she building her business and preparing for her next gig? I used to make self-deprecating jokes about being unemployed when I was actually trying hard to build up my freelancing business. I'd go weeks without a gig, and because I was my own harshest critic, I'd let other people's biases influence how I thought of myself. I discounted the hard work I was putting into building up a blog, carving out a niche for myself first as an event photographer, then as a conference photographer, and doing all the behind-the-scenes work that much of this book discusses, by focussing strictly on whether I had clients and how much I was making (or not making).

We are conditioned by external forces to evaluate ourselves according to criteria that are neither appropriate nor helpful when working as a freelancer. Even the concept of being a freelancer, for some, can feel like a failure if viewed through a lens of conventional thinking that only values outward signs of success.

We judge ourselves (and others) by what they do, how much they earn, where they live, their status in life (married or not), and all kinds of other criteria we impose (and have imposed) on ourselves and others. Freelancers need to be ready to set some, or all, of that aside to develop clear and productive ways of thinking.

Are you happy yet?

Money is a big one, and understandably, as so much of what we do, see and experience in the modern world seems to encourage the accumulation of as much wealth as possible and there is never enough. Although we live in an age when obscene amounts of money are held by a select few, we continue to invest tremendous energy — and struggle incessantly — in the pursuit of money for its own sake, rarely pausing to consider things like:

- How much is enough?
- What do I really need to live on?
- What do the things that bring me true peace and happiness actually cost?

Without veering off too deeply into the way money and happiness diverge, not being able to say how much you earn really is an issue for freelancers who have left paid positions, willingly or involuntarily, and are used to thinking of themselves in terms of the salary they once earned.

From the point of view of your ego, it is very difficult to earn less than you used to earn. There are countless studies that show humans experience loss much more acutely than gain. The same trader who earns a $10-million bonus one quarter feels a $1-million loss the next with pain that disproportionately outsizes the pleasure from his previous gain. For the same reason, it has been found that people whose friends are just a little less well off than they are feel better about themselves. It's not the absolute dollar value that matters so much as our perceptions of our past selves, our social context and where we think we should be. While really having no money and struggling to survive makes life less pleasant and more challenging, research shows that people living in the developed world need about $75,000 a year to live comfortably*. Above that figure, they don't gain a proportionate amount of happiness.

I've lost count of the people who've told me I have the best job in the world or tell me they wish they had the freedom I have to do what they want to do. Most of these are the same people I used to be embarrassed around because I was just a freelancer. They are generally richer than I am, have nicer homes, drive better cars and from the outside, seem to be doing very well for themselves. But even if they are cash rich, they are often time poor, and no matter how great their job may look on the outside, many of them have to show up and go to work every day at jobs they don't love all that much.

You are not your account balance

Money and identity are often tightly bound and it is difficult to prise one from the other. It's great when the money is coming in, but what happens when it stops? Many freshly minted freelancers are walking wounded, secretly carrying around within themselves a feeling of failure and thinking of themselves as frauds. Nothing can be more damaging to your self-respect and self-confidence.

Equating your self-worth to a dollar value is nonsense (pun intended), but people do it all the time. Say, for instance, you have two children. Is one worth more than the other to you? Do you not love and value each individually and especially because of their uniqueness? Assuming you are not sociopathic, the answer is, of course, yes. Yet we have trouble applying the same mindset to ourselves when we are no less valuable and unique.

* https://www.ncbi.nlm.nih.gov/pmc/articles/PMC2944762/

It is no easy task to change your view of yourself. It's even harder to do with age, as the older we are, the more fixed our sense of identity becomes.

But fluidity is important and keeping a more fluid sense of yourself is particularly useful in freelancing. You are worthy, not for the money you earn but for the fact that you are trying to be something.

Salary and wealth are false representations of worth. The richest person is not more likely to be a noble and good person than the poorest. These associations we hold between wealth and goodness are merely the result of advertising and marketing, both done for profit and through cultural mores passed to us via movies, stories and our own clouded perceptions.

"All that is gold does not glitter,
Not all those who wander are lost."

—J.R.R. Tolkien

Remember that if you find yourself beating yourself down because you're earning less than you used to. At some point, you may actually make more than you ever did, or even thought possible. Either way, your worth can't be reduced to the balance in your bank account. You're worthy because you are committing to yourself. You are deciding to do work that matters to you.

You are choosing yourself.

How to think about work

Now that you've got a handle on how to manage your time, and you've reset your perceptions when it comes to how you view money, you've got one final hurdle to overcome in your journey to becoming a freelancer: re-thinking the definition of work.

You're not getting into a suit and joining the commuting hordes, jostling for room on a crowded subway platform, or grinding your teeth as you stare into a sea of red brake lights on a congested highway. On your first day "on the job" as a freelancer, you may wake up naturally, pour yourself a cup of French-press coffee, shuffle a few feet from your bedroom to your home office, and press the on button of your computer. What's next?

Expect to see more crossover between your work life and your "real" life as a freelancer. In the beginning, the two may flow seamlessly into one. You may find yourself working at odd hours, and playing when others are working. Since you are the one crafting your own schedule and figuring out for yourself, over time, what works for you, you'll need to reconsider the notion of work/life balance. Rather than thinking of work time as opposed to playtime, start thinking of your whole life as fluid energy.

Rethink work

When you "work", what you are doing is applying your skills and effort towards a specific goal. You are actively and deliberately cultivating energy, then doing something with it. Think of work as a directed energy flow, one that you get to decide how to direct.

What's important is learning how to use your energy. It's up to you to discover your best, most creative, most important time to work. For many people, that's first thing in the (early) morning. But it doesn't have to be. Yours may be the hours between 12 and 3 am. It's up to you. What's important is figuring out when you are productive, and creative — when your energy is flowing and needs to be used — and using this knowledge to cultivate a lifestyle around your energy flows.

To be a freelancer, you need to let your ideas of how to work evolve so you work intelligently, using the tools technological change has made available and affordable to everyone.

It doesn't mean you shouldn't keep regular working hours, or treat each day as an opportunity to accomplish something and make progress toward your goals. It just means that those hours are, to a large degree, up to you. And the regularity, consistency and discipline you bring to them (which you'll develop over time) are what will make the difference between having a successful life as a freelancer, and one spent wondering why you're not getting the attention you believe you deserve.

This next section aims to provide you with a whole new way of understanding what work can be. It will show you how you can work smarter, more efficiently, more joyfully and purposefully as a freelancer and liberate yourself from the many negative aspects of working jobs that lead people to fantasize about freelancing in the first place.

It begins with recognizing that all work means serving someone.

Gotta serve somebody

Bob Dylan, who was awarded the 2016 Nobel Prize for Literature, expresses a truism about freelancing in his 1979 song, "Gotta serve somebody." At its core, freelancing is about serving someone (ideally, better than anyone else can). The sooner you recognize that, the better.

Many freelancers describe themselves as "working for themselves." But that phrase is only a placeholder. You may well be self-employed, but the term really only means something to tax authorities. In fact, working for yourself means you work for your client or, depending on your field, several clients. You have to serve all of them with élan.

Understanding that the freelance life is actually a life of client service is paramount. Naturally, if you are going to spend your life serving someone, you should choose whom you serve carefully. But this is one of the greatest gifts of freelancing: you get to choose your customers. You actually have the liberty to turn down work requests or seek to serve only the niche market that values what you have to offer and has the money and willingness to pay you for it.

A well-served client is recurring revenue

Thinking of yourself as someone who serves is helpful. Clients expect to be served. Keeping service first and foremost in your mind keeps you in line with their expectations and helps you correct your course as you grow and develop your practice. Treat all your clients with respect and give them a level of service that exceeds their expectations and they will remember you. When a client remembers you, they will come back and tell their friends and colleagues about you. A client who feels valued and well served by you is the basis for a lot of future revenue.

A returning customer pays you again and again. The ability to focus on the lifetime value of a customer is what makes the difference between freelancers who thrive and freelancers who dive.

How do you keep those clients returning (and recommending you) for future jobs? You deliver. To do that, you need to be organized and know what's happening inside and outside of the project you're working on. Your client should never have any reason for concern or doubt about what you are doing. That takes some project management skills, which we'll look at next.

Everything is a project

While this is not a book about project management, there are a few key project management concepts that are very useful for the freelancing life. But first, let's define what we mean by a "project."

What is a project?

A project is anything you do that starts, happens and ends. It can be large, with many action steps along the way, or it may be relatively small, such as running errands. Your health is a project. Training your new puppy is a project. Writing a book is a project. Selling your car is a project. Getting a gig is a project.

You can keep track of projects on a blank sheet of paper or by using your preferred software or app, whether that's Trello or Omnifocus or Basecamp, or a hybrid method you choose. Whatever system you decide on is fine as long as you can access it anywhere, at any time, and get in and out of it quickly. The point is to have a simple-to-use system that you can use and maintain without expending any mental energy (as previously discussed). Find whatever works for you.

Breaking down the project

The most important part of a project is the action step — the exact language that tells you what to do. And the most important thing to remember when developing your action steps is that each action is a discrete step that you focus exclusively on until it is complete (if you need a refresher, return to the chapter on units of time). Some steps must precede others (linked actions) and some can happen in parallel to others, but regardless, all action steps must be conceived and executed as discrete actions, to be executed one at a time.

Take the project "My health," for example. You want to be healthy,

I'm sure, as everyone does. Being healthy means staying fit, eating well, getting enough sleep, etc. It has a physical, psychological and even spiritual component. There's a lot to do. It's all one big project, but each part can be broken down into smaller projects as well. Take, for example, "eating right."

Action steps for the "eating right" sub-project could include things like:

• Research online healthy recipes.
• Make a meal plan for the week.
• Buy groceries.
• Invite a friend for dinner.

Your "staying fit" project might include action steps like:

• Do daily stretches.
• Take a CrossFit or Boot Camp class three times a week.
• Run 10 kilometres one day a week.

The same approach would apply to writing a book. The beginning part of the project is often the hardest, so expect that and give yourself more time for it. Your action steps might look something like this:

• Get started by writing down 10 different topics you're interested in.
• Write 500 words every day.
• Create an outline.

As a first-time freelancer, some of your top-line projects will probably include:

• Create a website.
• Find a space to work out of.

- Have a logo designed.
- Find customers!
- Make products.

Depending on the nature of your work, whether it's a product (like software you're developing or a unique work of art you're creating) or a service you plan to deliver (like being a photographer, graphic designer or web developer), the sub-projects will be slightly different. But all will require the same project-focussed mentality.

What is the structure of every project?

Every project has three things in common: time, money, scope. Each of these is like one side of an equilateral triangle. If you remember your geometry lessons from grade school, you'll know that you can't extend (or shorten) one side of an equilateral triangle without fundamentally changing it into a different kind of triangle. All projects — and as we will see, everything is a project — adhere rigidly to this one golden rule, and all are bound by the laws of the equilateral triangle.

For example, if your project is to build a deck in your backyard, the size of deck you plan to build (scope), depending on whatever materials you decide to use, will have a set budget (money) allocated for the purchase of materials and the labour required to assemble them. Your budget includes enough to pay your labour for the two weeks (time) that you have scheduled to build the deck.

You can easily see that if you want a bigger deck (increase the scope), you also need to increase the budget (money) and the length of (time) allocated for its construction. Similarly, if you decided to kibosh the deck and build a smaller balcony instead, you will reduce the budget and schedule by proportionate amounts.

By treating everything like a project, you subtly yet significantly alter your perception of how you will spend your time. You sharpen your focus on actions, which automatically engages the reward centres of your brain and pays the dividend of a sense of accomplishment as you proceed through your action list, which creates a powerful sense of progress and momentum that is a source of renewable energy. In effect, you create your own destiny, one small, discrete action at a time.

Thinking like a project manager also trains you to focus on achievable and measurable outcomes, the results of your actions and the end point of any project. Progress can be measured as simply as can your productivity. Your sense of time, too, will be shaped by project mindset. Without creating an artificial sense of stress or setting arbitrary deadlines (the remit of micromanaging bosses everywhere), you learn to treat time like a resource, drawing on it to move through your projects to their conclusions. And with every completed project, you gain both a measurable sense of accomplishment and, more importantly, knowledge of how to get things done that's in tune with how you live and work.

A freelancer of any stripe is ultimately the sum of all the projects he or she completes. There's no point in being busy for the sake of being busy. What you want is to have lots of projects with your attention neatly divided and metered out according to your own schedule and goals. That's rewarding in itself, and it pays dividends as you go.

Getting Things Done: A place for everything

After looking at and experimenting with a number of different organizational systems, I have finally hit upon a hacked, hybridized version that works for me. The key for you is to customize your system to yourself and how you work. What follows is a quick overview of some of what's out there, and some tips on how to build your own bespoke solution.

There are many off-the-shelf solutions available if you want to implement a time management system for your day. Let's review one of the most popular ones: David Allen's *Getting Things Done: The Art of Stress-Free Productivity* (and I highly recommend buying and reading this book in its entirety to really learn how this productivity system can work for you).

The problem: Work without edges

Perhaps the mother of all productivity systems, or at least the most well-known, David Allen's seminal work *Getting Things Done* (also known as GTD) has inspired legions of bloggers and changed the organizational habits of tens of thousands of individuals and companies. Underscoring Allen's GTD system is the insight that the modern knowledge worker — and aren't we all in some way now working more with pixels and bytes than anything else? — has no inherent boundaries. It is, as he calls it, work without edges. This lack of limiting factors means our work life creeps into our private life, and vice versa. Though the first edition was written before the proliferation of smart phones, the principle it expounds has only proven to be even more important and relevant in a world where most modern workers — at home or in the office — live under a constant deluge of pings, notifications, email alerts and reminders, not to mention good old-fashioned phone calls and interruptions. And that's not even considering the massive undertow sucking on your psyche from your various social media addictions (Facebook status updates, Twitter, LinkedIn, Snapchat, etc.). And if you're single and looking for companionship, you'll have to contend with an even greater, crushingly heavy workload of data relating to your pursuit of a mate.

The solution: Hunt down every single thing on your mind right now and capture it

The first thing Allen recommends is to do a brain dump (as discussed above in the section on thinking like a freelancer). Stop whatever you're doing, sit down and write an unmitigated stream-of-consciousness list of everything and anything on your mind. Do not try to edit this list or sort it or do anything but thoroughly exhaust the entire contents of your mind. The guiding principle here is that anything that's in your mind and not out of it on paper has a psychic weight. This weight translates to stress and becomes a little drain on your mind's (and thus your body's) finite physical reserve of energy. The emptier you can scrape your brain, the freer and lighter you will become. You need to be nimble, agile and ready for anything and to be in that highly productive state of mind, you need to trust that you have not left something undone, have no loose ends, didn't forget something, etc. Get it out of your head and onto paper or your easy-to-use, instantly available digital notepad.

Use your inbox

After your initial mega brain dump, you'll use the same system to stream whatever enters your mind — the constant flow of thoughts, interruptions, requests made of us by others via any and all communications tools available (your "open ports") — into your inbox. In GTD parlance, the inbox is now your single point of contact with everything coming at you. Everything streams through the inbox first. You will never miss anything. You now have a place to store things temporarily until you deal with them.

Decide how you will deal with it

Now take a look at the long list of "things" and for each and every single item decide if it is something you can do now, later or not at all.

Having fewer options is often better, so if the item on your list isn't actionable, chuck it, or save it for later if it's something you think you will need later for a project you are working on. When in doubt, throw it out.

If it is an actionable item, and you can do it quickly, do it now. If you can't do it now is it something you can outsource to another freelancer? Is the item really just something you are waiting for, like getting your new logo designed? If you need to do it later, assign it to the correct project it belongs to and mark it down as the next thing you need to do to move that project along.

Create a reminder system

Once you've captured everything and decided what you need to do for everything, put a reminder system in place to ensure you stick to your commitments. Set dates, schedule blocks of time for activities and use your calendar to hold yourself accountable.

Do it

Now that you have captured every niggling thought in your head, put every "to do" in its proper bucket, prioritized and scheduled all future actions on your plate and set up your reminders to make sure you stick to your commitment, there's only one thing left: do it. Take the first thing on your Next Actions list and do it. Don't move on to the next item in the list until you've done the preceding one. Adhere religiously to this rule. While you're working on your actions, don't also be checking email, answering texts, flitting around on Facebook or reading. Reserve a time for those tasks and only do them in the times you've scheduled for them. As you rip through your email, get into the habit of identifying whether it contains an actionable item, whether it's something you can do now or will do later, or whether it is something to be filed away. Do the same for incoming calls, ideas that come to you as you go about your work, actions and items that arise from meetings or conversations with collaborators or clients, etc. The GTD system is all-encompassing and if you truly embrace it, it can provide a robust organizational structure that helps you make tangible progress on your projects and organize your time (and life) effectively.

Review

Periodically schedule reviews. No matter how well you stick to the system, cracks will appear and work will begin to pile up. Some tasks will take longer than you think, some will prove to be less important and some more. Build in a regularly scheduled review period to recalibrate and tweak your system so you are always on track.

DIY productivity

Ultimately, a productivity system is subservient to you, your goals and working style. There is no system that can do the work for you, and no one system that is perfect for everyone. Explore and choose one that works for you, or cobble your own together out of pieces of separate systems. The only purpose is to free your creative energy and mind from unnecessary, time- and brainpower-consuming, non-value-adding anxieties and stress that easily arise from being overwhelmed, stressed or disorganized. In the end, it's only the work that matters. Your productivity system is simply a tool to let you do your work using your fullest potential.

The power of a short to-do list

Ah, to-do lists — the great "frenemy" of the hard-working solopreneur and office warrior/serf alike. There is nothing quite so satisfying as checking off the last item on your list and looking at a long list of accomplishments. It feels damn good getting things done. Lacking other forms of external structure, sometimes a completed to-do list is all you have to show for what you did in a day. Those tasks matter. They mark progress and are tangible proof of productivity. "Hey, I'm not just sitting around here clicking on video links in Facebook. I'm working. See?"

But it doesn't always work that way, does it?

Many freelancers are susceptible to the endless time and energy fallacy, so to-do lists become irresistible to them. While you can't control when someone says yes to your offer or gets in touch to hire you or buy something from you, you can control the things you put down on your list (or so goes the myth). When you need to feel like a superhero with all the time in the world, to really kill it, nothing feels more satisfying than loading that list up with everything you want to get done, now and forever.

Of course, what happens is you wind up with a huge list that you can't possibly get through in a day, or even a week. (I occasionally fall victim to the fallacy myself: I just spent the better part of an hour scrolling through the Task list in Gmail. I had tasks in there from as far back as three years ago, and in some cases the same email was flagged three or four times.)

And on that list you've got a jumble of different things — some of which are actionable tasks, such as "call fridge guy about the noise in the kitchen," while some are unspecific wish lists, things like, "start writing book today." Some are priorities, like "meditate!" and some are just whatever pops into your head when you write the thing (usually leftover, uncompleted to-dos from previous lists).

What a to-do list isn't

The problem is that most people use to-do lists like any other list. They run through all the things circling around in their brains, and with the good intention of cleaning house, they write everything down. This is an excellent method for staying productive — it's just not a to-do list. An exhaustive list of what's on your brain at the time you sit down to produce it is called a brain dump, as described earlier.

A to-do list should only ever be a list of actions you need to perform to move forward on your project, whatever the project is (and as you know well by now, everything is a project).

In David Allen's famous GTD system, your projects comprise a series of next actions, one logically preceding the other until the project is done. Every project is made of actions, but they can't all be done at once. A big error in how people break down their projects into actions is either to forget — or not think about — the order in which actions need to flow for real progress to happen, or not write down a real action in the first place.

For example, the problem with a to-do list item like "start writing your book" is that it is so unspecific as to be useless, since it does not give you any indication of exactly how or where to start. A to-do list should always and only be a tool. The reason you create one is to focus the thinking-through part of your work when you create the list, so when the time comes to do the things on the list, you don't have to.

It's all about effectively allocating the one truly precious and scarce resource you have: your attention. (Which is why meditation and mindfulness practices are so important because, like mining for Bitcoins, you are creating new reserves of focus and attention when you meditate.)

When you have a list with a set of detailed specific actions to take, you know at a glance what to do, and the order in which to proceed.

Using our "write book" example, what you need to do before you write anything down is identify the mental block that's preventing you from moving forward. Why haven't you started writing your book? Because you don't know what to say? Where to start? How to write? Or maybe you don't have the right software, or you haven't figured out yet where you will actually do the writing. The real reason you don't start is because you haven't given yourself a simple way in. Which is what an effective to-do list can do for you.

Instead of "start writing book today," put down "write seven topics that interest me." Or three, or one. Or take a step even farther back and say, "choose which writing software I will use to write my book: Word, Scrivener, Pages, Notes, or by hand." If you are farther along, you can simply say something like "write for 45 minutes today" and make sure you have the time blocked off in your calendar, with everything else turned off.

See how easy it is to get started?

What a to-do list is

Which brings me to the point of this chapter: once you figure out what a to-do list actually is (a set of clear, unambiguous actions that are the very next thing you need to do towards completing your project/achieving your goal/priorities), the trick is not to overload it.

Think of your to-do list as a thin sheet of cheap, single-ply tissue. Imagine someone holding that tissue between two hands, and your to-dos are stones that you place onto it — good-sized stones, about the size of walnuts, and heavy. How many stones can you place on that suspended tissue before it tears? That's about as many things as you can reasonably expect to accomplish in a day. How many stones do you think it will hold? Three? Five? Seven?

In other words, make your to-do lists short. Really short. As in, three to five items at the very maximum. And that's it.

Another idea is to use index cards. The size of an index card creates a physical limitation to how much you can cram onto it, which is a good measure of how much time and energy you really have available to you to complete whatever is on your list.

The Big Black Book

I like the idea of the cards, but in practice, I found keeping a stack of cards around messy and unwieldy. Which is why I prefer the Big Black Book.

The BBB is by far my favourite and most useful productivity tool for a number of reasons (and I highly recommend the blank page options, though you can use lined or graphed paper if you prefer):

- It is portable;
- It never needs charging;
- It can be used anywhere, under any conditions;
- The only accessories needed are a pen or pencil
- It can be easily reviewed;
- It doesn't need an operating system and never has any software updates or upgrades;
- It is very inexpensive;
- It has edges.

Here's how to use it:

Take a single page (I use one page for the entire week).

Draw a line down from top to bottom, about two-thirds of the way over. At the top of the left side (the bigger side), write TO DO

(Week of_____). Below this is where you're going to write your daily to-dos, a short list (no more than five) for each day of the week. (I write mine for the next day the night before.)

At the top of the skinnier side, you write down UNPLANNED. Here's where you're going to add things that creep up and hijack your time. It could be something urgent that happens or a response required to an unscheduled event. It could also be an action you need to take that pops up in a phone call or an email, or just an idea you get doing something else that is something you think is important enough to keep track of but that wasn't on your planned set of actions.

Two-thirds of the way down the page vertically, draw another line across the page. This section is for notes and ideas. It's your scratch-pad. You can doodle here, write down random, un-actionable thoughts or observations, or just leave it alone. It's free, unstructured space, there to reassure you that you won't lose a single one of your valuable thoughts but neither will you have to allocate any of your precious, finite mental space towards keeping it in place. You jot it down and out it goes, freeing up the mental energy it was consuming to latch inside your brain.

You can use this space for anything. I sometimes use it to track daily actions I am working on building into habits, such as meditation, working out, writing, etc. I simply create a small grid and run down one column listing all the habits I'm working on (or working to break), with the days of the week across the top. Then I just check them off as I go, and I can see at a glance whether I'm sticking with something or falling off track.

The real power of an effective to-do list is its ability to direct your attention to what matters next. Attention, which we look at next, is a scarce resource indeed and one that needs careful management and curation to work its magic.

If you can't give it your full attention, wait until you can

What is the scarcest resource a freelancer has to learn to deal with? No, it's not the obvious answer, money, or even clients (money) or equipment (money) or anything else that you think you need to acquire. It's not time either, which can be managed to provide you with enough time to get done what you need to get done.

No, it's your attention.

Are you still there?

Whether you believe human attention spans are shrinking, like the size of processors or state-sponsored pension plans, or that we are simply more adept at speedily dispensing with content that triggers our anti-B.S. alert system, the reality is that working alone, primarily with computers and connected devices, subjects us to a fairly steady stream of distracting interruptions. With the Instagrammification of our daily lives, our attention spans have been shattered into email checks (hundreds of times daily), social media news/drip feeds, and a steady bombardment of texts, Snaps, Facebook messages, WhatsApps, etc.

Without the controlling pressure of being in an office surrounded by colleagues who are ostensibly working and a boss who may periodically peer over your shoulder, it will be up to you, the fearless freelancer, to learn how to tune out the noise so you can concentrate on what you are doing. If you're coming from an office environment where you were used to being constantly interrupted by colleagues, or asked to join meeting after meeting while being simultaneously cc'd on hundreds of emails that only peripherally concern you, you're in for a rude, but probably welcome awakening.

You will be amazed at how much more you can get done when you work on focussed blocks of uninterrupted units of time and refuse to allow yourself to be drawn down the myriad paths of distractions that the tools of the digital era have spawned.

Don't multitask

Leave the multitasking to your computer. Human brains don't do more than one thing at a time very well. Just try patting yourself on your head with one hand and rubbing your belly in circles with the other. Do it for five seconds, then try switching the direction of the circle with your belly-rubbing hand... If you're like most other humans on the planet, you'll find the hand on your head has followed suit and stopped patting up and down. That's doing two things at once. Now try doing that while listening to a podcast, watching a show on Netflix, dictating an email response and thinking about the important work you are supposed to be doing, but just can't get a handle on.

There are several ways to achieve focus, and you can mix and match the ones discussed in this book until you find what works for you. Whether it's time constraints, quick deadlines, rules of engagement on when you can be connected to the Internet, how often you check your email or phone or whatever system you put in place, the goal is the same for them all: create chunks of uninterrupted time when you can do meaningful work alone without pausing and switching tasks. And do it every day.

Imagine how much more effective you will become. You can start small, dedicating just an hour a day in the morning to your most important work. Instead of doing what we all like to do — grab our phone and check email, news headlines and social media before we've even rubbed the sleep from our eyes — sit down and do your most important, most creative, most meaningful work first.

You'll find that the hour quickly becomes insufficient and you'll want to add another and another, until you're working in three- or four-hour chunks and powering through work like you've never done before. And rather than be exhausted and drained by it, you'll feel energized and excited.

One technique I have found helpful for controlling myself and reining in the impulse to constantly check my various feeds and streams is to simply shut them off for set periods of time when I'm working. I turn off my phone and mute the sound on my computer. If I really need to hunker down, I disable wifi from my computer.

For emails, I try to check the messages only at predetermined break times (at 10 a.m., again at noon and once more around 3 p.m.) You can do this manually or set up an app to run in the background on your phone or computer to automatically block distracting apps like email and social media sites for predetermined blocks of time in your day. Just search "distraction blocking apps" and try a few out.

Instead of losing your energy on switching and refocussing across an array of unrelated tasks, you are concentrating all your firepower on what matters most in the moment you are doing it. This one simple change will have a huge impact on how you do your work, and what you can get done without distractions.

You can even start to have fun with it, setting up a day without distractions once a week where you turn everything electronic off (yes, that includes your wifi router) and just do your work. Turn off, tune in and get focussed.

Focus

Sitting down to do any kind of professional work — whether it's writing code, designing flyers, building a website, stepping into the ring or getting into your scrubs — requires focus first. It's called getting into the zone. It's as if there is an invisible line between what you were doing before you start work and where your mind goes once you are in it. You need to learn how to get into the zone every day and stay there if you want to get anything done.

It doesn't get easier with time. But practice and habit do help make it more automatic. Inside the zone, you have an implicit set of constraints that are usually time-bound, but also linked intrinsically to the nature of your work. If you're trying to write, then you have the blank space, which is really the field you let your mind run out into. There is nothing of any importance outside these walls that matters. When you are deep inside, you no longer even realize that there are walls. You're just there, doing what you're doing and completely unaware of external distractions of any kind. This is the holy grail of focus.

Getting used to getting into it takes practice. You can try establishing rituals for yourself. I like to meditate briefly before I begin work. I also use timers and give myself targets and breaks. When the timer goes off, I take five minutes to tend to whatever niggling thing is trying to wriggle in and yank me away from the zone. I check emails, tend to some administrative task I've left for myself to do, get a coffee, whatever. Then when the break's over, I hunker back down and get on with it.

Getting on with it, regardless of how you feel, is critical. Professional work, the kind of work you want to share and can be proud of, doesn't wait for you to feel like doing it. It's there to be done, and your feelings on the matter don't matter at all. When you develop that respect for the zone, it starts to become more of a friend and less of the taskmaster it may initially appear to be.

Getting into the zone actually releases you from being held hostage to how you feel. You may be on a high or dragging your feet through an all-time low. It doesn't matter. (I'm not disregarding the impact of chemical imbalances that can make this kind of focussing difficult or impossible for some people, such as those who are depressed. If this applies to you, by all means, take your prescribed medication or follow the regime that you've discovered works for you.) But for everyone else — people with "normal" emotional lives — there are inevitable ups and downs. Few indeed are the placid individuals for whom nothing changes anything. But you can put yourself into a state of calm, concentrated workflow by focussing on one task, one thing only, and doing it for as long as it takes.

The one who focuses, wins

Without focus, the mind is like a dandelion puff, scattering its seeds to the winds. The mind without focus doesn't care what you do with its ideas. It just sprouts them and sheds them. If you want your ideas to matter — if they matter to you — then you have to guide them. You have to take hold of them and direct them into action. You need to gather up the ones that matter and plant them where they will take root and then keep at it, working the garden, loosening the soil, prying out the weeds, making sure that every day they get the attention they need to keep growing. That's focus.

It's never been easier or harder to get focussed. The modern workstation, which is a computer for most people who aren't engaged in some kind of manual labour, is a source of abundant distraction, but it is also equipped with tools for restricting yourself to the task at hand and for keeping other distractions at bay. Use constraints like periodically shutting off your wifi access, or going full screen with no other browser tabs open.

There are different kinds of focus. Short-term, task-oriented, up close and intense concentration. And long-term, sustaining, following a plan, working to a master vision focus. The two are distinct, and you are likely to be better at one than the other. The challenge is getting strong in both, which is required to execute any significant idea or project.

First, recognize which type of focus your mind favours. Leverage it to apply force to the other.

If you are better at short tasks, use one work session to create a big list of short tasks, all of which add up to a long-term plan. Plans can only be executed in bite-sized pieces anyway. But without some orientation and structure around a list of tasks, you put yourself at risk of being very busy, but not necessarily productive. This is my personal challenge.

Recognizing the limitations of a day is also crucial. I am always tempted to create lists that are too long to ever complete in a day. This results in the feeling that I'm constantly chasing things. To help manage this, I set aside some time every week to do the brain dump and indulge in the master list. Then at least I know it's taken care of and I can go back to daily plans, which are smaller (usually much smaller than you think they should be) and try to do that. Three things is a pretty well accepted and time-tested size for a list. Do three things. Every day. That's 15 things done in a week, with weekends off to do whatever you'd like. Forty-five things in a month; 540 things done by the end of a year. If each of those tasks, let's call them, takes two to three hours, and you break down a task into 25- to 30-minute periods of focus, you can get a hell of a lot done.

A day plan looks something like this:

Today I want to focus on:

1. Updating my online portfolio site;

2. Completing my marketing plan or the year

3. Writing my list of goals by category, short- and long-term and printing it out.

You will do other things, of course. You may have another set of activities, like a program that runs in the background. These would be your daily tasks or habits you are working on. Mine are:

1. Meditate.

2. Write 500 words.

3. Take a snapshot a day.

And then there are the bi-or tri-weekly activities, which for me are:

1. Work out three times a week.

2. Do weekly review.

And finally, the administrative/non-creative tasks that I use as productivity rewards or snacks, because they are usually easy to do and provide a satisfying check mark on the list. These include:

1. Update books.

2. Clean out inbox.

3. Declutter an area in my home office.

All the extra stuff gets stuffed into the day (or much of it does) and then there's all the stuff that pops up, creeps in, is not planned or expected but often has to be addressed. Pretty soon, you see your day get overloaded.

Getting things done takes focus, practice, constraints, personalized systems, honesty with yourself, discipline, good health and creativity.

Do what you can get done

One of the greatest hurdles you have to overcome when you work for yourself is managing Mount Overwhelm. That's all the work that lies in front of you, piled up as high as a mountain while you're still down at basecamp fumbling in the dark, looking for your hiking boots. Rather than feeling proud of your audacity for daring to go it on your own (which is not to say go it alone, as you will rarely truly accomplish something without the help of others in one form or another), you feel daunted, scared and probably doubtful of your ability to get things done.

These feelings are to be expected.

But just like a real mountain, the only way to conquer Mount Over-whelm is to focus on what you can get done, one step at a time.

Just as you wouldn't expect to climb to the summit on Day 1, don't expect the world to come beating a path to your door when you be-gin your freelancing career, just because now you're ready.

Conversely, don't be dismayed or make less of an effort just because you aren't getting obvious signs of success. The stress on "obvious" is deliberate, of course, because having read this far, you know by now that success as a freelancer has many facets, only one of which includes money and clients and all the things that are commonly associated with success. The fact that you show up, every day, at your chosen hour and your chosen place of work is a success. The fact that today you pushed forward on one of your goals, maybe something as simple as setting up your new Gmail address or buying the domain name for your planned blog, is success.

One step at a time

By focussing on what you can get done, which includes what you can do yourself as well as what you can get done for you by setting into motion actions that can be executed by others, you're guaranteed to make progress. And making progress is critical; however small the step forward, it is twice the distance from the same step backward.

Building your business is a long hike. There are milestones along the way, and stopping points where you can catch your breath and take in some spectacular views, but it isn't going to be easy. And why should it be? If you want easy, stay home and walk 20 minutes on your treadmill every morning while watching news stream across your flat screen TV. You're moving, but you aren't getting anywhere.

Freelancing, on the other hand, isn't about doing the easy thing. It's about doing the work you've chosen to do because you're driven to do it and you want to be the best at it. You do it because you want to be in control of your own destiny and not subject to the whims of a moody manager or victim to the next company reorganization.

That freedom comes at a price, and the price is paid in every small step you take towards accomplishing some of the big goals that lie before you. By valuing each step for what it is and doing your very best to focus on just that one, then the next, and the next after that, you will not only get there, you will also learn.

You will learn how to manage yourself, how to motivate and push yourself past limits you thought you had. You will learn how to break big projects down into small actionable steps. You will learn how to keep the big picture in mind while paying attention to the details at hand. You will learn how to do the work you've set out to do and continuously get better at it.

And at some point you'll be interrupted on that long hike by someone who wants to pay you to do what you do, and you will be ready for it.

Stop waiting

This is going to be hard for the perfectionists out there to swallow, but it's an important lesson to learn: it's better to put something out there that you're not totally happy with than to wait around till you feel you have something perfect to present to the world.

Take a blog post, for example. The first time you start writing for a public audience, it's tempting to hold back on hitting that publish button. You want to tweak the text, find a better image to illustrate your point, maybe add a section here or remove one there. Fussing over your work can become the focus and usually it just gets in the way. Good enough is better than perfect. (You can always edit after the fact.)

The first step in creating anything is to start doing it. You can start (and you probably will have to) before you believe you can do it. You may produce for years or even decades until you feel you're up to the task. But if you wait to feel right with it, you may never even get up to bat.

You'll wait for a lot of things when you are working as a freelancer. You'll wait for a reply to your beautifully crafted email pitch. You'll wait for likes on your posts. You'll wait for someone to call. You'll wait to get paid.

You'll spend a lot of time waiting for things to happen to you. And if you do that, you'll be waiting a very long time. Much longer than you are likely to have the patience to wait.

Waiting is not the way to carve out your niche.

Press "O" to speak to an agent

You cannot, of course, control other people, much as you may wish you could. You will still be waiting for an answer on any number of queries and pitches you have sent out to leads, prospects, friends and long-shot Hail Mary passes that are still worth doing even though they almost never amount to anything.

But the key to flipping the concept of waiting on its head is to be focussed, not on the results you are waiting for, but the actions that generate the waiting in the first place.

Yes, you want to see huge uplift to your latest offer online. But the important factor here is not waiting for the uplift. It's the fact that you actually put an offer online.

Keep changing up your offers to the markets through constant and repeated (focussed) experimentation, until you find something that hits. If/when it does, do as Sean McCabe (seanwes.com) once wrote: "you hammer it." Push hard on what works and abandon what's not working.

That's so important it bears repeating: push on what works; abandon what's not working.

If you are getting even the faintest whispers of a promise, put more effort and energy into that action. Conversely, if you've tried and found no response at all to something, then stop doing it.

Now by stopping, I don't mean throwing out the baby with the bath-water. But if something fails to elicit a response of any kind, then rethink what you're doing and your approach towards it. If you still think it's something important and meaningful to you and your business, then change something and try it again.

Take a blog post, for instance. If it doesn't seem to be attracting the readership you hoped for, maybe try republishing using a different headline or a slightly shorter text. Add an image. Take an image away. Try it on a different platform. Try sending it out at a different time of day. Repurposed content is still content. If after a few tries something continues to fail, drop it. You may not understand why it's not working. Be patient. It will come to you.

If it's something that's worth doing, it will resurface as you try new things and somehow, through the magic of the subconscious and the ever-changing nature of the Internet, at some point that core idea will emerge at the right time, in the right place, for the right audience, in the right format, and you'll have a win.

Just push the button

You're not sitting around after pushing the publish button waiting for a response. You're actively doing something with your idea.

The same is true whether you're making a sales pitch or reaching out to potential collaborators. Leveraging your bias for action, you keep trying and working relentlessly towards your goals. Responses, when they come — and they will, don't worry — will fuel you in information first and then, eventually, money.

First you do.

Then you learn.

Then you do again, applying what you've learned.

And repeat.

At some point, part of the learning yield includes money — people start responding to your offers with offers to hire you.

That's when you've hit the proverbial vein that gold miners search for. Once you do, work the vein. You may not be able to tell if you've landed on Smaug's hoard (as you may recall, that's the dragon in Lord of the Rings), or it will just drivel down to nothing. You can't predict the future. Keep doing what you are doing and with every attempt, you'll take something back with you that informs the next action.

Even if that lesson is simply do it again. Try doing it louder, wider, with more amplification.

Or maybe the opposite: do it with more precision, more targeted, more directly towards where you are seeing the growth.

Regardless of whether more is more or less is more, or more is less —

by doing, you learn the difference.

And you don't stop. You're not waiting around for something to happen to you.

You are what's happening to you.

You're the one making the waves.

Now is better than never

It's never too late to start, but it's always better to start as soon as possible. Let the inspiration come, experience it, feel it, and if you have the slightest inkling that it's worth acting on, just do it. Don't overthink it, don't try to get it perfect, don't even try to really get it right. Just get it out. Then look at it. Maybe work it over, revise it, reflect and republish.

But get it out first, real, raw and fast. It's better out than in. Once it's out, you have something to chew on. While it's still inside, it can only chew on you.

It took me several years to actually start blogging. Not because I didn't think it was a good idea, or believe it was necessary to promote myself. But because I didn't think that (a) I'd have enough to say and (b) anyone would care about what I had to say when I did. I was also worried that I didn't know how to do it or what tools to use and that I'd look foolish. When I did finally launch my blog, none of those fears went away right away, but I stopped paying attention to them. When I ran into a technical problem I couldn't figure out, I went online and looked for solutions. As I wrote, I discovered I did have a few things to say, and I noticed that having the blog up and running meant that when I was working gigs, I was looking for and thinking about ideas to write about. It's as if by making the blog a real thing, I opened up a door to my creativity that would have remained closed

unless I actually had a need for it. I think that's the most important reason to not wait on anything. Starting is just the beginning.
Whatever you do will change and evolve over time. You'll get better.
The market will change. You'll even look back at what you did in
the beginning and probably feel embarrassed about it ("I launched
with that???"). But that's the point. You never get past the awkward
starting stage if you're trying to polish and make everything perfect
before you start.

You just need to put it out there and begin.

Being there

Being There was a fantastically witty and entertaining Peter Sellers
film made in 1979, in which he plays a simple gardener who is mistaken for an upper-class gentleman and becomes known for simple
gardening wisdom that is rich in unwitting double-entendres.

It is also, and not for entirely unrelated reasons, one of the most important responsibilities any freelancer has.

Being at your station, ready to work, is the key to survival in the
freelance world. Where that station is, of course, can vary. It may
just be you and your phone, but what matters is that you are there,
ready and able to do work when it comes in and complete work that's
already there. And no less importantly, you need to be ready to follow
up on work that you've already delivered.

Be there...

- for the call from someone who found you online;
- for the referral from an existing client who's heard great
  things about you;
- for when your client asks for revisions or tweaks;

- for the after sale, when something goes wrong or your client just needs a little extra support.

Working when you want to doesn't mean you get to pick everything about how you work. Maybe one day you'll be big and successful enough to turn business away (but even that requires that you at least respond to the request). But that day is far from the beginning, and may not ever come. In other words, it's not something you should look forward to, and certainly not something you should be building into your workflow.

Answer the phone, respond to the email even if it's annoying, listen to the feedback. When you're starting out, the most important thing you can do for your long-term success is customer service. Be on the front line and take whatever comes your way. Learn to listen to the voice of the consumer. Only by talking to real customers will you ever learn about your clients. Sometimes they won't say exactly what they want. Often, they might not even know what they want. But if you are attentive, and actually care, you will learn how to decipher even the most inarticulate customer demand. You will learn to listen for the real pain points and be there to offer a solution to their problem. Do that over and over again, and you have a business that can't fail.

When your big break comes through, make sure you're there to open the door.

Harness the power of habits

This may be the most important chapter in this whole book, so if you take in nothing else, remember this. You are your habits. What you do repeatedly defines who you are and has the greatest impact on what you get done during your life.

Some habits form easily (like having that after-work cocktail) and some don't (like flossing every day). Unfortunately, the bad ones seem to be much easier to form than the good ones, even if the same principles apply.

So what are the useful habits that will serve you throughout your lifetime? Start with the core or foundational habits. These are the habits upon which others can take purchase and be built, and without which it's hard to make any progress at all. Not surprisingly, the core habits for your successful freelancing career have nothing to do with business.

Foundational habits

1. **Meditate:** A daily practice of as little as just one or two minutes a day sitting, focussing on your breath and clearing your mind can develop into a superpower. There are lots of reasons why and how meditation works and brings health benefits, which I won't go into here as they are easy to find. The only thing to remember here is that meditation is perhaps the core habit from which all others will grow. It is the Ur-habit, and it is so beautifully simple that you can do it right now. Just stop reading at the end of this sentence, set a timer for one minute, sit straight, breathe in deeply, then out. Close your eyes if you want to, but you don't have to. Your mind will keep whirring like a fan unplugged. That's okay. Just focus on your breathing. There, now you know how to meditate (check out Leo Babauta's excellent blog ZenHabits, which can help you get started on meditation and learning more).

2. **Sleep well:** Keep regular sleeping hours and get enough sleep. You may need more or less to feel refreshed, but for most people seven hours is the ideal. Sleep lets your mind wash itself out with dreams and fills your bones with rest. You cannot live without good, regular sleep. Pulling all-nighters and sprinting to a deadline can pull you out of a slump when used sparingly, but these are not long-term solutions. By prioritizing good

sleep you are investing in your long-term health and well-being, without which neither you or your freelance business will survive.

3. **Exercise:** You know you need to. Just do it. Start with any small effort. A walk around the block. Five squats in the morning. A yoga class. Find ways to bring exercise into your life on a regular basis. Aim for at least three vigorous workouts a week. If you aren't sweating, you're not working hard enough. Get your heart rate up and keep your head focussed on doing the exercises, whatever they happen to be. The clarity of mind and focus you gain post-workout is more than worth the price in pain it costs you, not to mention the benefits of having a healthier, stronger body to carry you through. Exercise also stimulates creative thinking. (I often get my best ideas towards the middle or end of a workout session.)

4. **Eat consciously:** This usually means more veggies and smaller portions, but since you already know that, the main point here is to be mindful of what you consume. Think about the food you are putting into your mouth. Where does it come from? Who made it? Is it clean and free of toxins? Is it fresh? Is it full of sugar? Is it processed? Pausing briefly to think before you eat anything will fundamentally alter your relationship to food and provoke positive changes.

With these core habits in place, you will have the strength of mind and body to develop other habits that will help you work intelligently and productively. These are just a few of the ones I've found most helpful. You may find others that work better for you, so feel free to add to or modify the list, but consider implementing some version of these habits into your life to truly engage your latent super powers and unlock your real potential.

Productivity habits

1. **Set your main priorities and keep them visible:** Whether you call them resolutions, goals or priorities, these are the major projects you are working on and what you want to accomplish. Keep the list short and doable. (Warren Buffet recommends writing down the 25 things you want to accomplish in life, then striking out the bottom 20 and concentrating on the top five for the rest of your life.)

2. **Plan your day the night before:** At the end of each day, I write out a short to-do list for what I want to accomplish tomorrow.

3. **Use brain dumps regularly:** As noted above, a brain dump is a powerful mind-cleansing technique that frees your mind from being a storage space and allows it to think and create. Get familiar with doing brain dumps and make them a part of your regular routine.

4. **Use timers to measure your units of time:** As discussed previously, there are various schools of thought about the ideal length of time you should allocate towards a task. Just experiment with different lengths until you find an ideal amount of time that allows you to focus and get work done. Somewhere between 25 and 45 minutes is a good place to start. You get far more accomplished with five chunks of time than you would simply sitting at your desk for eight hours straight of "working." Setting a simple timer to let you know when you should be working and when you can take a break to check email, futz around on Facebook or make yourself a cup of coffee trains you to work in productive bursts without burning yourself out.

5. **Take frequent breaks:** Build in lots of mini-breaks throughout the day and one or two longer (20-minute) breaks to really

relax or even power-nap. Everybody's energy levels spike and dip during the day. While most people tend to feel most energized and creative in the morning, some people get their best work done after midnight. Choosing how you manage your "work day" is one of the benefits of working as a freelancer — so long as you do it with an understanding of what your natural circadian rhythms are and work your productive sessions around them accordingly.

6. **Don't switch tasks:** When I worked on construction projects with my brother the project manager, I remember him always telling the guys to do one thing at a time and not to switch over to another part of the job until the part they were working on was complete. If they didn't listen, they made mistakes. Period. Multitasking is simply an excuse for working in a distracted, unfocussed manner. Study after study has proven that jumping from task to task or doing more than one thing at a time simply diminishes the quality of the work so it takes more time to accomplish everything than if the task had been done with focus and concentration. That doesn't mean you can't do more than one thing in a day or work on more than one project at the same time, it simply means focussing on one task at a time. You could use the first two 45-minute chunks of time in your day to work on a piece of writing and then switch over to another project for a few chunks, then switch back. That kind of switch enhances your productivity by allowing you to put your energy towards tasks you are engaged with and giving yourself a break when your mind or attention starts to sag a bit. Checking your emails or Facebook every five minutes is not productive and simply disrupts your flow and distracts your mind, fracturing your concentration and the effort that follows.

7. **Have a frictionless information management system in place to capture and track actionable items:** Work today is multidimensional and comes without neat edges.

Work tools, like email or the phone, are also often sources of entertainment, pleasure and personal contacts that have nothing to do with work. You need a system that you don't have to consciously think about to help you triage information so you don't waste time sorting through all the different sources of information and tire yourself out before ever actually doing the work that lies buried within. Actionable items can come from within emails, fall out of conversations with friends, clients, colleagues or collaborators, or be the result of your own ideation process. Have a simple system for capturing and tracking actions and make it a habit to parse any information feed for the action items that lie within. If there are none, delete it.

8. **Perform weekly, monthly and annual reviews:** Keep an eye on your progress by periodically scheduling reviews in your calendar and then actually conducting them. How are you doing on the projects you are working on? Where are you slipping? Where are you farther ahead? Identify where you need to put more time and where you can peel back a little. I sync brain dumps with reviews, doing the brain dump first, then moving on to a review with a clear mind.

Creativity habits

Working productively is how you get stuff done, but what you work on that matters to you often flows from your own creativity. Developing habits that train, exercise and maintain your natural creativity skills are just as important. Here are a few of mine:

1. **Do something creative first:** Practice creativity every day, ideally first thing in the morning. A creative practice (whether that's writing something in your journal, taking a photo or drawing) is an important tool for keeping your mind agile and helps prepare it for the day's work ahead.

2. **Write down 10 ideas a day:** I've recently begun this habit (which I got from James Altucher) and while it is sometimes difficult to come up with one, let alone 10, new ideas a day, I am already feeling the benefits of the practice. Simply sitting down and focussing on coming up with ideas is a form of mental workout that seems to loosen the soil, as it were, for other ideas to sprout throughout the day.

3. **Write daily:** A daily writing habit, like a journal or blog (for public or private viewing), is another way to build up a superpower. Writing is a flow-conducive activity. The more you write, the clearer your mind begins to become and the easier it becomes for you to think more clearly. Writing helps you process emotions, deal with situations, think through problems and come up with new ideas. If I had to choose one habit to try from this list, it would be this one. And don't worry about making your journal entries neat and tidy, or always try to be clever, clear or even concise. Just write. A sentence, a word, a list, a random thought. It doesn't matter what you write and you never have to show it to anyone if you don't want to, but doing it daily will build your mental strength and create a fertile ground in your mind for all kinds of other forms of creativity to take hold.

4. **Capture your ideas:** Use a notebook, your phone or whatever system you can easily work into your lifestyle that is easy to access. (I prefer a small notebook and pen.) Ideas often occur to me in places like the gym or on walks or during conversations. If I don't write them down right away, I often lose them. Like little fairies, they seem to flit away moments after they present themselves. Having a quick-access, no-friction system for capturing ideas helps me remember them and gives me a stress-free way of seeking them out because I have eliminated the anxiety I used to feel about losing an idea that I didn't immediately write down.

Leverage constraints

Sometimes the most difficult job is the one where you have complete and total freedom to do whatever you want.

While having total freedom over your work may sound like a dream opportunity to the office-bound worker who is used to being harried by bosses and colleagues to deliver on one of the several projects she's managing, in practice, total freedom is one of the most challenging aspects of working as a freelancer.

The power to create is driven in large part by constraints placed on the act and execution of creation. As a creative worker (which every freelancer is in some way or form), your first and most important job is to build for yourself the constraints you require to produce. We all need them. If you are doing the kind of work you have chosen to do — writing poetry, interviewing strangers in the streets and taking their portraits, or whatever — you are not going to be paid right away. You may not have any place to send or show your work but your own personal blog, and you may never get any feedback, good or bad, from anyone on what you do. You can give up. You can quit. Move on to something else. Try to find a job.

Or you can recognize that you are choosing to do this one thing because something in you compels you to do it. That being so, you have an obligation to yourself, and to the people who will eventually, one by one, find their way to you for the quality of the work you produce, to do your very best work.

To do that, you need self-imposed constraints. Your constraint may be a daily word limit, a specific block of hours in the day, a publishing schedule that you commit to on your blog. It may be a commitment to paint only with blue for a year, or write standing up, or photograph the same tree in the same frame every day. It may be a promise to email your subscribers a completed story every week or a finished painting every day.

Many famous writers have had routines of some form that act as a self-imposed constraint. Haruki Murakami gets up at 4 a.m. and writes for four or five hours, then does a 10-km run or a 1500-m swim. Ernest Hemingway wrote standing up, as did Virginia Woolf. For many, the morning hours serve as the constraint that spurs their creative writing.

Whatever your goal, having the constraint will spur you on. Rather than acting as a limitation, the constraint is actually the driving force, the gateway through which your energy and creativity are channelled.

Recognize your limitations

As much as constraints can keep you working creatively and productively, knowing your limitations is also important.

Knowing your limitations is part of becoming great at what you do best. Frittering your time and energy away on doing too many things beyond your purposeful core activity is counter-productive, demoralizing, and it never pays off anyway.

For example, I used to say yes to pretty much any kind of photo job I could get. At first it was because I needed the money — something a lot of first time freelancers can relate to — but then it also became about pushing myself to try new things and expand my skill set. As I became known for my event photography work, I went after conferences and started winning more and more business covering conferences, until that became a big part of my business. I did the same with taking corporate portraits, and then editorial shoots, and my practice continued to grow and expand.

Then came my first product shoot (every time you scroll through an online store, the photos of the items for sale are the result of a product shoot, usually shot against a white background with the goal of making the product look its best). "I can do product," I thought,

"Why not? How hard can it be? The subjects don't move!" It was for a gift basket business run by a nice lady out of her apartment. The gift baskets had things like stuffed teddy bears, bath products, chocolates and balloons that said things like "It's a boy!" or "Just Married." I remember visiting the client in her little kitchen, then going into her garage to load up my car with boxes of various gift baskets and their contents. I was to shoot them against a white seamless background and return the products with the edited photos.

I was inexperienced with lighting at the time, and rather than set up in a studio, because I'd grossly underpriced the job, I decided to try to save a bit of money and do it in my living room. It was hell trying to get that white look the way I wanted it, without shadows, and then the edits were a whole other kettle of fish, trying to parse out the individual hairs around the furry teddy bears or crisply trim around the weave of the basket handle. I spent a weekend shooting and editing and when finally I delivered the products and photos to the client, I got nothing. Silence. Three days later, a phone call, with a litany of complaints about the images. While most of the complaints were unfounded, I soon realized that product photography was different from shooting live events or doing portrait work. Alas, it was the first of a few such encounters before I finally learned that I don't do product photography. I'm not great at it, I don't like doing it, and I find the work tedious. Recognizing my limitations here, I avoid taking on product shoot mandates now, or outsource them to people who do them better.

Say no more often

Another kind of limitation is the one you need to set for yourself when you realize that the work isn't worth the effort. You may be great at doing it, but if it doesn't satisfy you, isn't what you like doing or doesn't pay well, you're better off saying no to this kind of job every time.

Real estate photo gigs are this kind of job for me. When I bought my first house, I spent a lot of time on real estate sites and was appalled at the low-quality images I used to see there. (It's much improved since.) I thought to myself, "Hey, I'm a photographer. Here are a bunch of agents whose names and telephone numbers I know and their photos suck! Easy money!"

So I went after them. I dropped off postcards in real estate offices, called up every real estate agent I could find on listings sites, and soon had a lot of clients willing to hire me to come out and shoot their properties.

I priced myself fairly low to get the work, at $100 per property, which at the time seemed pretty fair considering that it took about 30 to 40 minutes to shoot the properties (inside and out). In my inexperience, I underestimated the time it would take to help move furniture around inside to stage the rooms, edit and load the photos to the client's listing service, and drive to and from the properties, which were all over the city.

Remarkably, though the average selling price of the homes I was shooting at the time was well north of $500,000, I received a lot of pushback on the price. Now, considering an agent makes 2.5 to 3% on the sale, even if they have to kick back half of that to their broker, they're still taking in a cool $6,000 or more. And they thought my price was too high?

I pushed on, blogging about the gigs I was doing, showing my best images, and before too long I was the top ranked real estate photographer in my city. I got calls all the time. I raised my price to $150 per property. The clamour of complaints I got from callers grew ever louder until finally I decided it just wasn't worth it. I wasn't going to drive around town, schlepping couches across rooms and primping bowls of green apples on tables, and haggle with agents who thought that $150 was too high a price to pay for photos that would help them sell their high-end properties.

So I started saying no or quoting prices at $300+ to anyone who called asking about real estate photography. I stopped blogging about it. And pretty soon I fell off the map as a real estate photographer. I couldn't have been happier about it.

Develop your bias for action

Whenever any kind of information comes to you — whether through your own directed efforts like researching something online or reading a book — or through email, a phone call, a conversation or just a spontaneously generated idea, you have a choice.

You can parse the actionable part out of that information, you can tell yourself you'll do it later (and hope to remember) or you can ignore it.

Almost all the work we do today is based first in some kind of information source. The information may not always be textual — it can be a conversation, an image, a political movement forming — but the notions present themselves to us as information. When it does, what you do with the information (habitually) defines the kind of freelancer you are and is an important factor in determining your future success.

Taking action is a choice. Looking for and then taking note of the actions you can take is what you do with information.

When you have a bias for action, you have a purposeful way of treating any information you come across. You scan it for its actionability and then can decide to act on it now, save it for later or delete it as unhelpful and un-actionable. When you develop this mental habit, you can quickly spot those who don't. These people will waste your time, send you rambling pointless emails, call you for no particular purpose and generally eat up the precious resource of your attention.

What can I do with this?

Having a bias for action means you want to get things done. You want to work on projects for which you can determine the outcomes, projects that you will move forward by constantly looking for the next actionable step. It also means you aren't sitting around waiting for something to happen to you. You're making things happen for yourself, and likely for others around you.

A person with a bias for action doesn't wait for the phone to ring. He or she identifies who potential clients are and where they can be found, then goes out and contacts them. An action-oriented person sometimes says yes to opportunities to meet and network with prospects. More often than not, an action-oriented person also says no. No to distractions like whiling away time on social networks or accepting requests to participate in projects that aren't part of their core purpose and won't help them achieve the goals they've set for themselves.

When you're freelancing, your time is one of your most valuable resources. Whether you're billing it out directly to clients or it's an imputed input cost in the production of goods you're selling, you need to protect your time and use it wisely. When you have a bias for action, you implicitly think in terms of the time it takes to get something done. The combination of a bias for action with an awareness of the value of your time puts you in the optimal position for creating and developing projects that matter to you and serve the interests of your clients.

The alternative is to accept whatever happens to you, to react, to wait for other people, to hope and pray your phone rings or someone emails you for a job. Being the one who acts and seeks out action is, not surprisingly, far more rewarding.

Think of any successful freelancer you can name off the top of your head. Chances are you know their name because of what they do, and you can point to a recent example of their work or know of a recent client of theirs whom they helped. That's the result of an action bias.

GIGGING

part four

GIGGING

....

Where to work when you can work
from anywhere

WAY, WAY BACK at the beginning of the digital age, in the mid-to-late nineties when the Internet first became a thing, stories appeared online about people making a living off their blogs, or their Internet business, upping stakes and becoming "digital nomads". You see the same stories today, even in print.

The idea of living and working from anywhere — because the tools of a laptop, an Internet connection and a website enabled it — became the holy grail for a lot of freelancers, as well as people hoping to avoid or escape the rat race of the office/desk bound 9-5 work regime.

Images of people sitting on the beach, laptop literally on their laps while they gaze at some azure blue shoreline in Thailand or Bali suddenly became popular. And a raft of first-movers — creative, nomadic souls who had the right time, offer and mindset to produce some kind of content that hit the zeitgeist of the times — started "sharing"/advertising their recipes for how they left office routine behind for a life of adventure on the road. Their blogs boasted stories, pictures and news from remote outposts in Costa Rica, Laos or maybe Austin, Texas, and countless other off-the-beaten path destinations most people dreamed of going to.

People like Tim Ferris were out there advertising their formulas for working a four-hour week, and breaking their lives down into little monthly challenges or modular learning experiments, learning how to tango in Buenos Aires one month, mastering four foreign languages the next. All because their awesome Internet businesses paid them tens of thousands of dollars a month and they could go anywhere, do anything and live free.

It was — and still is — a captivating illusion and powerful fantasy that cons a lot of people into thinking it can happen to them too. All they need to do is save up a few months living costs, find a country where they can live cheaply, launch their blog/web-based business and presto! The dollars start piling up in your PayPal account and you're free.

Of course, this is rarely how it works out. And while there will always be the persistent few who moved first, or faster, or simply had the luck and advantages you need to make this kind of lifestyle work out, the vast majority of real freelancers will discover that working from anywhere isn't all it's cracked up to be.

Home is where the heart
~and likely your first customers are

Having a home base (which can be literally a space in your home, or a co-working space, or sublease, or table in a local cafe...) brings a lot of advantages you won't get on a sandy beach in a foreign country. Freelancing in the same town where you grew up may not feel glamorous, but it has many advantages often erroneously discounted by the digital nomadic set.

To begin with, working from a home base likely means you have a built-in network around you. This probably includes friends, family, former colleagues and eventually clients. Do not underestimate the power and value of this network. In addition to the tangible financial benefits it can confer through referrals, introductions and actual contracts from people you know who want to see you succeed, there are equally important, intangible benefits like feeling a part of a community, being close to family, and maintaining and developing long-term relationships with friends, or romantic partners.

I can't count the number of times I've benefitted from referrals through friends and clients who bring me with them when they change jobs. I was hired by my accountant to shoot his wedding, by my dentist to do her office portraits and by my child's daycare centre to shoot the class photos. I got one of my best clients from a client who went to work for a new company and brought me with her. Being local just creates so many opportunities to build and develop long-term relationships with clients that it's hard to beat.

I got most of my business because I built up my local network and let people know I was available. Not all kinds of freelancers have businesses that are as closely related to being a local supplier as mine is, but most freelancers benefit from being in a place long enough to develop a local network. Even if your business model is based on offering an online service, it is still incredibly helpful to have people you can meet and network with locally who can give you that early support when you are just starting out. Despite the ease with which many kinds of jobs can be outsourced to anyone with an Internet connection, many clients still prefer having someone local whom they can call (in the same time zone) and meet in person if necessary. Just knowing that their supplier is not too far out of reach gives them psychological comfort.

Working from a home base also grounds you and helps you through the hard times when it seems there are no contracts coming your way. It gives you closer and more immediate access to more traditional employment should you decide you want to return to working a regular job and makes it easier for you to do a lot of little things you may forget are important when you live a constantly nomadic existence.

Things like growing some of your own food in a garden and cooking at home, or having your own, high-speed connection to the Internet you can rely on and pay for. Things like building a workout regime into your lifestyle that keeps you active, fit and energized and gives you the mental breaks from your work you need. Things like feeling confident and vital from knowing that you are in a place where you have strong connections you can actively develop and maintain.

Ultimately, you can choose to try out both. Maybe you are living in a city with really very few economic prospects and no valuable networks to speak of. Maybe you are still in search of your tribe. Definitely go out and find it. It is out there. But at some point in time, when you find a place in the world, and a few people around you that you can work with and who make you feel positive and happy and optimistic about your life and prospects, you can consider stopping awhile.

Travelling is one of the best ways to open yourself up to the world. Exploring, getting lost, having adventures, meeting new people, experiencing and learning about new cultures, languages, foods, customs is exhilarating and energizing and acts like growth hormones for your soul and your mind.

But even the lightest, airborne seed eventually needs to find somewhere with a bit of soil to take purchase and grow.

Working from home

This is not a paean to one of those fluorescent paper flyers you see posted on telephone poles shrieking: "Earn $12,000 a month working from home!" But there are many salient advantages to setting up a home office, from tax benefits to optimizing your time by sparing you the daily grind of a long commute. And the reality is that you will likely be working from home, at least when you first get going as a freelancer. Here are a few tips on how to make it a productive and positive experience for you, along with a few things to watch out for.

One of the most important things you can do for yourself when you're setting up your home office is to keep the space sacrosanct and dedicated to work and nothing else. For the same reason you don't bring work into the bedroom, don't bring the comforts and distractions of home into your office. How you choose to decorate the room is up to you, but whether you are a minimalist or love to fill your wall with crayon drawings by your kid (who really is going to be the next Picasso), dedicate whatever space you've allocated to being your home office purely to work. This is not only important for figuring out what portion of your household expenses you can justifiably write off for tax purposes, it also helps you do better, more focussed work. Both your body and mind will, in a short time, associate the space with doing work, which means that just being in the space will become a supportive habit for getting things done.

Optimize your space

Keep whatever system you've adopted for staying organized at hand. This may be an application you always have running on your computer, like Omnifocus, or just a simple Notepad, or it could be the more old-school (and eminently more portable) never-needs-charging solution I use, which is the aforementioned Big Black Book with unlined pages.

Don't share the space

You may have an arrangement where both you and your partner work independently from home, or together. But you need to have your own dedicated personal space. No matter how small your home office is, if it must be shared make sure that each of you has your own computer and desk. This will keep your mind focussed and free from having to do any kind of unnecessary searching when you sit down at someone else's desk and don't find things exactly as you left them.

Keep regular business hours

Even if no one is ever going to knock on your door except the FedEx guy bringing you your latest Amazon purchase, set up a work schedule and stick to it. Because it's your home, your business and your time, you can choose whatever schedule best suits your situation. Maybe you work in two shifts, one early morning to noon, then another later on once the kids are in bed. Maybe you stick to the conventional 9-to-5 with a one-hour lunch break. The actual hours you choose should correspond to the hours your customers like to work in, and you should be disciplined about sticking to that schedule every day. Just because you no longer have a "boss" doesn't mean you should start working half-days or taking boozy three-hour lunches. Whatever it is you're trying to do — write a book, build an online business, become an expert financial planner — you need to put in the hours. If you've read Malcolm Gladwell's book *Outliers*, you know about the "10,000 Hour Rule," which states that to become expert at anything requires at least 10,000 hours of practice. Even though this theory has been challenged and mastery is more than just practice, you will benefit from developing and maintaining a professional approach towards your own work. You'd better get going.

Write it off

Having a home office also confers tax advantages that give you the right to expense any reasonable portion of your household costs that can be attributed to the proper functioning of your business. Check your local tax ordinances for specific details, but this will certainly include things like computers, Internet access fees, telephones, office supplies, as well as the portion of electricity and other utility costs your office represents in your house expenses. You can even write off the portion of your home or apartment dedicated to running your business, meaning that even a percentage share of the interest on your mortgage is tax-deductible. When you run your own business, every dollar saved is a dollar more you earn. So it would be careless and foolish not to take advantage of whatever tax breaks you can get by operating out of your home. Take the time to learn what those advantages are.

Finally, working from home means that yes, you can work in your bathrobe, though I wouldn't recommend it. Especially in the beginning, as you transition from going out to work and get used to not having colleagues around, dressing as if you were going to work, even if no one will see you all day, is psychologically important to help you develop a sense of professionalism and confidence in yourself. Call it the "fake it to make it" approach to becoming a successful freelancer: getting up early, taking a shower and dressing as if you were going to meet with clients helps create a sense of purpose that pushes you to work harder to achieve your goals.

Working in cafés

It's called that third space — neither home nor the office — and it's where creative conversations and fruitful collisions are more likely to happen. It's also where a lot of freelancers find themselves working when the burden of solitude becomes too heavy, or when they just need a change of scenery from their home office.

(I'm writing this from the hotel lobby of the Omni Hotel, where I have a gig starting in about an hour. I'm listening to someone's idea of lively music, accompanied by the sound of the cappuccino machine frothing milk. The chair is comfy, but not great for writing. The marble cocktail table is a bit too high and there's no plug in sight, so I'm working off my battery. But when I look up, I see strangers. And I like working around strangers. Because to me, strangers = possibilities — a potential new connection, friend, colleague, mentor. I've always valued meeting strangers, and working in public/third spaces is a simple way to make that happen more often.)

As you embark on your freelance life, you'll begin to explore parts of your city you may not have encountered before. You'll work in places where you used to play and only visited on "sanctioned" time off, like before/after work or on weekends. The effect can be a little jarring at first. You might experience a sense of dislocation or not really being where you are supposed to be. You may feel like you're an impostor, or that if you're sitting around in a café you're not really working. Get over it. If you're able to focus and do the work, you're not a fake. You're trying to be something, and as Miguel de Unamuno, the Spanish philosopher and author, once said (in a note I taped on the inside bottom of my desk drawer): "Just because you haven't made it yet does not mean you are not great. The fact that you are trying to be great makes you great."

That said, some kinds of work lend themselves more readily to working in a café than others. To help guide you through the process, here's a list of pros and cons I've developed after spending more than a decade freelancing (and downing hectolitres of black coffee).

Pros and cons of working in a café:

Pros

- A refreshing change of scene — good for stimulating creativity.
- An opportunity for networking — you may meet a stranger, a friend, a potential collaborator or future client.
- It can be enjoyable in itself.
- Lower cost than renting office space — for under $5/day you can "rent" a table and get a cup of coffee.
- Offers more variety. You can work in a different café every day if you want to.
- Background white noise can help you concentrate.

Cons

- Tables too high, chairs too short — mismatched furniture is hard to work on.
- Access to plugs can be limited.
- Owners may not like you hanging around all day drinking one cup of coffee.
- Can be too noisy/distracting.
- Time wasted travelling/parking/finding a place to set up.
- More expensive than staying at home.
- Not private enough for many professional conversations.

Office space: Share, rent, own?

The final rung in the freelancing ladder to working is, of course, having your own away-from-home office. You may never get there, and that's okay. Just as the home office space can be anything from a basement nook under the stairs to a stand-alone separate studio structure in the backyard, your out-of-home office can take many different forms.

Ultimately, the primary purpose of working outside your home is to break out of work habits that reinforce isolation. While certain kinds of focussed work require, or benefit from, the elimination of distractions and the effect of isolation, the very best ideas and work you produce will come through interactions with others. You can achieve this in any number of ways in our connected age, but one shortcut to interaction is simply working in the same physical space as other creative people.

Look into sharing office space with other related freelancers — perhaps people who do the same kind of work you do, or better yet, complementary work. A photographer may pair up with a videographer, copywriter, graphic artist, maybe a translator and a web developer. The obvious advantage here is that you've got a de facto digital marketing agency should you land a client looking for additional services, but more realistically, you've got creative people around you with whom you may discover the opportunity to collaborate. Working alongside other independent creatives allows you to take advantage of what Steven Johnson, author of *Where Good Ideas Come From*, calls the "adjacent possible."

Creative collisions

The adjacent possible is a concept originally drawn from the work of a biologist, Stuart Kauffman, to explain the biodiversity on the planet. While studying molecules and the origins of life on earth, Kauffman arrived at the theory that things evolve only within the bounds of the adjacent possibilities. Transformation occurs, but not without influence from what is in the nearby vicinity of the possible. Each new facet of an evolving life form creates different possible interactions. Multiply the interactions on a massive scale over millennia, and you have an explanation for how life on earth has evolved by encountering and exploring not the vast potential of the universe all at once, but simply the next nearest thing at any one time, continuously.

Steven Johnson took that insight and applied it to how ideas evolve. Having and developing a good idea is a process that involves searching for the next, nearest ideas to your own. In other words, what happens when you share ideas in conversation with someone else? You are, effectively, exploring the adjacent possible. Sometimes your ideas are improved, sometimes you improve each other's ideas, and sometimes your exploration leads you to abandon your original idea in favour of the newer one reshaped by the collision of thoughts and words with another.

Steven Johnson writes: "The trick to having good ideas is not to sit around in glorious isolation and try to think big thoughts. The trick is to get more parts on the table.... figure out ways to explore the edges of possibility that surround you. This can be as simple as changing the physical environment you work in, or cultivating a specific kind of social network, or maintaining certain habits in the way you seek out and store information."

You can find shared office space through Craigslist ads looking for co-workers, by walking through loft-style buildings in your city where you know there are clusters of people working the way you work, or by joining one of the popular co-working spaces, such as WeWork or SharedDesk or Breather. Just do a search for "co-working space YOUR CITY" and you'll quickly find a space that suits your specific needs, budget and location.

Planning: Begin with the end in mind

If you read Stephen R. Covey's seminal work, *The 7 Habits of Highly Effective People*, you may recall the concept of beginning with the end in mind: it's his second habit. The concept is simple: engage your imagination in visualizing what the outcome of the endeavour you are about to embark upon actually looks like. In this case, it's your new life as a freelancer. It is a powerful technique for allaying your fears and anxieties, and providing you with an internal compass as you find your own way forward.

All this requires is using your imagination. I've noticed that imaginative capacity is not something that people exercise often enough, if at all. Using your imagination, however, is a core skill anyone seeking to invent a new life must develop. So you might as well start practicing as soon as you can.

Luckily, imagination and the creative faculty it is fuelled by are inherently human features. If you are lucky enough to have contact with any young children, you will see that their minds are incredibly inventive and imaginative places. Take away the tablets and the devices and as soon as the complaining stops, the kids will be on to a new game using whatever items they have at hand. They will invent worlds to play in and fill them with the creatures from their imaginations.

I will let you in on a little secret: freelancing is fun. It's a lot of fun. It's varied, it's flexible, it's engaging, and no matter what service you are delivering, it requires you to use more than just one dimension of your intellectual capacity. Yes, work can be enjoyable and fun and there's nothing wrong with thinking of it that way.

But to get there, from wherever here is for you, you first need to imagine it. See yourself doing it. Imagine an ideal day. Imagine what your clients are saying about you. What do you most want to be known for? What will they say about you when they refer you on to others?

Beginning with the end in mind is how you get to a strong starting point. When you are running your successful freelance business, where are you working from? Are you alone, or surrounded by colleagues and other freelancers? Who are you connecting with? How are your days structured? The more you can imagine what the successful outcome of your freelancing experiment looks like, the more likely you will be to actually convert that vision into reality.

I am not implying that your future it will come to pass just by imagining it. I am not recommending you purchase some crystals and expect to be successful because you have a positive attitude in life. Having a positive outlook is helpful, of course, and I don't think you can really transform yourself without it, but it's not how change happens. Positive thinking is a precondition for change.

Success doesn't "happen" to anyone. It is something that proactive people make happen, and key to its eventual arrival is first having visualized what it looks and feels like.

But don't be fooled by the word "end". You're never really finished at this task. It is simply a way of placing a focus just a little past your present reach. As you develop and grow, return to your vision. You can enhance it, calibrate the colours, and make adjustments according to your now new reality. Your imagination is your buffer, an invisible force field gently pushing away the obstacles just ahead of you. The more you use it, the stronger it becomes.

We often hear stories about "visionary" leaders. These are simply people possessed with a powerful imagination they have cultivated and developed through discipline and practice. We call them visionaries because their visions are so big and encompassing they carry us along with them. We can literally see the world they are imagining, and through their organizations they co-opt our help into making their vision a shared one.

So take a breath, sit somewhere comfortable and before you do anything else, close your eyes and begin imagining what you want to become. Build out the new world you are going to inhabit. Imagine in as much detail as you can, what you look like, who you are talking to, how you are reacting and going about your day as a freelancer.

View it from as many different angles as possible — you are in effect creating a 3D model for your future self — until it is so clear in your mind it that it feels as real to you as the chair you are sitting on right now, or this book (or e-reader) you are holding in your hands.

If you can see it clearly in your mind, you've already begun building your business.

Forget the business plan

Despite what you may have read, seen in movies or heard about from business coaches and gurus, a business plan for a freelancer is virtually worthless — at least, in my opinion.

A lot of people spend an inordinate amount of time trying to cobble one together, thinking it somehow provides a guarantee of success.

It doesn't. It's just a bunch of words and numbers you put down to make yourself feel good, most of which you invent. If you have ever applied for a government grant or bursary to start up a business, these words and numbers are paramount. To me, that's a clear signal that business plans are largely irrelevant to the actual development of a business, and mainly important to bureaucrats.

I'm not saying you shouldn't think about what you're going to do and how you're going to do it. You've already done that in Part II of this book, and most of what you're reading is about doing just that. What I am saying is that in nearly all cases, but especially for freelancers who are unlikely to be looking for an investor, writing a business plan is largely an exercise in creative writing.

If your business is about work you've chosen to do because you recognize a need and because you're passionate about doing it and being an entrepreneur, a business plan won't help you. (And by the way, neither will an MBA.)

What is a business plan for?

Okay, so before I can convince you to abandon traditional wisdom, I should prove to you that I know what I'm talking about.

A business plan is supposed to help you define your business idea/proposal. You're supposed to be able to articulate clearly what it is you're planning to do, how you're going to do it, and most importantly, why it's a good idea. What problem are you solving? What solution are you bringing to the market that doesn't exist yet, or that you can do better than what's already out there?

These are good things to think about, and by all means, you should write the answers down. But this process is not really going to help you actually get your business up and running.

Starting a business is work. It's action. It's all about execution. A business plan is not execution.

Places that support entrepreneurs and government websites will often lead you to online templates for writing business plans. I know, because I tried to complete several over the years before I realized how useless they were.

Besides the above, the other components of a business plan are:

1. Problem identification and definition

2. Business structure (e.g. sole proprietorship, partnership, corporation)

3. A detailed description of the business structure, management team (ha ha), assets, etc.

4. A detailed look at the competitive situation around you. Who else is doing what you're trying to do? How do they operate?

5. A description of what you're going to do and how you're going to do it.

6. A description of your target market: who they are, how you're going to reach them, what you're going to do to make it work.

7. A financial plan. How much is it going to cost you? How are you going to fund it? How much money is it going to start bringing in and when?

That last point is probably the most ludicrous. You won't know how much money your business will bring in until you start doing it. If the business plan is supposed to help you decide whether you should do it, then you're going to have to make that part up. If it isn't, then you don't need it because you're going to find out the hard way. The real way. By adding one client at a time and learning, in real time, what they care about, what they don't care about, why they chose you and what they want more of.

Writing a business plan won't teach you anything compared to what you'll learn from having 10 conversations with people in your target market who you think might become your customers.

And that's the point. Everything you do should be focussed on getting real feedback and making real connections with real people.

You can talk about target markets and operations management and supply chain and all that stuff, but the only thing that matters to a business is having customers who care enough about what you have to sell to find you and give you their money. No matter how big your addressable market is, it's made up of individuals. You need to think about and connect with as many as possible, one by one.

"But wait," you may respond. "I'm not setting up a business-to-consumer (B2C) type business. I'm starting up a business-to-business (B2B) company. I'm selling to businesses, not individuals."

Think again. Behind every business is a group of real people. Behind every "yes" is someone you have successfully connected with.

A business plan won't help you get there.

Understand how you're going to set yourself up? Fine, go out and get 20 customers, then figure out whether you need to register as a corporation or not.

Understand your management team? Well, it's just you, so unless you have a multiple personality disorder, you don't need to write it down. You're going to be responsible for everything. Check.

Understand the competition? Fine. Worth looking into, but it can, and often does, lead you to the wrong conclusions. Having a lot of competitors can be the sign of either a healthy market with strong demand or a saturated market with diminishing returns. In either case, it's what you do with the information that matters most.

Understand your market? You don't know until you meet them. You need to meet them. Period.

Understand your financial situation? Expect lumpy uneven costs and revenues. You'll spend more in the beginning, then even more when you're doing well. Your revenue will come in fits and spurts: at times it will be less than you think you need, then it will surprise you with a bonanza from more clients than you can handle.

Not having a business plan doesn't mean you don't think about or plan for your future. Freelancing means recognizing and accepting that you live in an unpredictable world. I personally don't think it's that different than having a regular full-time job. The difference is, rather than being concerned with the future stability of your employment status, you are concerned with getting your next gig, and then the one after that. You ensure your future better by doing your work, and executing daily on your projects, by doing, rather than investing a lot of time and energy in a document that at best can only deliver a false sense of security and a best guess at the future.

The real danger of a business plan is that you begin to operate based on its initial assumptions and fail to maintain the critical engagement and response to the actual operating environment you find yourself in. The best business plan you can have is to stay alert, stay active and stay focussed on building your business, one client at a time.

Trust yourself and the new habits and processes you build into your daily life. These are going to help you and your freelancing career much more than any fill-in-the-blanks business plan template ever will.

There is no blueprint for your success because only you can decide what success is. I believe that as long as you can keep going, you're already well on your way to success. So don't fear the future, and don't feel naked because you've launched a freelancing life without a business plan.

RIGHT PLACE, RIGHT TIME

I once had a gig doing business development for a start-up that had developed an app for the travel industry. I was hired by the founder, who had been grounded due to some health issues and was looking for someone to be her legs in the field. Having experience in travel (my adventure tour leading days) and as a co-founder of a (now defunct) start-up in online art sales, I felt reasonably qualified to take on the contract. One of the pressing issues for the company was an upcoming travel show being held at the Bellagio in Las Vegas by the Virtuoso Network, a network of high-end luxury travel agencies with 1,700 preferred partners — hotels, tour operators, cruise lines, etc.. Every year the group hosts Virtuoso Travel Week, always in Las Vegas, always at the Bellagio, bringing together the entire network for a mad week of meetings, selling, networking and partying and doing billions of dollars of business. In short, being present would be a major coup for this company: the people attending were exactly the ones we were trying to connect with and sell the app to.

Members Only

There was just one catch. Virtuoso is a private, invitation-only group, and the event is closed to non-members. The company that hired me was not a member, and was unlikely to become one before the show, which was only a few weeks away. We knew one or two people at some of the member companies, and through them, managed to get our hands on a directory of attendees. We spent the weeks leading up to the event doing cold calls and emailing to prospects. We managed to line up about 15 confirmed meetings by saying we'd be onsite and happy to meet them to demo the app in person if we could.

There was no room at the Bellagio, but luckily there was a room available in an adjacent hotel, the Vdara, with a passageway connecting the two hotels. Calling ahead, I asked the receptionist where in the Bellagio I could meet someone, and found out that a popular piano bar was centrally located in the middle of the casino. So we booked our meetings for mid-mornings at the piano bar.

Only later did I realize how lucky that location would turn out to be.

The way Virtuoso Travel Week works, the days are spent in 90-second meetings, beginning at 8:00 a.m. and running straight through to 4:00 pm. Inside a giant conference room, the world is laid out before the network. At one side of the table, travel agents representing Europe sit in one long line, agents from South America in another line, and so on, for every region of the world. Down the other aisle sit the sellers — the tour operators, hotel owners, cruise line promoters — pitching their particular products to targeted travel agents with the hope of securing new partners who will then re-sell their tours, or hotels or cruises.

As you can imagine, the days are exhausting.

But not for the boss, of course. The boss or owner of the company usually shows up with staff who do the heavy lifting in these speed-dating meetings. So when someone like us calls ahead to ask for a meeting at the piano bar in the Bellagio, they agree because they've got the time. The piano bar is a nice place to hang out, and, as it turns out, a very popular after-hours watering hole.

However, the piano bar is missing a few essential things, like enough chairs and tables to accommodate the hordes that descend on it after the meetings. I set up at a large table there as my office for the day, so I found myself in the enviable position of having something that all of my prospects really needed: table space and an extra chair. Suddenly I was the most popular guy in the bar. All I asked for in return for sharing my space was a chance to show them the new app I was there to promote.

In other words, just being there was all it took to double the number of meetings I was able to arrange, and increase my reach into the exclusive, members-only pool of Virtuoso Network. Access is everything, and sometimes, all it takes to get that access is a comfortable space to sit down and enjoy a drink after spending a long day on your feet.

Most problems aren't really problems

Here are a few objections that I consider fake problems:

- You don't have enough money to start.
- You don't have a good enough idea.
- You don't have the time.
- You don't have a place to work.
- You're missing X piece of gear or equipment.

Adopting a "start early" mindset can help you get past this kind of self-defeating thinking.

The "start early" concept is the antithesis of the thinking that holds a lot of people back from ever even beginning to do the work they want to do. It is the opposite of thinking that you aren't ready, don't have enough money, time, ideas, space, gear, creativity to start. It is grounded in one solid belief: you can only get what you don't have now once you begin and are on your way.

First, recognize that the "problems" that are holding you back are really just a form of procrastination. Stop waiting for the stars to align perfectly. They won't. Now is the time for you to begin living your life the way you want to live it. You need to start first, before you have proof it's possible. You become the proof by doing it.

Believe that you have enough now to start. You don't need to know the full length of the journey. All you need to do is put one foot in front of the other and have the strength and drive to keep going.

Start with an MVP (minimally viable product) — the most basic version of what you can offer. Get it out there, test it with real customers, ask for and take feedback (good and bad), reworking your idea with the knowledge you gain from your current (and future) customers.

It's never too late to start anything... so why not now? (There's a pod-cast all about doing just that by Amy Jo Martin, amyjomartin.com.) Belief precedes action; you have to believe you can do something before you can make it real.

> "Tough physical training aside, there aren't many disciplines where it's truly too late to start. Mathematicians, painters, writers, playwrights — there are always people that didn't start making great work until their 60s or beyond. If you want to do something, you can."

—Charles Chu (The Open Circle)

Want to write a book? Just do it, little by little, every day. Whether you aim for a certain word count (750 words a day), or decide to write it chapter by chapter, just plugging away at it (ideally in the morning when the mind is fresh, creative and your time is uninter-rupted) will get it done.

Start a blog? Don't research yourself into paralysis. Do you have a topic you care enough about and think about every day? Can you write a sentence? Do you want to communicate with others and share insights and ideas? Get started. It's never been easier to launch a blog. You may not be have any subscribers. That's immaterial. The trick is to just do it and keep on doing it. It builds into a strong habit that underpins many others.

Whatever you intend to do, you can start much sooner than you think.

Be clear with your objectives and set simple goals to get started. Don't talk yourself out of moving forward and making progress towards your goals, regardless of how ready you feel. Fake problems have a way of creeping up exactly when you are about to make a break-through. It's as if the mind wants to slow things down and keep you where you are just as you are about to grow. Challenges will come and continue to come along as you grow from nothing to something. Expect it, adapt to them, but acknowledge that what look like problems rarely are. Just put your shoulder into it and push forward.

Freelancer strategies: What kind of freelancer are you?

There are many different ways to get into freelancing. Taking a moment to figure out what kind of freelancer you are will have a big impact on how quickly and how successfully you build and develop your freelancing business.

Take a moment to ask yourself how and why you came to be holding this book in your hands:

1. Are you an accidental freelancer? Someone who fell into freelancing because you suddenly found yourself without a job?

2. Are you a hobbyist turned professional freelancer, who slowly and steadfastly has developed a skill and passion for making or doing something that people need and are willing to pay you for?

3. Are you a portfolio manager freelancer, looking to generate some side income in parallel to your day job? In other words, are you looking to start a "side hustle"?

4. Are you a pirate freelancer, prioritizing your personal autonomy and freedom over all other options and deliberately seeking work that supports and enables your choice?

5. Are you a nomadic freelancer because it is the only way you can earn income while satisfying your larger goals of travelling and living on the road?

6. Are you a lifestyle freelancer, choosing to work fewer hours? To spend more time at home with your family? To have no boss? To work on your own schedule?

7. Are you a freelancer-for-fun, doing something in your spare time or to keep you busy in your retirement? Do you feel that getting paid is a nice-to-have bonus, but not essential?

8. Are you a "kind-of" freelancer, hanging your sign on the door and hoping that someone will come by and give you some business?

9. Are you a freelancer of last resort, with the choice thrust upon you, because there are no good jobs around and you need to do something to survive?

10. Or are you a purposeful freelancer, choosing among a set of viable options that include salaried jobs, because the work you have chosen to do offers the best balance of autonomy, wealth creation and opportunity for you to fulfill your purpose?

Being honest with yourself in the beginning will help you understand what you can hope to get out of reading this book, and ultimately, what you can get out of your freelancing practice. A large part of how well you develop your freelancing business is determined by how much it matters to you. And that, in turn, is linked to why you are doing it in the first place.

Why you shouldn't just say yes to everything

When I first started working as a freelance photographer, all I thought about was getting gigs. I wasn't thinking of what my clients' problems were, or what I could bring to help them solve them. I was letting them do all the work. I figured that if they were looking for a photographer, they knew what they wanted and all I had to do was respond and be available. As a result, my approach to clients was reactive. I was just doing what I thought all photographers/freelancers did by saying yes whenever anyone contacted me about some possible work.

Do you do weddings? Yes!

Product shoots? Yes!

Events, conferences, headshots, baptisms, bar mitzvahs, anniversary parties, real estate photography, family portraits, birthdays, pet portraits? Yes, yes, yes, yes!

This kind of thinking is common to first-time freelancers. And while it's true that being available is part of the solution, it's really just the beginning and it's not enough to set you apart from your competitors, which is essential for making your business work in the long term. Being available is table stakes in the gig economy, especially at the outset, but as a strategy for developing your career as a freelancer, it's just the first step.

Saying yes to everything is not a great strategy because it means you never get known for any one thing. You get known as the guy/girl who says yes, which means you may get a lot of volume but you are always vulnerable when it comes to pricing, since your clients will always discount your work against what a specialist might charge.

Understand your client's problem — and solve it

Everything changes, however, when you recognize that you are not in business just to say yes to everyone; you're there to solve a specific problem. When you start thinking in terms of problems your clients have, the solutions you propose automatically become more valuable.

For example, I began to realize that events and conferences were really where I shone. I understood that these clients were different from, say, a bride hunting for a wedding photographer or a company looking for someone to do a series of headshots. What made them different was what they needed me for, which translated into what their problem really was.

Event managers and conference organizers have one main problem that a photographer can help with: making their event look like it's worth attending. Whether the event is a product launch or some kind of experiential marketing concept or a conference for IT managers, the issue all these organizers face is the same: they need people coming in through the door to sell as an audience to their sponsors, or to pay for the event itself. Audiences for my clients' events are spoiled for choice, so the way event organizers differentiate themselves is by investing in cool locations, offering great content and a chance to meet people their audience cares about, because it will help them expand their professional network or provide them with business or learning opportunities. Ideally, their conference will appear to promise all of the above. All of these needs need to be communicated well through images that will accompany emails, websites, ads and other marketing collateral that will be sent out in anticipation of the event as they are marketing it. Photographs showing happy smiling people looking engaged and networking in interesting venues are small but important pieces of the marketing kit that help my clients do their jobs better. I solve a simple problem. But knowing that, I can work that solution into any conversation I have with a prospective client. Offering a solution to a problem I understand always makes a client feel better and instantly creates a better rapport. They feel understood. You win their trust. And usually the business follows not far behind.

So I specialize in event and conference photography. Sure, it means I do fewer weddings, where there is also good money to be made, but the clients I do serve, I serve very well, and they know it. I focus on solving their problem. When they call me, they know we can talk about how I will solve their problem.

Another advantage to this kind of "solution selling" is that price is no longer the top discussion point with clients. Of course, you still have to offer competitive prices, and you will still be asked to quote, but your price is not the deal-breaker it would be if it was the only way you could distinguish yourself from the competition.

Think of your own freelancing business in terms of the problem it solves. Who are you helping? How exactly? Spell it out for yourself and then look for the clients you know have the problem you can solve.

In the best-case scenario...

Most of the time when people think about the future, they think, "In the worst-case scenario..." Then they map out all the things that could go wrong before deciding whether they will do whatever it is they are considering doing.

"Worst-case scenario thinking" is a way of assessing the potential cost of any action taken, trying to balance out the potential gain against the worst possible outcome if everything goes wrong. We all build plans to accommodate that worst-case scenario, so we are prepared and don't have to worry about it.

There is merit in being prepared and having considered possible outcomes from any course of action. But why start with that? Why not assume the best-case scenario first?

Doesn't that just feel intrinsically more exciting and interesting? When you think "best-case scenario," you activate optimism and the energy that goes with it. You greet your future with open arms and a smile. You're still getting ready, but you're preparing for success. You're preparing for things to go really, really well.

Beginning with a "best-case scenario" sets the tone for you to see things through the filter of success, rather than the veil of failure. Once you've done this, you can review the other possibilities. Of course things could go wrong, but probably not as wrong as you think they could, and in the wrong there may be a few things that went right.

Optimism and cautious pessimism are ways of perceiving reality. Both serve a purpose and have their adherents and believers. And like everything else, it's up to you to choose. But why not choose an encouraging outlook that raises your optimism and positivity?

Start small

Most projects are stillborn. You get excited about the idea and then fall into the drop-off zone when your initial excitement wears off and you have to swim through a channel populated with doubts, fears and inertia. Many don't make it across.

When you think about becoming a freelancer, the same thing happens. You get excited, maybe a little bit scared, nervous, happy — and then it hits you.

What the hell am I thinking?

You're filled with dread. Your stomach turns and sinks. You suddenly realize how much work you have ahead of you. I have to update my LinkedIn profile. I have to get on Twitter! I hate Twitter. I have to stop wasting time on Facebook. I have to learn how to run ads on Facebook? I need a new profile picture. I need a website! SHHHH-HH!

The tyranny of your unchecked to-do list overwhelms you, and stops you in your tracks. For days, weeks. Months even.

Don't let this happen to you.

The best advice I would give to 10-year-ago me is to start small.

Yes, you want a gorgeous website, with a suite of fully automated marketing tools embedded, that will run itself and just deliver hot leads who are desperate to send you money. But in the meantime, you're stuck with a sort of okay-looking WordPress theme you got for free and aren't quite sure what to do with. That's okay.

Useful first, pretty later

Here's another piece of very useful advice I wish someone had told me 10 years ago: be useful first, pretty later. Launch a workable, useful product/service out into the world as fast as you can and start bringing in revenue. When you get more revenue, you can invest in getting prettier things, fancier websites and more expensive gear.

But start small. Build a basic, simple website that has just enough about you and what you do for people to get interested enough to send you an email or actually call you. Put a clear, simple but value-adding proposition on your site telling people how to get in touch with you.

Small, simple steps, one after the other, will lead to greatness.

But worrying about looking great before you get started will leave you stranded on the desolate plains of high hopes and little action.

Better to do one thing well than lots of things not very well at all.

Be clear with your objectives, and set simple goals to get started.

And keep going.

Start with a slash

There's a proven strategy for getting your feet wet as a freelancer without diving right in: start a side business. Sean McCabe (seanwes.com) refers to it as "overlapping." World traveller and blogger Chris Guillebeau (chrisguillebeau.com) calls it a "side hustle." I call it "slashing," as in, "I'm a photographer/writer." It used to be called "moonlighting," but that term seems to have gone out of fashion. Regardless, it all means the same thing: starting out small, then working in off hours, weekends and/or evenings to test out your ideas and aptitude for starting your own business.

The advantage of this strategy is that it lowers your risk by giving you a chance to fail while you still have another job paying your rent or mortgage and putting food on the table. Building something slowly and cautiously this way suits a more risk-averse personality, though it also means the endeavour may take longer to get off the ground. For some, having a sideline (or two, or three) is great in itself, and that's okay too if you can make it work.

One of the things you need to watch out for if you take a side hustle approach to freelancing is complacency. By definition, your freelance career is not your central focus, so you may feel less pressure to work through the hard parts. It can feel a little too safe. Even if it's just something you are doing on the side for now, for a little spare change, if you can see yourself doing it full-time one day, then it's best to treat it that way from the start. Just because you're doing it in your spare time doesn't mean it should only get spare attention. When you're doing it, all the same things I've talked about earlier in this book apply. Focus, determination, stick-with-it-ness and drive are just as important, if not more, when the gigging is less frequent and your time is split between working somewhere and your project.

Instigate, or work for someone who does

In his course on freelancing, Seth Godin talks about being an insti-gator, making a ruckus, being the one who acts instead of the one who reacts. As an approach to life, this puts you in the driver's seat and casts your life not as a series of events that happen to you, but as a set of experiences you engineer and curate to add purposefulness to everything you do. For a freelancer, it represents the choice between going after business and letting (hoping) it comes to you.

To instigate doesn't necessarily mean you are going to run a start-up or lead a million-person march (though, of course, it can). It is fun-damentally about taking a stance. An attitude. It means embodying the belief that you will take and provoke action instead of just being acted upon. Instigating may mean, for example, writing a blog post with a call to action that requires that the reader either do something or purposefully ignore you.

And ignore you, many will. Because that's almost always the easier path for most people. Ignoring something or someone is how people insulate themselves from change. Ignore, deny, avoid, and ultimately defend against.

Luckily, these people are not your customers. They may become your customers one day, when the tide of inevitability has washed com-pletely over them, but for the time it matters, your task is not to seek to convert those who ignore, but to spark reactions and enlist the support of the change-makers — the ones who will try something new if it holds the promise of being an improvement on the old way of doing things. The ones who are actively looking for solutions, who know they have a problem, and who are willing and able to pay to have the problem solved — these are your customers.

You can choose to lead or follow

If you choose not to instigate, you are effectively choosing to follow those who do. In the beginning, you may tell yourself you don't have anything to instigate; you're too inexperienced, too shy, too uncertain. How you feel may matter a lot to you, but the audiences you are trying to reach don't care how you feel. What they care about — what all customers care about — is their problem, their want, their need being solved, met or fulfilled. Your feelings never enter the picture.

A successful freelancer is one who has customers. Once that trust is earned, that customer will probably return. As an instigator, you have the opportunity to enlarge the relationship. What else does the customer need? Does your customer have colleagues in other departments who might also need what you have to offer? Do you, as a freelancer, know other freelancers who sell what your customer needs? The trick, of course, is to look. And keep looking.

Ask questions, listen, pay attention. Seek to understand the business your customer is in. Anticipate changes or problems they may face. Apply proven solutions you've learned from other customers like them. Probe. That's what the instigator does. That's what an instigator strategy looks like. Waiting for the phone to ring is a strategy, but not a very good one.

Be the hub

As you embark on your freelance journey, you will soon encounter other freelancers. Getting to know them — what they specialize in, how they operate, what their rates are — will help you, whether they are your direct competitors or potential collaborators or, as often happens, both.

Ultimately, being connected to a large pool of people like you who offer similar and complementary services enables you to bring more value to your clients. Who you know matters as much as what you know, and provides you with an avenue for growth that allows you to break free from what I would call the "hourly constraint" that many freelancers face.

Let me explain. There are only so many hours in a day, and only so many of those you can actually allocate to revenue-generating work and get paid for. Having a curated list of people you know, trust and can establish a good working relationship with is a way to marginally increase your revenues. If you get good at getting work, you may soon find you have more work than you alone can handle. At that point, you have a few choices to make: hire an employee, partner up, outsource or refer.

Let's look at all four possible scenarios.

Hiring

Hiring someone to join your freelance business is a big step. With the additional resources you can, of course, take on more work, but now you're also responsible for keeping that workflow going (and growing) to maintain the cost of the new hire and the additional profit he or she brings in. There are many factors to consider when making a hire, not least of which is anticipated revenues and a time frame that justifies the additional cost and hassle factor involved with bringing someone on board. Here are some things you will need to consider:

- Cultural fit. Even if it's only the two of you in the beginning, that's enough space between people to create a culture. Do you get along? Does your hire reflect and share your values and epitomize the key aspects of your brand as the freelancer that you are? Will he or she project the same level of professionalism, enthusiasm, competency and passion in front of a client as you do?

- How and where will you work? Will you be sharing a space or be a virtual team working in your separate home offices?

- What are the legal requirements for hiring an employee? How will you handle processing for taxes, insurance, etc.?

Giddy up, partner!

You may find someone out there who thinks a lot like you do and who is also in a phase where they are looking for a business partner. Successful collaborations — which all good partnerships must be based on — are engines of growth and can drive your freelancing business to new heights. But if they don't work out as planned, they can also be a major drag on business and in the worst case, drive you out of business altogether. Choosing a business partner is in many ways akin to getting married, and the decision should not be taken lightly. Some factors to consider:

- Do you work well together? Does each of you offer complementary and necessary skills that combine to make your businesses stronger together than either of your businesses alone?

- Do you enhance each other's skill sets and bring greater value to a client when selling yourself as a team vs. a solo operator?

- Do you like working in collaboration with each other? Having a partner means more time spent discussing things and coming to an agreement on decisions you were previously able to take without asking anyone's opinion. Does having to do so now result in better decisions, or give you access to new realms you could not otherwise access?

Outsourcing

Outsourcing work to sub-suppliers, with you maintaining lead status and being solely responsible for the complete job, allows you to maintain an optimal level of control while still growing your mandates beyond what you could handle alone. While a new portion of your time will be spent on managing the project and acting as a liaison between your client and your suppliers, this is much less of a demand on your time than doing all the work yourself, if that were even possible. A few considerations to keep in mind:

- Do you trust the people you are outsourcing to? Will they have direct access to your client or will you always be the intermediary? Depending on the nature of the work, presenting your suppliers directly to your client can facilitate the overall functioning of the project (e.g. video production). This can work fine, provided you have in place some kind of agreement (ideally an independent contractor arrangement) whereby your client and your supplier both agree (in writing) to work through your collaboration, and neither is allowed to work with the other without your involvement for a defined period of time (at least two years). This is especially important if your suppliers are in client-facing roles or performing tasks that require a lot of client interaction.

- Have you vetted your suppliers? Can you vouch for them? Is their work up to your professional standards? Ultimately, anything you sub out and in turn deliver to your client as part of a larger service offering has to be on par with your brand. You are only as good as your weakest link, and if one of your sub-suppliers does a shoddy job or fails to deliver on a key client requirement, in the end you're the one who is both responsible and the ultimate loser, as your client is not likely to trust you with that kind of mandate again, if ever.

Referrals

Referring work to fellow freelancers or other businesses can also yield an incremental increase in your revenues. However, even more importantly than with an outsourced resource that you manage, you need a written agreement in place that defines the terms of the referral and explicitly spells out what you will be paid, for how long and on what terms. A standard referral fee, depending on your business, should be somewhere between 7 and 15% of the final value of the invoiced service, and include a term for how long the referral remains valid. Remember, referring a client to another freelancer or business is effectively a way of sending that client away. A client may wind up going back to your referral over and over again. You want the agreement you have in place to cover repeat business for at least a year, at the same rate or a negotiated rate that makes sense for both entities. Of course, you can, if you wish, simply bank a favour with a friend and leave monetary compensation out of it, but even with that kind of friendly arrangement you should at some point have a way of cashing in on the favour and a mechanism in place for ensuring you get the fair value of your referral, either through referrals back to you or a service you need or value.

Growing your network will always benefit your freelancing business in some way. For all of the above strategies, don't forget that you may also be on the receiving end. You may be the one having work referred to or being offered outsourced work on behalf of a fellow overloaded freelancer. Knowing who these other hubs are can be as important to your business as becoming one yourself.

Working with friends and family

Should you choose to work with a friend or family member when you start out freelancing, or go it on your own entirely?

Well..."that depends."

Ultimately, the choice is yours, and having done both, here are a few of the things I think you should watch out for.

Keep it in the family

If you have a strong and stable relationship with the family member(s) you've chosen to work with, good. You're going to need it. You can expect to get into a few screaming arguments and have at least one episode of the silent treatment.

I have often worked successfully with family, but not without some growing pains. A couple of my brothers and I started a business called Cocobros, selling and distributing coconut water throughout the city. We'd purchase excess inventory from an importer, usually a few pallets of coconut water (about 400 to 600 cases), and sell them to local stores, restaurants and hotels. It was an exciting business, mainly because it gave us a chance to knock on a lot of doors and really learn how to sell. We spent a lot of time together, either driving around in our delivery car or working the phones side by side. Working with family can be very rewarding. You know you can trust each other, and personally I take a special kind of pleasure from knowing I'm helping my family earn some money. But it is certainly not without its challenges.

Good communication is key, and if your family members aren't great communicators, then you'd better be or you could wind up in very awkward and uncomfortable situations that could have a limiting effect on your success. Frustration builds in silence, and you can expect a few blowouts now and then. One of my brothers and I once spent six hours in a car side by side not speaking after a particularly heated argument over how our business was going. You need the kind of relationship that can recover from that and bounce back relatively quickly. Otherwise, you may be putting too much strain on the relationship and you may be better off finding a non-family related partner.

No matter what your relationship, you need to establish right from the start who does what. Let's say you decide to set up a partnership and split everything 50/50. How does that work out in real terms? Usually the benefit of working with a partner is that you each bring something different and complementary to the arrangement. That likely means one person is going to spend more time doing sales, for example, and another will spend more time on the bookkeeping. Understand that everything has to get done between the two of you and be clear about playing to your strengths while not taking on more than your fair share of the work.

The best way to splinter a partnership and damage a relationship is not to be specific early on. Ask anyone who has ever had a partnership go wrong, and the first thing they will tell you is to sign a partners' agreement in the beginning that spells everything out. This should include what happens if/when one partner wants to leave early, or wants to bring someone else into the arrangement.

And remember, whatever happens, you're still family in the end. You can't just walk away and never look back. Well, you can, but it would be a terrible price to pay for what presumably began as an experiment in optimism.

If your partner also happens to be your wife/husband, you have even more factors to consider. What happens if it doesn't work out? How secure are you financially? Can you both afford to put all your eggs into one basket and work on the same business? And that's not even getting into what happens if you break up in real life. Will you stay together as a working couple if the marriage dissolves? Do you even want to think about that right now?

Best friends forever?

Working with friends entails similar risks, but also runs the risk of destroying the relationship if the enterprise fails to live up to expectations. One good idea could be to start out maintaining each other's independence and working collaboratively on projects when and where it makes sense to do so. While there is an advantage from a client's perspective to dealing with only one supplier on projects with a few moving parts, you can still work together and share ideas, space, software etc. without actually becoming business partners. And in most cases, that's probably what you should do.

I was once hired by a friend to be the co-founder of his start-up. It began very well and I think we both really enjoyed the experience, but as the business faltered and we struggled to find a good market fit for what we were trying to do, frustration crept in on both sides and communication broke down. Eventually, he wound up moving away and taking the business with him. While I was ready to keep working on it, he told me he was shutting it down. I accepted reluctantly, only to find out that after he left town he handed over my job to his (then) girlfriend. I was angry, embarrassed and felt betrayed. Luckily, we did have a contract in place and I was able to sell my shares in the company, but sadly the friendship didn't survive.

If/when you do decide to take your friendship up a level and form a small freelancing business together, then the same rules apply as they do for working with family.

Sign a partnership agreement, be clear about your expectations of each other and have the uncomfortable talks about money, ownership, equity, etc. up front. It wouldn't hurt to speak with a lawyer and an accountant.

And remember, no matter how awkward or uncomfortable you may feel about discussing what could happen if x, y and z go wrong, it's a whole lot worse doing that after x, y and z actually have gone wrong.

Embrace technology: Think digital

It's not (just) a slogan.

Even if you run an organic co-op, grow organic vegetables and sell them locally, delivered by bicycle, you'll still use technology to get the word out (email marketing), post updates about what's fresh (blog) and accept payment online (PayPal) for members to join your coop.

No matter what form your freelancing takes, it will involve digital technologies in some way. Rather than perceive the digital age as a threat or a problem, embrace it for what it can be — the best possible opportunity for you to genuinely thrive as an independent worker. This is a uniquely modern phenomenon, unthinkable just a few decades ago. Even today, many people still have not fully grasped how much powerful technology is available at very low cost, and how technology can unleash the virtually unlimited creative potential of individuals and societies as a whole.

There is no part of your business that will not be affected by digital technology. Everything from how you are structured to how you market, sell and deliver your services or goods will depend on digital technologies in some way, shape or form.

Mobile handsets (what we still anachronistically call "phones," though they are rarely used for talking any more) are how the vast majority of people interact with companies today. They browse, message, create and connect with companies, friends and lovers with that device in their hands. No matter what your business, you need to build it for a mobile world.

If it's not, it's already obsolete. Whether you think you're in a technology business or not, you are. Technology is pervasive, and will become increasingly more so.

I contend, with no hyperbole, that digital culture is human culture, and it is —and will continue to be — as transformative an influence on our world as the invention of language, agriculture and the industrial revolution.

You can choose to avoid it, ignore it (at your own peril), minimize its influence or embrace it. I think you already know which I would recommend.

How to learn any new technology fast (tip: don't read the manual)

It's hard to keep up with technology. No matter what field you're in, there are hungry tech entrepreneurs out there innovating in your space and creating new apps, gizmos and workflows that can make everything you currently do obsolete in six months. Aside from being a little overwhelming, it can be downright discouraging. You go to the trouble of learning a new software and before it's out of the box (anachronistic, I know), it's already outdated and you need to upgrade.

So how do you do it? The trick I've learned, mostly by emulating younger people, is go and get what I need, and no more.

It's a simple switch and makes perfect sense. I just wish I'd made it sooner. I've only just begun to realize that the way I learned when I was in school is now completely dépassé and not applicable to the way we learn anything today.

Let's back up and remember how we used to learn things

If you're not a millennial and were born any time before the advent of smartphones, you may have gone to school and done a research project using old-fashioned things like real libraries, encyclopaedias, sticky notes, pens and paper. You may have actually learned the Dewey Decimal system or had to follow around a librarian to show you how to find a book on a shelf somewhere in a room full of books. You may even have queued up to get access to the microfiche machines to peer through a tiny lens and stare at the super-magnified text from old newspapers and you may have thought that that was really cool. Weird, I know.

Let's say you were doing a history project about the causes of the First World War. You would rummage through index cards to find out where the books were that had stuff written about the topic you were looking for (what you'd call a hyperlink today), and then you'd walk to where those books or periodicals were, physically take them off the shelf and carry them back to your comfy cozy little nook in the library where you were camped out for the day (preferably near a window and across from a cute art history major).

It took energy and time to actually go and find the books and carry them, so to optimize, you took as many books as you could carry and made a huge pile on your workspace so you could go through each book and cull the tidbits you'd need to fill your paper with appropriate quotes and prove to your professors that you actually did research the subject you were writing about, and maybe even learned something.

Researching then looked a lot like this:

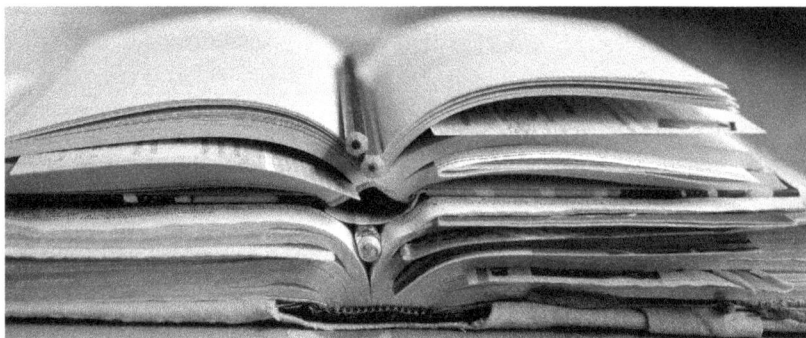

The whole process took forever, and you'd waste a lot of time poring over irrelevant text (what we called learning way back then) to unearth the one or two nuggets around which you'd build your thesis, and then you'd spend a lot more time trying not to copy what you read word for word by struggling to translate what you read into your own words. I'm not even going to go into the types of word processing machines you'd use, or what a drag it was to correct typos.

Get rid of your bookmarks

One of the bad habits associated with this kind of learning was a hoarding mentality. Gather more than you need, then winnow it down and parse it into something useful. The digital analogue to that today is bookmarking and wasting hours of your life organizing your bookmarks into folders you never revisit because it's always easier just to Google the thing you're looking for now rather than try to remember where you buried the nut you wanted to save for later.

And that's the point. You don't need to save any piece of information for later any more. First of all, later never comes because whatever tidbit or treasure trove of facts you squirrelled away can more readily be found by simply tapping out your search query again. More than likely, your find has been eclipsed by a newer, more relevant piece of information; if not, it will pop right back up where you can click through to it.

More importantly, how we consume information has completely changed from how we learned how to consume information before everything was digitized. Today we live in an era of information abundance. So we graze constantly. Access to the answer to every question is available anytime, virtually anywhere. Consider the implications of that statement. You can get the answer you need right now without moving more than your thumb and some slight stimulation to your optic nerves.

Where once you had to actually move your body, go to where books were stored, arduously decipher coded organizational systems to locate books, then risk paper cuts and allergic reactions to dust mites while leafing through pages, actually read something and then either photocopy it or transcribe it with your own hand to save it, now you just whip out your phone and look it up. With voice recognition, you don't even have to know how to write any more. You can just press a button, ask a question, then choose the best answer from the results delivered to you.

It's grab and go time

That's how learning happens today. It's fast, it's efficient and it's focussed on one thing at a time. Forget foraging and filling your basket full of all the roots, tubers, nuts and berries you can find 'cause the hard times are coming. We're never running out of food. You can just take a bite out of that apple and toss the rest. We're living in a resort where the buffet is always open and it's always all you can eat.

You don't need to save anything for later, you don't need to read through the manual and try to understand something all at once.

Just as you wouldn't tackle a huge project without first breaking it down into manageable tasks, you don't learn a new technology all at once. Whether it's image editing software (in my case) or a new customer relationship management (CRM) system, running an ad campaign on Twitter or just trying to figure out how the hell Snapchat is more than just a way to send gaggy animated videos of yourself doing stupid things, you need to treat whatever tool, app, program or device you have to work with like a project.

Just do the first next thing. Learn it, then repeat. What is the first next thing you need to learn to do right now to do what you have to do with the software or tool? Turn it into a question and Google it. You will almost certainly find pages full of results with links to (mostly free) YouTube channels, online courses, tutorials, infographics and step-by-step guides on Pinterest explaining how to do that one thing.

Throw away the manual

Forget trying to read technical manuals or help guides all in one go. It's pointless. You'll never remember anything past the third page (if you're particularly alert) and even that you'll probably have forgotten by the next day if you manage to stay awake long enough to get there. Reading a manual is basically like peering through the entrails of a disembowelled database. Every single potentiality is denoted and defined. Japanese tool, camera and car makers all seem particularly afflicted with the need to write confusingly detailed manuals that never seem able to answer the one question you need answered now. Which is really all you ever need.

"Just in case" is the death of learning

I used to try to learn everything at once. I am the kind of learner who wants to know it all. It's most likely a form of some undiagnosed obsessive-compulsive disorder. I have this need to put a fence around a field of knowledge and plough through it all, try to cram everything into my head at once just in case...just in case....(those words are the death of actually learning anything), just in case... I might need to know how to do this one thing some day.

You never get there. You never finish. I have hundreds of Google docs and spreadsheets I created trying to map out every social media tool out there, every online GTD software that could help me be more organized, work smarter, have it all covered in one place. And they are all incomplete, abandoned or so minutely detailed I can't even look at them without feeling stressed out.

Learning any big software app works the same way. If you get too fussy or too focussed or too stressed about trying to absorb it all, you fail. What works best? Ask the question about the one thing you want to learn now, then go now and learn that one thing and put it into practice right away. You may find you need to go back and relearn the same thing a few times before it sticks, but once it does, you're done. You've got it and now you can move on to the next niggling problem that you need to solve, and so on and so on.

It never ends, the changes keep coming, but by taking a bite-sized approach to learning (and life, really) rather than the impractical and unwieldy gather-as-much-as-possible-at-once, in time you will steadily build up a knowledge base in the one database you can't do without — your brain. And that little computer in there is still the most efficient, effective and productive tool you'll ever have in your arsenal of GTD hacks.

Technology for "non-techies"

There are technophiles and technophobes in the world, and without splicing the demographics too thinly, if you were born when phones still needed to be plugged into the wall and came with big curly tethers to a base, you're more likely to be on the technophobic side of the equation.

While that's understandable, given the rapid pace of change and the massive influence technology has had on just about every aspect of human life, freelancers can't afford to recuse themselves from learning something about technology with the excuse, "I'm just not very techie." You don't have to be a techie to use technology and you don't have to be born after 1989 to let technology into your life.

Technology does wonderful things for us, saving us time and effort and providing us with entertainment and frictionless experiences that once were onerous and tedious. Like fishing for coins to use a pay phone, or actually having to get up and change the channel on a TV. The horror.

Unlearn your fear of technology

"Fear has big eyes", my German father-in-law Otch always says when recommending how to approach a new challenge. So let's break down technology to its basic definition to help you understand what it is, and what it can do for you.

As with most words ending in "-ology", "technology" is a word with Greek origins:

Technology ("science of craft," from Greek τέχνη, techne, "art, skill, cunning of hand" and λογία, -logia) is the collection of techniques, skills, methods and processes used in the production of goods or services or in the accomplishment of objectives, such as scientific investigation. Technology can be the knowledge of techniques, processes, and the like, or it can be embedded in machines which can be operated without detailed knowledge of their workings. (Source: Wikipedia: Technology)

The important bit in that definition is "...technology...can be embedded in machines which can be operated without detailed knowledge of their workings." That means you can build a beautiful website using Wix or SquareSpace or Wordpress or Photoshelter without knowing how to program or code. In fact, there are really very few tools you need to master in order to use almost any piece of software (or software as a service) or app today. These are:

- Control A (PC) or Command A (Mac) to select all
- Control X (PC) or Command X (Mac) to cut
- Control V (PC) or Command V (Mac) to paste
- Control Z (PC) or Command Z (Mac) to undo
- The "Redo" button or command in the file menu

And how to use a keyboard, and a mouse or trackpad.

Just as knowing basic addition, subtraction, division and multiplication will get you through 80% of real life's math problems, even if you consider yourself "not a techie," knowing these basic shortcuts and tools on your computer will get you through 80% of your use of technology.

Here are some examples of how you "non-techies" are probably already using technology to improve workflow and your business as freelancers:

- Adding a calendar entry to your calendar
- Entering someone's contact details in your phone
- Googling anything
- Taking a photo or video
- Sending an email with a photo or video attachment
- Posting an update on Facebook or LinkedIn

Obviously, technology is so deeply embedded in how we live our lives that it has become almost invisible to us. If you're not doing any of the above, then you're probably not reading this book either. So, assuming you are doing those kinds of activities, you are using as much technology as most non-developers ever use and you already have all the skills you need to write a blog (in other words, your website), market yourself online, connect with and sell to prospects and find out anything about what you need to know when you need to know it.

Stop labelling yourself a "non-techie." Not knowing how to write code isn't a sin. More importantly, knowing how isn't a necessity. You can learn how to if you want to (check out Code Academy for an intro), but you already know everything you really need to know about technology.

Leverage automation

It may not seem important in the beginning, but at some point (maybe sooner than you think), you will find yourself busier than you want to be and looking for ways to reduce your workload. You can always turn clients away, but that will reduce both your current and future revenue, since clients don't like being told no.

Another thing you can do is look for ways to improve your workflow so you get more done, more efficiently, in the same 24-hour period. Automation can help.

Tech entrepreneurs would have you believe that everything can be automated, but there is no such thing as a successful freelancer who runs their business entirely on autopilot. As tempting as it is, for example, to schedule posts to your social media or let a chatbot handle your communications, these tools only really add value when you have such a large following on social media and so many clients that you can't feasibly respond on a one-to-one basis. And even businesses in that situation risk losing customers if they aren't properly staffed to give people the opportunity to speak directly with a human if they want to.

But there are still ways for smaller outfits (e.g. solopreneurs like you) to leverage automation — and technology is the solution.

Leverage blog posts for frequently asked questions

For example, take managing your customer communications. Unless you offer tailor-made solutions that require intense customization for every new customer, you are likely receiving the same kinds of questions and queries over and over again. Take advantage of downtime between contracts to draft texts that respond to the most commonly asked questions, or deal with the most routine issues that may arise.

For example, some of my clients would sometimes have difficulty understanding how to download the photos I send through my site once a job is done. No matter how clearly I thought I had explained it, there would always be one or two who just couldn't get the hang of it, and then I'd be dragged into a long phone call having to walk them through the process step by step. When this happened to me while I was away on vacation one time, I decided I'd had enough and sat down to write a blog post, with screen shots, illustrating in painstaking detail exactly how to download photos from my site. Then I stuck that link into the email signature of the email template that gets sent to clients with the link to their photos.

The result? While I still sometimes get the question, now I simply forward them the link to the post and no longer have to engage in a long support call for which I am not earning any extra revenue.

Put your email on auto-pilot

Auto-responders can also help if you receive a lot of email from your website or have a sales funnel in place that is doing its job of capturing emails from prospects. An auto-responder is simply an email that is preloaded with content that is automatically sent based on some trigger. The trigger could be filling in a form on your website or clicking on a specific button or image you've put in place for the purpose of driving engagement on your site.

You can even set up a series of auto-responders or schedule a bank of emails to send out over a period of time to prospects on your list, segmented based on their behaviour. For example, you could create a series of emails aimed at people who have expressed some interest in your product or service but haven't ever gone all the way and bought from you. The frequency with which you try to entice them back to you has to be carefully calibrated with their presumed interest levels and tolerance. Send too many emails too fast and customers might just unsubscribe, but if you pace the sends correctly (perhaps only one a year around the holidays, as Naked Wines does to me), they'll help generate sales for you with minimal effort after the initial email is crafted.

The very basic tools of automation, such as calendar reminders, can help you stay focussed and make sure you don't miss any important appointments. Most people already do this for meetings, but you can also use your calendar to schedule blocks of time for yourself to work on specific tasks or projects for which you don't have a hard client-driven deadline, like writing a blog post or working on a long-term project such as writing a book. I schedule writing blocks and automate a calendar reminder to publish something on my blog every Tuesday and Friday. While I may not always follow through, at least I keep myself to a schedule and don't have to wonder when was the last time I posted or whether I'm a little light on content this month.

Work smarter, not harder

Some of what you do can be "automated" to a mechanical "turk." A mechanical turk is a form of human-automation (used by Amazon) in which one or multiple steps in an automated process are done by an actual human. For example, you may run a data analysis consultancy that produces reports for your clients on the efficacy of their social media campaigns. Some of that initial data analysis can be generated automatically from the various software services you or your client are subscribed to, but a portion of that report may entail someone combining various outputs from a few different computer-generated analyses into a single report. That part of the process is handled by the mechanical turk.

You can hire or outsource a portion of the creation of your product (or all of it) to suppliers you've found who can do the same kind of work for less than what you can charge your clients for, in which case you earn the difference. Take website design, for example. Today, there are many designers in countries with lower labour costs to whom you can outsource work that will cost you much less than doing it yourself. If you are in the business of making websites for clients, you may find yourself spending more time finding and winning clients (so increasing revenue) while a lower-cost provider takes care of the actual creation process.

However you structure your workflow, it is good practice to check periodically to see if there are any parts of what you are doing that can be outsourced to a lower-cost supplier or replaced by a piece of software or app that can get the job done just as well.

Freelancers tend to assume that working longer, harder hours is the only way forward, but that attitude puts your health — and the sustainability of your business — at risk, as it invariably leads to burnout. Finding ways to increase your productivity through strategic uses of automation — either through software or outsourcing — is the only way you can grow a business that is inherently delimited by time (as many freelance businesses are).

Ultimately, the more time you can free up to focus on the parts of your job that cannot be replicated by either a machine or another human being, the better you will do what you do best.

Using technology to learn the habits and preferences of your tribe: Analytics 101

I will preface this section by stating up front that I am far from a master at data analytics. I use the most basic of tools and have only a high-level understanding of how to use most of those. There are far more detailed pieces of content out there that can teach you everything you want to learn about analytics and more. But I would be remiss in writing a book on freelancing without mentioning analytics and their vital importance to your work. Even a smattering of knowledge will be useful to you as you embark on your journey, so here goes.

Data — as you've probably heard so much the word makes you queasy — is everything. All the biggest, most valuable companies in the world are swirling through unimaginably vast troves of data, like digital tea leaves of near infinite depth, from which they glean everything there is to know about the creatures on the front end of that data trail: you, me and everyone else alive on the planet today who uses the Internet and therefore has a digital signature.

Leaving aside that portion of humanity stranded on the other side of the digital divide, you are probably reading this book on the kind of handheld device we still anachronistically call a "phone." That tool in your hand — your prosthetic brain — connects you to all the knowledge in the world available today with a few simple taps of your fingers, or simply by responding to your voice commands. As we've seen, it has fundamentally changed the way we think and behave, and how businesses everywhere interact with us.

With every website you visit, every message you send, every physical place you visit, every app you use, every search you conduct, every contact you make and communicate with, you are generating data. That data is trackable and measurable, though it comes showering down out of each and every one of us in such volume and velocity that it requires sophisticated parsing tools and technology to transform it into sense and make it actionable.

While the artificial intelligence abilities of Alphabet's DeepMind or IBM's Watson are beyond the grasp of most of us[*], there are tools available that an everyday non-techie freelancer can learn to use with a modicum of effort. To ignore them and their gifts of knowledge is to wilfully choose to operate blindly when the world around you is constantly listening, watching and recording.

The most accessible, though by no means the only tool available, of course, is Google Analytics. By copying a small piece of code that it provides you with onto your website, your business benefits from

---

[*] But worth a look. https://www.ibm.com/watson/

Google's enormous reach and ability to teach you about who's coming to visit, what they're looking for, what keywords they're using to find you, what type of content most resonates with them, and where you are losing their interest. It's free to use (all you need is a Gmail address) and powerful. Learning how can take a while, and you may wish to go farther than the basic level by taking an online course on Udemy or by simply poring over the thousands of YouTube videos out there on the subject, but even without investing a huge amount of time in learning the interface, you can gain insights into the behaviours of your audience and the effectiveness of the things you are doing to reach them (e.g. posting blog content, running ad campaigns, etc.) by looking and paying a bit of attention to what you are looking at.

Getting good at analytics is a specialized skill set and therefore requires time and effort to master. Most freelancers (except, of course, those who are freelancing as data analytics experts) will not have the time or inclination to do so. The task can be outsourced, of course, to experts in the field, but it is worth the small amount of upfront effort it takes to peer into the basic level of data an analytics platform like Google Analytics provides, if only to understand the volume and type of traffic you are getting on your web assets and whether that is translating into any actionable response you can take to influence it.

Of course, as we'll discuss in the next chapter, what we track and measure has far more significance than the tools used to do so.

Marketing matters: Getting found

Your audience needs to be able to find and follow you easily. Understand this one fundamental truth, and you will understand all there is to know about marketing yourself as a freelancer.

Modern digital marketing is mainly about getting found. Yes, you still need to try to find your audience, your tribe, your market, but the bulk of your marketing efforts should be spent on creating valuable pieces of content that matter so much to your audience that they will seek them out.

Whether you are wrangling it single-handedly (as most will be at the outset), or paying a consultant or digital marketing agency, the single goal of your marketing efforts is to connect you to your audience.

Your audience includes your prospects, past, present and future clients, and evangelists (people who love you so much they can't help but talk about you with their friends). Once they find you, your goal is to keep them engaged long enough for some of them to convert into paying customers.

How you do it that would take another book to explain, but fundamentally, the point of your marketing should be to attract the kind of people who need what you have to offer, and provide enough information once you've grabbed hold of their scant and fleeting attention, to convince them to pay.

Win their attention first, and the sales follow.

You are the new CMO

The CMO, or Chief Marketing Officer, is the person who sits on top of the whole marketing team in a company. Everyone who does marketing — traditional, digital, in-house, agencies of record — all ultimately report to her. It's a big job, and in big companies it's more than enough for one person to handle.

But in your company of one, you're it. That doesn't mean you get to stop doing the other stuff you need to do to make your business thrive. Unfortunately, it doesn't work like that. It means that you have to do it all and always be thinking of how to continuously keep your brand top of mind to your customers.

No matter what you're doing, whether it's selling, making or sharing, your number one job as a freelancer is marketing. You are always marketing. It will never stop or let up. So learn to love it, learn to do it well, and learn to live, breathe and think like a marketer. Your life literally depends on it.

Hacking PR for a $100,000 Sale

A great way to help you get found is to do a little content jujitsu and be part of someone else's content needs.

While there is a plethora of self-publishing platforms available now (e.g. Medium, LinkedIn Pulse, blogs, etc.), there are still lots of "traditional" media outlets and paid journalists producing content for their outlets. They need stories and ideas for stories, and you and your business could be just what they need to fill a content block.

It's worthwhile canvassing your personal and business networks to see if you have any direct contacts with any media outlets. You can also just scan the local media around you and look for the journalists who cover stories your freelancing activities might fall into — a business journalist, or someone covering tech or the arts page editor. Anyone who has written stories or covered topics that have any overlap with your area of expertise or field of interest is worth making a pitch to.

I know it works, because the single largest sale for an art start-up I co-founded was the direct result of a media story our little fledgling start-up was featured in. Through a writer friend, I was connected to a journalist who wrote for the Business section of the Montreal Gazette and was looking for stories about local start-ups. Ours fit the bill and provided some good visuals too (which helps), because our business was to connect local artists with local businesses, provide a platform for the two to connect and let business owners "try out" the art on their walls for a month before deciding to buy. We sometimes served as a holding area for the artwork and so had some art available onsite when the paper sent over a photographer to do a photoshoot with us.

The story was eventually published as the front page of the Business section, and since most "local" media are owned by national or even international conglomerates, the story was shared across a number of different media properties around the country. That included Toronto, where the executive assistant to the CEO at the Canadian Standards Association happened to read about us. And wouldn't you know, they'd just completed a multi-million dollar renovation on their facilities, had acres of wall space to fill and wanted to feature works from local Canadian artists.

And so we got a contract that eventually turned into the sale of over 87 individual artworks from little-known to unknown artists, for a total sale worth more than $100,000.

Cost of advertising? Zero.

If you have any kind of story to share (and if you don't, you need to develop one fast), you've got something of value. In addition to learning about the journalists who cover your area, you can submit story ideas to sites like Help a Reporter Out (HARO, www.helpareporter.com) and become a source. Reach out to other bloggers in your space, attend local meet-ups and make use of every available contact and you'll likely end up with more than one piece of coverage.

Grab that username

How many people in the word have your full name? 10? 100? 1,000? Way, way back when the Internet first started and people were all agog at new things called "websites" and "e-mail" (the hyphen was ditched a while ago), you could get pretty much any user name or domain name you wanted. All you had to do was spend a few dollars and register, if it cost anything at all. If you didn't, by the time you realized it, you wound up with an email address like yourname000001@gmail. com. That's okay, but I bet you'd rather have the name you wanted than the name the system picks for you when you try to register, if only because it's worth grabbing your username of choice on new platforms that come out.

I bought my name domain in early 2005 (to the chagrin, no doubt, of Dr. Julian Haber, MD) and did nothing with it until I found a hosting site with some templates I could figure out enough to put up a rudimentary site with a very basic design mid-way through June 2006, with the goal of getting hired as an event photographer and selling artsy photos online.

I also got my email address on Gmail around the same time, and ever since, whenever the earliest tendrils of a new platform start appearing, I immediately register a username. Sometimes the platforms arrive with much hype and disappear (remember MySpace? Friendster? Peach?), but some of them stick around (e.g. Facebook, Twitter, LinkedIn). Will Snapchat be here in ten years? Maybe, maybe not, but the possibility is strong enough that it's worth getting registered for it early on just in case you ever decide you want to start using it, or it emerges as the indispensable platform to be on (which I doubt, but you never know.)

Whenever a new technology emerges, there are people who jump all over it and hype it as the next best thing (the early adopters), and people who wait until all the bugs and kinks are worked out and it's established, safe and cheaper (the mainstream). As consumers, it's fine — maybe even a good idea — to wait a while for a technology to prove itself and be tested in the real world by more adventurous users so you don't have to be the guinea pig. But creators and producers, which all freelancers are, are always going to be better off learning a new technology and growing with it, if only to watch it evolve and already be familiar with it if it happens to blow up into the next big thing.

(*Mark Suster, a venture capitalist and prolific blogger, writes a very good summary of the reasons for trying out new tech in a post on his blog, BothSidesoftheTable. It's a worthwhile investment of three minutes of your time to read.)

Blogging and writing

I hope you like to write, because despite what Twitter's 140-character limit did to sentence structure, and the apparent Instagrammification of everything, there is still no better tool to tell your story, communicate who you are and connect with your tribe than the written word.

Writing teaches you to think clearly, distills your emotions and provides an automatic pathway into the minds of people who care to learn about what you do and who you are.

Regardless of how non-verbal your product or service may be— my main line of work is photography, also known as stills — the people who buy from you are still people. And people thrive on stories and narratives, which words are perfectly designed to convey.

Of course, words are not the only means of communication. You can use photos or videos or music or soundscapes or any combination thereof. You can create experiences and you can feed people savoury and delicious meals. However, you cannot escape text, if only to serve as captions and headings.

You may think that because your freelancing business is based primarily on selling to businesses directly, blogging is a waste of time. You may think that, but you would be wrong.

Inside the business-to-business model is really a person-to-person model. The person on the inside of the business you're attempting to connect with is the same person who is interested in learning and getting better at what he or she does (and probably wastes a bit of time every day on Facebook). That person will seek out information they trust and believe in if they feel it can help them improve themselves, deepen their knowledge and understanding about their business and their industry, and let them add another notch to their expertise.

Where are they going to find that?

They'll look for it online and stop at any blog or site that offers them something of value. If you are there, offering to share your insights, your knowledge or your wisdom on the subject you care most about and around which you have designed your freelancing business, then you are that person. And long before any business gets conducted, your words may have already opened up the door to the opportunity.

Blogging is hard work, there is no doubt. It requires a strong conviction and belief in yourself and a commitment to showing up and delivering a post (at least once a week and many would argue, once a day). It means you expose yourself. You may say something stupid or get your facts wrong. You may look like you don't know what you are doing. But if you are honest with yourself and your audience, you will grow and learn, and they will grow and learn with you. And they will appreciate you for it.

Whether you have an audience of one, or even none, doesn't matter. Blogging is as much about honing your craft and testing out your ideas as it is about connecting with your audience. You can use your blog to gather email subscriptions, but don't be alarmed or depressed if few or no one signs up. You may only have four subscribers to your list — if that. It doesn't matter. Write for them, and know that for every one reader who subscribes, there are many who care and value what you have to offer but just don't want to commit to receiving yet another thing to read in their inbox.

Over time, maybe a long time, your audience will find you. But that can only ever happen if you write, and keep shipping, as Seth Godin would say, regardless of the response or lack of response you get.

Nothing could do more for your long-term success and the audience that wants to hear from you than building up a huge library of content around the issues, subject matter, keywords and focus of your freelancing life. By trying to discover and write about topics that you believe your audience will care about, you learn and can improve. See what sticks and gets some attention, see what gets liked, shared, tweeted. Do more of that. Try new things. Test out concepts and float ideas about projects. Share your posts through your social media channels. Give yourself a publishing schedule you can handle and stick to it. If you slip up and miss a day, make it up. Slow and steady wins the race. While a post a day can accelerate your uptake and impact, if that's not feasible for you (and it is not feasible for many), then choose a formula you can commit to. (I post once a week to my photography blog, occasionally more often — it's not much. I should probably do more, but it's all I can commit to while keeping up on my work and other projects).

Writing is a free and simple method for discovering what works, what resonates, what your audience cares about, and what you have in your mind. It keeps you focussed. The discipline required to regularly write and post is a transferable skill helpful in everything else you need to do with your freelancing practice. Along with meditation, exercise, good sleep and healthy living, writing is perhaps the core skill that may not be directly related to what you do, but that has the most profound and significant impact on your long-term success.

But where do I begin?

Don't know where to start or what to say? Have writer's block? Worried that everything's already been said about your topic? Shy? Feel like an imposter or a fraud pretending to be something you're not? Having trouble getting started?

Sorry to break it to you, but that's all par for the course. You're going to have to write anyway and push past those feelings. Remember, you don't need to know it all — you just need to know a little more than the person reading your posts. And you will learn and share your growth as you do, which many readers value for its authenticity. They are learning and growing with you.

Sit down and create a list of topics you think you could write at least a few hundred words on. Don't edit or limit yourself, just pour out the contents of your heart and mind into a massive list of writing seeds you can later plant in the fertile soil of your mind and produce from. (For a longer description, use the brain dump technique referred to in the section on GTD.)

Set yourself up to produce by turning off all distractions. The only tools I use to write are Scrivener and a timer. Pick a time in the day when you are most creative and energized and which you can commit to regularly. (Most people choose mornings, but find whatever works for you.) Start small, but start. Don't move on to another task till you've written something. Anything. Even if it's just a single line. Get into the habit of staying put and starting your fingers moving, even before you know exactly what you are going to say.

Having a rough idea and a general sense of what you want to end up with is more than enough to write on. Sometimes you need to write just to discover what it is you want to write about. Write. If you don't like it, chuck it and start over. But keep writing and commit to publishing something at the end of it. It doesn't have to be perfect. Check it for errors and typos of course, but don't let your fear of failure or of exposing yourself to the world prevent you from sharing you work. Push the publish button. Let it go. Breathe in, breathe out.

Do it again tomorrow. Eventually it becomes second nature. You'll even miss it if your day gets hijacked by work or something unexpected that takes away your writing time. That's when you'll know you've picked up the habit.

Get your marketing kit organized in a day

A little advance work on your marketing kit at the outset will save you from scrambling around trying to cobble something together when a prospective client asks to see your portfolio. The ideal time to put together a basic marketing kit is before you get too busy. It's job, of course, is to present prospective clients with enough information and "sizzle" to induce them to either engage further or hire you right then and there. Don't worry, your marketing doesn't have to be perfect out of the gate: once you build it, it will grow and develop with time.

What you need to get started

Everything I'm proposing can be created in a hard day's work. One day dedicated to creating your marketing kit is not a lot when you think that the payoff will be paying work and new customers.

1. **An email account:** While this seems obvious, make sure that your email address is not still something you've had since high school. If it has the word "rocks" or "sexy" in it, for example, and ends in "Hotmail," get a new one. I recommend Gmail, as you can set up other emails like yourname@yourdomain. com to redirect there, keeping all your email in one place and accessible from any device anywhere.

2. **A website/blog (ideally simply yourname.com or yourcompanyname.com) with the following sections:**

   a. About: explain briefly in plain language who you are, what you love to do, the kinds of projects or mandates you love, why you do it, and who you do it for. No more than one or two paragraphs. Include a good professional headshot photo of yourself, and if relevant, your product or workspace. Remember that people hire people — they will look to this section to get a sense of who you are as a person and if they like what they see, they'll move on to the rest of your site to check out your work. If you work with a team (either actually or virtually) you will want to include their bios, headshot and specialties here as well.

b. What we do: (You can change the "we" to "I" but even if you are a solopreneur, it's worth considering presenting yourself as being part of a team, even if that team is only brought together for specific mandates or certain projects). Include in this section a clearly written explanation of the services you offer and the kinds of projects or mandates you work on. If you have any examples or case studies, link to them here, or include a link to a curated portfolio of your work that represents the kind of work you are going after.

c. Pricing: You can include as much or as little detail as you want here. There is a case to be made for including price information up front, or requiring customers to reach out directly to you through an email or form. I am of the mind that if you are going to show pricing information, you should provide a range and descriptors that specify what the range covers. You don't want to price yourself too high in the beginning, nor do you want to price yourself too low. You may also not really know yet what works well, so identify a range with an attractively priced starting point, then work out where on that range specific scenarios fall on. For example, I offer professional headshot sessions as one of my services as a photographer, and I charge less for a private headshot to another freelancer or artist than I would for a corporate headshot in someone's office.

d. Contact: this is the main purpose for your website in the first place - to be found and contacted by prospective clients. Make contact information clear, obvious, dead-easy to use and accessible on every page of your site/

blog. You may include a form to gather information but since some people hate filling in online forms, be sure to also include an email and phone number where you can always be reached (and respond quickly!). Include here as well links to your social media footprint (e.g., Facebook, Instagram, Twitter, LinkedIn, Pinterest, etc.)

3. **Email signature boiler-plate text:** For email: a succinct, brief description culled from your "About" section that you can use to send to anyone on a second's notice who asks what you do. Include an email signature with links to your site/blog, social media presence, phone and contact info and a short link requesting a review on Google+

4. **Your social media presence:** First of all, decide which sites you will focus attention on and invest time and resources in. Social media can be a huge time sink, but it doesn't have to be if you set yourself up wisely in the beginning (more on this in the next chapter: Social media as a tool - not a distraction). You don't need to be on every social media platform, but you do need to be where your customers are likely to hang out. For example, if you're a caterer or preparing ready-to-go meals for customers by delivery or pickup, you will need to be on Pinterest, but maybe not have such a strong presence on LinkedIn. As a minimum, you will need a Facebook page, YouTube/Google+, LinkedIn, Twitter, and probably Instagram and possibly Pinterest. It sounds like a lot, but you can leverage the same information you create for your blog for most of the setups, and then automate blog posts to publish in LinkedIn, to your Facebook page and Twitter account, limiting the effort you need to put into creating content specific to each channel. There are channel-specific content needs (i.e. Instagram requires you actually take and post a photo) but these can often also be linked back to your Facebook page, or be automated feeds in your blog (using freely available built in widgets) that allow you to leverage you content widely. You

can also use tools like Hootsuite or Buffer to create, plan and schedule posts to fire out through multiple accounts.

a. Set up your Facebook page: filling in the necessary details on who you are and what you do, cribbed from the content you created for your website. You can modify the tone (should be friendly but still professional), and include photos and any videos you have.

b. Set up a Twitter account: useful if only to make connections and be found. Twitter can be a very fertile ground for finding other people and for real-time updates if your business relies on staying current. It's also still pretty popular at conferences where tweets are aggregated by the conference hashtag and often displayed on walls or the screen at general sessions. It can be a great way for you to get your name out there. No need to obsess over follower numbers or retweets or anything like that for now. Just put your short bio in there, again a link back to your site and create the necessary connections to your blog to allow for links to automatically be generated and sent when you publish a post.

c. Set up a profile on LinkedIn (if you don't have one already): There are lots of articles about how to create a great profile on LinkedIn, but as a minimum you need:

    i. A professionally shot headshot (I recommend using the same headshot everywhere so people recognize you and your brand across platforms)

    ii. A strong and clear summary section that indicates what you do but focuses on why people choose you. Put yourself in your customers' frame of mind.

    iii. Links to your website and other social profiles

    iv. Updated contact information so people you are not linked with can still contact you

All this may look like a lot of work, but as you can see once you start doing it, most of what you are doing is re-purposing the same content across a few key properties with only minor tweaks or adjustments.

What you don't need right away

Over time you'll add to, edit and remove elements from your marketing kit. You'll regularly update it, tweak it and keep it relevant and reflective of you, your business and your evolving market. But at the outset, there are a lot of things people get hung up on having that aren't really necessary to just get going.

You'll note, for example, that I've left out one "major" thing that a lot of freelancers waste an inordinate amount of time worrying about: a logo. While a logo is an important visual representation of your brand, it is not as deadly serious to have at the outset as many people think (take a look at Apple's first logo). By all means, if you have the logo developed, then use it, but if you don't yet, don't stress about it and let it hold you back from getting started. (One of the advantages of being small and unknown is that few people, if any, really pay much attention to changes you make to your look, logo, website, etc., in the beginning). You can always start with something and re-place it with something better once you have more time, money and understanding of who you really serve.

A few other important but not mission-critical marketing pieces you don't need immediately are:

- **Business cards:** nice to have, useful and worth spending some money on for the real-world, face-to-face networking you're going to have to do, but not something you need immediately. You can always ask for a business card and simply mail the contact your details.

- **1-800#:** for some reason a lot of first time freelancers seem to think it's important to look like you're a really big business that can be reached from anywhere at any time. While responding quickly and accessibility are important, the fact that you are a small, independent, local supplier is a strength and not a weakness. If it's just you answering the phones, don't try to hide behind a 1-800#. Use your own number (or have two — your local clients will appreciate seeing and using an area code they recognize). Put it out there just like you're putting your name into the world. Embrace your smallness and uniqueness.

- **Trademark protection:** if your business entails some kind of intellectual property or innovation, you may fret a lot about "protecting" your idea. Let me tell you something a lot of entrepreneurs learn the hard way: you can't really protect an idea. An idea — that ephemeral wispy strand of consciousness that manifests around an insight, thought or observation — is not something you can put a fence around and keep away from the world. It is the opposite — the more you share and spread your ideas, the more likely they are to actually happen and have an impact. Trademarks are cumbersome, expensive, have to be done in multiple jurisdictions and eat up a lot of time and money that would way better spent actually making your ideas happen and putting them into action. Putting all your steam into protecting your idea before you've actually gone and done the work of turning your idea into action is like buying house insurance before you've found a house to live in.

Get this all in place and you are officially ready to roll.

Social media as a tool, not a distraction

Attempting to write anything about something as fluid and fast-moving as social media, in a format as old-fashioned and unmoving as a book, is arguably a pointless and Sisyphean task. Platforms come and go, and the big ones that appear to have staying power like Facebook, Instagram (owned by Facebook), Twitter and LinkedIn are constantly changing and altering their internal workings such that any specific advice about how to use them will soon become dated and useless. So I won't do any of that. Rather, I will simply address the issue of social media from the perspective of a practicing freelancer who seeks to understand its merits and avoid its many pitfalls.

First of all, social media is here to stay. It is not a fad, it is not something just for kids and it is not all just cat videos and celebrity selfies (though it is a lot of that). At its core social media is about a network talking to and about itself. It's a one-to-many and a one-to-one model for transmitting stories, information, ideas and emotions. It is where billions of people spend billions of hours every day. To ignore it because it is noisy, distracting, stress-inducing or time-consuming is to cut yourself off from the richest pool of potentiality for your business that exists in the world today.

It is, like it or not, a feature of the marketing landscape that your little freelance business needs to participate in. That said, you don't need to hand it the reins to your life. Your approach to social media can radically impact your effectiveness on it and determine how much, or how little, you get out of it.

Create content and share value

Your first commitment then, needs to be to adopt the stance of a creator/producer. Social media is your free publishing platform and it is the tool through which you will connect with your audience. They will use it to connect back with you, but your role is primarily one of producing and sharing value — not idly passing time reading other people's feeds and watching silly videos.

Use social media, don't let it use you. Stream your blog posts through it to the various pages you set up (i.e., Facebook page, LinkedIn profile). Try out platforms like Medium.com or Pulse (LinkedIn's native publishing platform) to share thought pieces you craft around your areas of interest and focus and establish yourself as an expert in your field. Look at who follows you and connects with you. Research your prospects and their interests. Learn about the people you are trying to connect with by reading what they post, watching what they share and interact with. Constantly gather information and build up your knowledge and understanding about your market through observations of the people on the network.

And be aware that you too will be observed. Don't post or publish highly contentious things. Avoid getting too political unless you are seriously committed to the cause and don't care that you may alienate the other side of whichever debate or policy you align yourself with. Keep your personal information protected while not hiding everything there is to know about you behind a wall of fakeness and inauthenticity — the likes of which can be spotted a mile off and can do immediate and lasting damage to your "social media" brand.

Your presence on social media platforms requires time and commitment but it does not need to be something you obsess over. There are businesses who light up on social media and who become hugely successful through building a following. Yours may well be or become one of these businesses, but don't despair if it doesn't happen right away, if ever. There is an ever-deafening roar on social media channels and cutting through that noise takes greater and greater amounts of effort. For many it will not be worth it.

What matters is simply being there, responding to queries or comments that are directed at you or spotting opportunities to create a connection, correct a misperception or offer some education. Sharing your content and other content you believe will resonate with your audience is a healthy social media habit. Obsessively counting likes, shares and re-tweets is not.

What you don't understand, you can learn

Look at the analytics tabs on your pages and learn how to read them. It may seem like reading tea leaves, but there is sense to the data. Whenever you encounter something you don't understand, look it up. There will almost certainly be an online tutorial, and a YouTuber somewhere explaining in great detail whatever aspect of social media you don't understand.

You don't have to learn everything all at once. Just like everything else, take it in small bite-sized doses. Fiddle around with posts, ask questions, look around at what other people in your space are doing and copy whatever you like (adapting to your own brand and voice, of course).

Look up!

Constantly checking your social media feeds is a kind of disease. We all know someone, possibly someone we spend a lot of time with, whose head seems permanently bent down staring into that little screen in their hand. Human brains seem easily addicted to the endorphins that get released when we see someone "like" our content or comment on or about us positively. Don't let yourself get sucked into the rabbit hole of social media to the exclusion of developing and maintaining your focus on the work that really matters.

Social media is the agora of the modern world. It's where ideas get exchanged and voted on. You, your freelancing business and the content you produce, all reflect your ideas. Some will be absorbed, some will be ignored and some will influence behaviours, sometimes, in your favour. But what matters with idea sharing is not the ideas themselves so much as the actions they inspire.

Leverage social media to give your ideas maximum impact, but don't confuse busyness on social media with the real work that comes from busily dealing with client needs. Remember that social media is a tool for you to use to further your aims and objectives. Don't lose yourself there, staring into its black mirror, falsely comparing yourself to others or stressing about how relevant or not you may think you are.

It's a tricky and ultimately inchoate space. There will be constant updates, and what worked before may just stop working for no apparent reason. Things that used to yield results may suddenly dry up, but then a whole new field you never expected may present itself.

Staying current with social media requires nimbleness, adeptness, attention and alertness. You need to dedicate some time and focus to it — but keep it in perspective. Ten minutes a day may be too little, an hour too much. Find the balance that works for you and generates a slow but steady uptick in people following your posts or reacting to them online in some fashion.

And learn how to tune it out and turn it off when you need to do your real work. Social media is characteristically needy and distracting. It will always be clamouring for your attention. Give it out sparingly and on terms that work for you, or risk becoming a slave to its ravenous hunger for more.

DIY advertising on social media

Running an ad campaign for your fledgling freelance business may sound like a daunting task, but when you break it to down into doable pieces, it's no different than any other job you're already more than qualified to take on. Approach it like the project that it is and you'll have your campaigns up and running in as much time as it takes you to craft a thoughtful blog post.

The key criterion to consider when planning a campaign is where your audience is likely to be hanging out. You may not know the answer yet, so make some assumptions. Are they young or old, male or female or both, do they live in cities, in rural areas, are they interested in snowmobiles, organic food or industrial machinery? If you don't know where to begin, consider that roughly 70-80% of all online ads will be distributed through two major platforms: GoogleAds and Facebook. You can pick one or the other, or run small test campaigns on both and you're probably hitting the majority of your market. Start there.

Facebook Ads

Just google "Facebook Ads" and countless self-described (and sometimes acclaimed) Internet marketers/social media strategists will fill in your search offering some kind of guide on how to do Facebook Ads. You can also look on online learning platforms like Lynda.com, Udemy.com or Udacity.com for more detailed, hands-on courses. Or you can log into your Facebook account and see how much you can figure out on your own. As of the time of this writing, Facebook Ad Manager has a fairly comprehensive system for helping you design your first ad campaign.

The starting screen (in early 2017) asks you to identify your marketing objectives with options for awareness, consideration and conversion. Basically, getting found (awareness), stimulating interest (consideration) and convincing some people to actually click through to your site (conversion).

To prove the point, I'm going to create an ad campaign in real time as I write this section.

First thing, I'll choose my objective. I'm going to choose: Lead generation. I then have to choose an audience based on:

- Location (e.g . Montreal, Canada, etc.)
- Age bracket
- Gender
- And I add further detail to include people with "Marketing and Events Manager" in the title along with "Event Manager"
- I also include Connections of people who have Liked my page

Next I have to choose how much to spend, and on what kind of spending schedule. You can choose either a daily limit of say $20, or a lifetime budget within a specified time frame. In this case, I go with a lifetime budget of $150 CAD.

Now I have to find a few photos that would work for my ad (which in my case was easy as I have a pile available, but if you don't, you can browse stock images right from the "ad creation panel"). After selecting a few — you can run up to six on a campaign and then rotate automatically, giving you a chance to see which ones do better and drop the ones that don't perform — I have to come up with some copy for the ad.

Writing pithy, attention-getting copy for ads isn't everyone's forte. It's harder than it looks but with a little focus time you should be able to come up with a headline and some body text that explains what you do and why someone should click on your ad. Here's what I came up with: "Work with a professional team equipped for all your photo and video needs. Get in touch today for a quote." Not perfect, I'm sure, but it should do the trick. I'll know more in a month's time, once ad campaign has run out.

Before going any further I get a review screen, which summarizes everything I've done. On the review screen I can check the name of my campaign, make sure I am targeting the location and groups that

I want to target, verify the campaign objective (i.e. Lead generation), and importantly check my overall budget for the campaign which in this case is just $150, which will be automatically spent bidding for impressions over the duration of the campaign which I've set to last one month.

And that's it. (I also created a form to capture emails, but you don't have to do that — I just figured I'd give a whirl since I was there anyway.)

That took an hour. Pretty time-effective. With my billable rate, plus the cost of the ad, if I land a single prospect that turns into a paying gig this ad will more than pay for itself. And if not, I got the content I needed to complete this chapter. Either way, a win-win.

Leverage search

Everything a prospective client learns about you/your business/your product/your service will come either because they searched for information or because information that is targeted to them reached them. The information — your story, your reputation, who you are and why you are worth finding — will appear on multiple platforms, on multiple devices, and in pieces, some of which is paid (as in, ads you made or had made and paid to distribute), and some of which is organic (as in, you wrote a blog post someone found, read, liked and started developing an interest in you as a result of).

The modern marketing landscape is complex, but if you can grasp this one distinction, you will have the key to unlocking your marketing potential.

Then the real work begins, of course. Because reaching customers, and making sure they find you, is not easy. The secret is working at it every day. It will take up a lot of time but it is a necessary and fundamental part of whatever you do.

What can you pay for?

- Ads on social networks like Facebook, LinkedIn, Twitter and Snapchat
- Online ads directly with Google
- Digital marketing / Ad agencies to help you create and place ads.
- Writers to write blog posts for you
- Photographers to take professional images for you
- Infographic artists to create infographics for you

What can (should) you not pay for?

- A real reputation
- Authentic reviews from happy customers on Google, Yelp, etc.
- Being top of search results for your category (well, you can, but the best way to be there is to actually be there...)

Leveraging searches, then, is about crafting and delivering a story about who you are, what you do, and why it matters to the people it matters to.

So how do you do it? It starts with having a story to tell, of course, and then getting really good at telling it in the formats and styles that have the most impact on your audience. You only learn that through trial and error. That, of course, means you need a way of understanding what your impact is, and how to measure it (analytics, which is touched on in the section on what to measure and why).

But to get started, let's take a look at creating content.

Why content marketing is key to winning in the gig economy (putting the 'free' in 'freelancer')

You've probably already heard the modern mantra "content is king" too many times for your liking, so I apologize for saying it again. Unfortunately, it remains true and will almost certainly continue to be true as long as you hope to be in business. So it's best to get a handle on it from the get go.

Regardless of what you are selling — whether it's your time, your expertise, your up-cycled Patron bottles on Etsy, or your new app — you need to wrap it up in lots of content (that you give away for free). Content is today's eco-friendly package. Or if food metaphors are easier to swallow (ha, ha), think of content as the sausage you're selling stuffed inside a Turducken (which is a sausage, stuffed inside a deboned duck, stuffed inside a deboned chicken, stuffed inside a turkey and then deep-fried).

What is content marketing, exactly?

According to Wikipedia, *"Content marketing is any marketing that involves the creation and sharing of media and publishing content in order to acquire and retain customers."*

Content can be:

- a photograph
- a hand drawing
- a video
- a sound clip
- a gif
- a cinemagraph
- a 360 photo or video clip

- a song
- an icon
- an infographics
- a pdf template
- an e-book

Content is basically what most of the Internet is stuffed, or some might say clogged, with.

Isn't there enough of this stuff out there already?

Yes and no. And in the time we took to get this far down the page, another petabyte of data just materialized into existence. Because, even though we're drowning in content (information), which has given rise to an entire industry of life editing/minimalists and declutterers (sending you content on how to cut down on the content you consume), content, like the poor, will always be with us.

Never before in human history have so many of us had so much time, capacity for distraction and access to such a variety of content. In an always-on, always hungry, always distracted age, people need to feed on content constantly. Whether you like it or hate where it's taking us, whether you believe it's a transformative opportunity or just making us all stupider, having near- instant access to virtually anything we want to see, hear, read or know anything about is how humans behave now and it's only going to get better — or worse, depending on your point of view.

How is content, marketing?

The expression content marketing first started creeping into the digital marketer's lexicon around as early as 1996, but really gained traction around 2013. By 2014, Forbes was reporting on the top seven ways to use content marketing, nicely illustrating its own point with a listicle title.

Content marketing is basically a response to the ad-weariness that emerged as the Internet brought a flood of clickable advertisements (advertisers thought they were awesome until they realized that people hated them, stopped clicking on them, and even installed software on their devices to block them).

If you're in the business of selling something (and if you're not, you're not in business), how do you get the word out to prospective, increasingly savvy customers who may have a visceral hatred for ads?

You change the way an ad looks, of course, by transforming it into content: something interesting, educational or entertaining. Which is not to say everything you read, watch, listen to and share with your friends for free is advertising masquerading as content, but more of it might be than you have paused to consider.

Like a Trojan horse for your brain, content lets marketers in until you stop treating them like invaders and start inviting them into your homes. If you are the marketer, this is a great thing. Saturate your prospects with enough familiarity and that part of your brain that makes judgements — the mental gatekeeper — stops looking at your content and gives it a pass. From there, it's just a short hop, skip and a click away from some kind of purchase.

Instead of using an ad to bait your prospect into finding out more about you or just making a purchase straight off, now you need to give your customers free stuff — lots of it — before they even think about becoming a customer. Most of the people you reach won't become customers, but because of the scale of the Internet, you don't need most of them. To have a successful business, you just need a tiny percentage of most of them.

Content is marketing today because nobody is ever going to find you, let alone pay any attention to you — yes! even you — if you don't pump out enough content to enable that discovery to happen.

Is it more work? Yes. Does it mean learning new skills? Yes. Does it cost you more in time and effort than just doing your thing online and hoping people will stumble across you and make you super rich? Yes. But it can also be fun, help you connect with people who will love what you have to offer and actually help you grow and develop into a successful independent entrepreneur.

Because you, dear freelancer/modern day gigger/artist/photographer/ writer/start-uppy dude/organic food maker, are just not that big a deal to most people. And that's okay. It's how you get to be known that matters and that's where the fun is at. And a big part of that is making content.

Understand why you are creating content

All content needs to be created for a purpose.

Take a blog post. Before you even begin writing, know how it relates to your brand. Every piece of content you produce should ultimately have a clear reason for taking up one more spot on the vastly cluttered shelf of Internet wisdom.

Are you trying to make friends? Get known? Establish yourself as an authority on X? Do you want to give something valuable away in exchange for an email address (create a "lead magnet") or a share or repost? Or are you simply hoping and praying that once you hit publish, it will magically start surfacing on the Internet and make you an online sensation?

You're building a library

As far as your content marketing strategy is concerned, you always need to keep the long tail in mind for the long term. You are effectively creating a constellation of clickable, link-rich portals, with all links leading back to your current work and your current raft of permanently rotating offers.

Another way to think of it is like farming. Every piece of content you create is like a seed you are planting. You make your best guess — informed with as much data as you can reasonably get hold of and understand — about where to plant, what to plant and how much to plant. Then you tend to it. You water it. Make sure it stays clear of weeds (occasionally resurfacing the piece with a new twist or simply to remind people of its existence). And you leave it to grow.

Something you published initially years ago may turn out to be your greatest source of leads, even if at the time nothing seemed to have happened.

Curate your content periodically

You need to consider your work as part farmer and then part curator. Review the content you've created and prune the duds. Kill off threads that are no longer on brand, or have no relevance to your current audiences. Be aware of your tail and always keep it in line with where you are going now, not where you were heading at the time of its creation, which may have changed since then.

A few tips for content creation today

- Provide something that is both useful and easy to share.
- Keep the content short and illustrate it as much as you can with powerful photography and imagery.
- Use fewer words.

- Use more pictures.
- Make it entertaining.
- Match your audience's level of attention.
- Then match your audience's level of intelligence.

Attention is the scarcest resource on the Internet today

Your content needs, first and foremost, to capture people's attention. That's why you see so many click-bait article headlines and listicles on the Internet. But just as importantly, once you've captured people's attention, you need to hold it.

How often have you clicked on an image or a headline only to be driven to a piece of content that either doesn't show the image again or mutates into something entirely different from what you expected to see? What do you do next? You usually move on to something else, feeling irritated at being conned.

Packaging content is all about creating and fulfilling an expected outcome.

Intention matters — yours and your audience's

We search for content that we need at a given moment. A quote to bolster our post, a fact(oid) to strengthen our thesis, a proof point to settle an argument. When people search, they are literally telling you what they want to find.

Good content will answer that immediate need but also offer something more nuanced, of more or equal value, and induce people to linger.

For example, say I want to look up 360 cameras. I find this post on julianhaber.com about 360 cameras but I also see there's a bit about time-lapse cameras, and since I'm organizing a trade show, that could be kind of useful too. Let me explore...

Content is a path and your viewers/readers are on a journey. Your job is to connect the paths and lead them somewhere useful. Allow them to explore, and make the exploring easy to do and worth their while.

Create content for the full journey

A first intention (e.g. a key word search, request for referral, etc.) should lead to that bit of content that meets that immediate need. Inside that content there should be a way into another piece of content with two links: a link to the immediate solution (some form of conversion: book me now, contact me now, etc.) and another link that lets them keep exploring if they aren't ready to buy.

Here's how it works: Let's say, for example, you were looking for an "event photographer in Montreal." The first thing you'd do is run a search on Google, using that exact phrase. If I've done my content marketing well, you'll find julianhaber.com, because he's an event photographer in Montreal, and maybe you'd land on an article about "What to think about when hiring an event photographer." In an unobtrusive but very easily accessed place (like the top menu where people expect to see it), there should be a link to a BOOK NOW button, if the searcher has seen enough and wants to move quickly to their next intended step. Or a link (or set of links) to the next thing they might reasonably be expected to want to see from this kind of content, such as:

- See relevant Event Photography work (targeted portfolio link, which will also have the BOOK NOW option, and further directional links).
- An article on Venues in Montreal = "Check out the most

photographable venues in Montreal."

- An article about photo booths: "Add some photo booth fun to your event."

Think the way your reader / content consumer thinks and produce as much content as you can that satisfies any and all questions you can conceive of that they might have. Always produce for intention.

- Who is my audience?
- What are they searching for?
- What might they also be interested in?
- What do they want to do when they find me?
- What do I want them to do when they find me?

Remember, the content you create takes time and effort to make. So invest your time and effort creating content that has the highest likelihood of leading customers where they are most likely to connect with you. So ultimately, they'll hire you. It's not an exact science, but there are ways you can make your content more "findable" and ultimately more clickable.

Use your analytics to find out what search terms led the most visitors to your site, and then orient your content around those keywords. If you don't get the traffic you hoped for, do your own searches online and see what kind of content you find, then copy it. Not exactly of course, but there is no reason why you can't use other people's good ideas to help your business out.

Finally, don't give up! Content creation is an ongoing, permanent part of your marketing efforts. It can take a while for you to hit on the right formula and frequency of posts. Iterate frequently, do more of what works and less of what doesn't. It may seem like all you're do-ing is shouting into the wind, but little by little, if you're really creat-ing useful content that speaks directly to your audience and provides them real value, you will eventually see positive results.

Content creation vs. content distribution

So now that you've made it, what do you do with it? How do you get your valuable piece of content in front of the highest number of eyeballs?

Sharing, posting, reposting, repurposing, scheduled posts, publishing...where to begin?

Not to mention all the other things to think about, such as how long it should be, what kind of content you should be creating, how frequently and how regularly you send it out into the world.

That's a lot to contemplate, so let's get started.

Getting your content out there

You've got a piece of content in hand, ready to go. It's been polished and you think it's as good as it's going to get and now you want to get maximum use from it. The first thing to do is to clarify in your own mind where and when you want to publish it. You can use an editorial calendar to help you plan this out. (HubSpot offers a few for free, in exchange for your email, of course.)

Ask yourself: why am I sending out this particular piece of content at this particular time, and for whom is it intended? Most importantly, what do you want your target audience to do with what you are publishing?

The Internet is like a giant soapbox. There's no shortage of self-proclaimed experts lining up to preach to you about how to convert your content into leads, how to pique interest and then transform someone's curiosity into a sale. The answer is out there — but how much will it cost you in terms of time and energy to parse it out?

There is a better way. It's a combination of KISS (Keep It Simple, Stupid) and trial-and-error.

Pick your platform:

- Social media: Facebook? Instagram? Medium? LinkedIn? Snapchat?
- YouTube? Vimeo?
- Pinterest? SoundCloud?
- Your blog or someone else's?
- Traditional media / publication?

The online world is full of platforms, but the ones everybody knows and uses are also the most readily accessible and probably the ones you should start with. Each has its own unique audience, but few are truly exclusive. The same user is likely on all or many of the different platforms and will switch between them countless times throughout the day. What you need to think about is why your customer is on a given platform at a given time of day. What is he or she doing there that they don't do on another site? Are they on Pinterest shopping for ideas, but only getting recommendations from friends on Facebook? Are they on LinkedIn reading articles, or spending most of their time spinning through Instagram?

What you should consider, when thinking about your content distribution strategy, is how your audience behaves (and like to be seen as behaving) on a given platform.

We know that people share content that reflects positively on them, and don't share things that might expose them to judgement. Most people want to align themselves with good causes and show their best, idealized versions of themselves in public.

Do as I do, not as I say

On Facebook, this behaviour is likely to relate more to how they want to be perceived personally: as someone who is smart, funny, goofy, clever, creative, etc. One person's idea of insight is another's conspiratorial fantasy. Knowing who your audience is — how old they are, how they like to show themselves to the world, what they show public concern for — will help you craft content that is meaningful to them.

People behave differently on different platforms, and there are norms and social mores intrinsic to each. It's hard to imagine anyone successfully sharing a video of someone twerking on LinkedIn, though it may end up streaming through your news feed on Facebook.

Develop content that corresponds with how people behave on a given platform and who their audiences are and you will have a greater chance of being seen, and distributed.

Catching waves

I was never that excited by surfing. I didn't grow up near any kind of ocean. The nearest body of water was Montreal's Lachine Canal, which smelled like horse urine, with dark waters covering up rusty bicycles and beer bottles. So when I was invited on a surfing vacation to celebrate my brother-in-law's 50th birthday, I accepted, but with no great enthusiasm for the surfing part.

The truth is that other than one failed attempt to surf decades ago, I didn't really know what I was avoiding.

When it comes to hanging out on beaches, I am about as lazy as they come. At best, I stretch out my right arm to get my next beer from the cooler. I don't even bother trying to read. Only rarely do I walk farther than from my chair to the shoreline to peer down at whatever shells the waves throw up.

But on my brother-in-law's birthday trip, I decided to give it a try. I dutifully strapped the tether on my left leg and plodded into the ocean. The beach, Playa Guiñones in Costa Rica, could not have been a better place to learn, I'm told, with its long shoreline and gentle break close to shore. Farther out, there are much bigger waves where the pros zip across the waves like frolicking seals. But where we beginners were, the waves were just strong enough to lift you up, nothing more.

I listened carefully to what my brother, my tutor, had to say about positioning yourself properly heading out to the waves. Pick your wave, turn the board around, lie down on the board and keep your feet together, he said. Then, just before it hits, start paddling furiously to work up your speed. When the wave hits, you deftly pull yourself up onto the board, standing up in one smooth motion, with your arms out for balance, and you let the power of the wave carry you in to shore.

At least that's the theory. In reality, you spend a lot of time waiting, then getting rolled by waves. Most of the time, you're paddling and flying off your board, arms and legs spread like starfish as the waves crash down around you.

Surfing, I realized, is a lot like sending content out into the world. You are always hoping to "catch a wave," hoping your hand-crafted content will rocket off when you hit the send button.

But just like surfing, it's a lot harder than it looks. Here, then, are how surf rules apply to making your content take off:

1. **Position yourself correctly:** You can't catch a wave if you're sitting on the shore. You need to grab your board and get yourself out to where the waves are breaking. In the content marketing world, this means you need to be creating and publishing on those platforms where your content has a chance

of being seen and shared by others.

2. **Choose your wave:** Once you're in the water, you need to choose the right wave. It's an intuitive process. The waves will keep coming at you and other surfers are all doing the same thing. The nice thing about waves is that they can be shared. More than one surfer can be riding the same wave at the same time. Picking the right wave in content marketing may mean choosing the right platform for your specific content once you've tried out a few and can see where you are getting the best response. For some, that may be LinkedIn Pulse, or SlideShare or a submission to Reddit. While you can try on Facebook or with your own blog, you need the power of re-distributors — people who will boost your content for you by sharing through their networks and across the platforms they use — to really get your content out there.

3. **Get on the board and start paddling before the wave hits**: Once you've positioned yourself well and picked the right wave for you, it's time to start paddling to give yourself the help you need for lift-off. In content marketing, this means you start building up pre-release demand for your content. That may mean boosting a post or sending out a pre-email to your list announcing a forthcoming post that you're really proud of. You're trying to bring yourself up to the same speed as the wave. So you do whatever it takes to get there. There is no time for doubt. That wave is coming and you need to be already moving when it hits if you want it to rocket you off.

4. **Stand up!** Once that wave hits, pull yourself up onto the board as smoothly as you can. In other words, get ready to double down and push out that post. Tweak the headline and publish it again on a different platform, or cull a few infographics from it to repurpose content you now know is working. It takes a lot of practice to develop that fluidity of motion, but as our surf coach said, you're probably going to fall off anyway, so you might as well fall from a standing position rather than staying

low in a false sense of security.

5. **Roll and repeat.** It's going to take a while. You may be out there all day and never get up on your board (like me). But if you can get it all right just once (even if you can't stand up and just boogie board it in), with those rocket jets under your board, you'll know what it feels like to really move. It's tiring, and you need to practice, practice, practice. Your body will get weary, your arms will get sore, but if you keep at it, with patience and determination, you'll catch a wave. And maybe one day you'll be riding with the giants.

Building a sales funnel

Having developed some content and published it, you have effectively seeded the top of what is known as a "sales funnel." Picture a funnel with the wide open mouth part up top and the skinny narrow funnel part pointing down. Your content is what's rolling around up at the top of the wide mouth like bait fish, with the sole purpose of attracting prospects down deeper into the funnel to where you can convert them into a sale.

What you need to begin

- Content: Articles you create or curate, such as photos, videos, e-books, webinars, etc. Anything related to what you create and/or the service or product you are selling.
- A platform: Somewhere to publish your content that prospects can easily find and access.
- A form: A simple mechanism to get your prospects to give you some information about who they are (usually an email address). (sumo.com offers a number of free tools).
- An email marketing tool (MailChimp or something else).

- A PayPal account or some other way of getting payment information securely from your clients.

What a sales funnel is

Your prospects, whether they are consumers (B2C) or other businesses (B2B), are out there somewhere. There are many more prospective clients than people who become clients. The process through which they pass from the world into your business is known as a sales funnel, because it's wider at the top (so it can accommodate all the people who are drawn to you for one reason or another) and narrower at the bottom, where the smaller percentage of prospects actually become paying clients (in sales jargon, these are known as conversions, because they convert from being a prospect to being a client).

There are several online courses and countless blog posts written on how to build a sales funnel. Developing a detailed sales funnel for your own specific business is beyond the scope of this book, but the structure and essence of what one is and how to design your own are described below.

How a sales funnel works for freelancers

As a freelancer, you are responsible not just for doing the work you get, but for getting it in the first place. Getting work is often much harder (and less fun) than doing work, but you can't do work (or outsource to other freelancers) if you don't get it first, so you need to hunker down and crack this nut.

The good news about a sales funnel is that it works for you. Rather than doing direct one-to-one sales sending emails, making cold calls or being out there pressing the flesh (which is not something everyone loves doing), your sales funnel is on 24/7, doing the one thing it's meant to do: drawing in prospects.

The simplest way to get a sales funnel up and running is a blog. You can put one up with very little cost, and start producing content that matters to your clients today. Every blog post you put out there is a piece of content that will attract some prospects to you as they search out information about what interests them. Every piece of content you produce, in whatever format (text, photos, video or other), can be considered a lead magnet, drawing prospects to you.

While much content is made to be given away and consumed for free, no strings attached, some people who really like what you have to offer will give you their email address so they can get more such content from you. Maybe that's content you've created and keep behind a premium "subscribers only" wall, or maybe it's an e-book you've written about your area of expertise that your prospects want. How you develop your content library and what you choose to give away, vs. ask for something in return for, is up to you. But once you've established a basic system of publishing content, requiring an email address to be given in exchange for more content, you've effectively created the top of your sales funnel.

For example, I run a blog (www.julianhaber.com) where I publish articles once a week about photography. Sometimes it's about gear, sometimes about conferences, or events or corporate portraits. Essentially, I try to create content that speaks to my expertise in photography, but that also can help or educate my target audience (people who hire professional photographers). The scope is very limited and the content, though varied, does not stray too far from the general categories that are relevant to my audience (event or conference organizers, people looking for headshots, corporate communications, PR companies, experiential marketers, etc.). My blog posts are my lead magnets. Clients find me by searching for things they're interested in (ideally, topics I've written or posted content about), and if they accept me as an expert and need to hire a photographer, they contact me. In other words, they start at the top of the funnel and start moving toward the bottom.

Not everyone who enters the funnel stays there. That's why it's wider at the top and narrows to a small tube at the bottom. Some prospects lose interest or change their plans or find an alternative to your solution. Some just stop — the equivalent of putting stuff in your online cart, then flushing it by closing the browser tab. If you haven't captured the prospect's email address, you don't actually know if you have anyone in your funnel until (or unless) they contact you.* (There are more specialized tools that will actually track this level of engagement, but I think they're beyond what you need when you're starting out). That's why it's important to have a means for soliciting and capturing an email address while you've got their attention and critically, their trust. If they appreciate the content you've supplied and trust that you won't abuse the privilege, some will give you their email address. This is the gold you're after. If you don't abuse it, it will turn into dollars for you.

Moving prospects through a sales funnel — from their initial contact with you to them buying something from you or hiring you for your services — is the art of the sale in freelancing. You need to understand what makes your prospects want to buy from you and what turns them away. It takes time, diligence and patience. You learn by trial and error. But it is the most important job you have to do. If you figure it out, you're like the farmer who wakes up one morning to find a goose that lays golden eggs.

Nudging prospects along through your funnel can be done by sending timely messages with offers of access to more resources or to a support person (in most cases, that's you) who can talk to prospects directly, answer their questions, provide help or whatever it is your prospects are looking for in that moment. With each contact, you have the opportunity to strengthen the trust bond that keeps your prospect moving down the funnel. If you push too hard, you risk blowing it up.

While formulas for how to do this abound on the Internet, I don't believe there is a one-size-fits-all approach. What works for a freelance graphic designer may not work for someone running a home renovation business. You need to learn and understand your audience intimately. The more you understand who they are, what they like and need and what makes them tick, the closer you get to a sale.

* That's not precisely true, of course, since you have data analytics like Google Analytics that can tell you the kind of traffic you are getting on your posts, where along your sales funnel they go and where they abandon course, based on their IP address and other data they leave behind as digital exhaust. But from a direct content marketing point of view, without having received any indication from the prospect that they are interested in hearing from you, in the concrete form of their email address, you haven't really drawn them close enough to sell to (yet).

There is more than one kind of sales funnel

Keep in mind that this online version of a sales funnel, while the most common, is not the only kind of sales funnel there is. As you begin the continuous process of attracting prospects to your business consider trying some of these other approaches as well:

1. Building or joining a referral network:

    a. Start with friends and family — tell them what you're doing and ask them to tell their networks about you.

    b. Align yourself with other freelancers to whom you offer a complementary service or product that helps them sell.

    c. Become a sub-supplier to a larger version of yourself who already has a steady stream of clients, or more work than they can handle.

    d. Align yourself with large companies or associations that can refer you to their clients or partners.

e. Ask for referrals from your existing clients: If you've been freelancing for a while, they can help you find new business.

f. Join local meet-ups, business networking groups or associations, etc., where you can be included in their directory of members/service providers.

2. Hiring a virtual assistant to do lead generation for you:

a. Hire someone to research your market and contact prospective clients on your behalf, who will then deliver to you a vetted list of qualified "warm" leads that you can then approach.

3. Run ad campaigns online:

a. Use Google AdWords or through Facebook (the Goliaths of online ads) to run small test campaigns putting out offers repeatedly directing those who click to a landing page on your website that then delivers on the ad offer, and guides them in though some kind of form capture.

4. Participate in trade shows.

5. Post flyers in relevant locations you know your prospects frequent.

6. Use larger platforms like Amazon or eBay or Etsy to sell, and take advantage of their built-in online promotional tools.

A sales funnel ultimately relies on both inbound leads (those who find you) and outbound efforts (prospects you find and reach out to directly). The right balance of inbound vs. outbound will be determined by the type of business you're in, your audience and your effort and inclination. As nice as it would be to sit back and have customers come to you simply on the basis of your reputation, that is unlikely to happen quickly, if ever. You will need to drum up business regularly and sustainably using these techniques, and others you discover on your own journey through freelancing.

But whichever method you end up using, remember that all freelance businesses begin with a single client. And you build that client list one client at a time by doing good work, delivering on what you say you will deliver on, being consistent and sticking to it.

Email marketing only works if your audience trusts you

An email address is easily given and easily taken away. But if you can use the access it provides to build an audience that cares about the work you do and trusts you to keep delivering on it, your email list will produce revenue. The key is maintaining the integrity of the list by treating the privilege of the communication as sacrosanct.

With a means of connecting with your prospects, you can write to them (or set up a series of auto-responders that go out in timed releases) triggered by actions the recipient does or does not take.

Here's how it works from a prospective client's perspective:

Your prospect comes across an article you've published that resonates with them. They click and read it. At the bottom of the article, other links appear with related content. They click on another headline. They read a few and just as they reach for another slice, up pops a window asking for an email address and offering something in return (a free e-book, a guide, limited-time unrestricted access to the full site, etc.).

If you've done your job well as a content provider and your prospect feels they can trust you and wants the content you are offering, they pop in their address and within a few minutes they receive an email (the auto-responder), delivering on the promise from the pop-up (a link back to the free digital product or credentials to log into your site for unrestricted access, etc.).

Now you've got the email address of someone who has demonstrated they're interested in the kind of content you are producing, which presumably is related to what you have to sell.

Respect the inbox

Where you go from here depends on your audience's needs and tolerance for further emails. Less is more, in my opinion. I've subscribed too many times to count to sites I initially enjoyed and found useful, only to unsubscribe after receiving an onslaught of too many emails right away.

Preserving the trust that someone's email address confers is critical. Use your next message to make an offer, but include access to free content. Seth Godin, who writes and publishes a blog post every day, periodically weaves into his emails offers to join his AltMBA program or buy his books or sign up for one of his paid online courses. Maybe 10 or 15 such emails come through in a year, but the rest of the year he supplies a steady, consistent stream of quality content so I never feel he's trying to sell me something. Sometimes when the offers do come through, I click and buy.

That's how effective email marketing works. Your prospects never feel like you're selling to them — rather, they feel they're getting a deal, being given value, and are happy to pay you for the service.

Whether you're selling a digital product or a service, the reputation you gain by providing content your audience finds useful, that adds value — even meaning — to their lives, ultimately becomes your strongest asset. Build and maintain that trust and you have a business for life. Break the trust by spamming, or diluting your content with too much low-quality junk, and you've killed the proverbial goose that lays the golden egg.

What to measure and why

If you've attended a conference in any industry in the past few years, you've heard the term "data" or "big data" so much it sounds like the robots have taken over and the world is being run by one giant super-computer called Google or Facebook.

Everything we do online and much of what we do offline generates data points that are traceable and can be used to build a profile on each one of us. What we like, what we don't like, who our friends are, what our political views are, the kinds of books we read, the places we go to — everything we do, ultimately, leaves a trail of data behind. It's this data — the new oil of the digital age — that drives e-commerce today.

It may feel a little overwhelming if you are running a one-woman shop and the biggest data point you have on your business is how many Likes you have on your Facebook page.

How do Likes help you do more, be more, sell more? They don't, of course. Not on their own, anyway. What you need is a way of understanding what actually matters for your business, and what signals (another word for "data point") you need to look out for and recognize that convey some kind of useful and meaningful — and ultimately actionable — information for you.

It's both tougher and easier than it looks. Let's start with the "why" part.

Why measure?

You need to measure data, or signals, from your market and presumed or actual target customer base to better inform your decisions about who your customers are, how they behave, what they like / dislike, and ultimately, what it is about you that piques their interest and especially what induces them to connect with you and sometimes hire you or buy from you.

If you knew exactly what your customers valued about you and why they chose to work with you every time they did, you could simply do more of that and get more and more customers infinitely.

Of course, it's not that easy. Customer types vary and therefore the reasons they choose you will vary too. And if you offer more than one service, then you need to do the same kind of thinking and research for each and every service you offer.

To begin with, think of why you choose to work with a given company or purchase a given product or service.

- Is it because of price?
- Someone referred you?
- You got a bonus or some kind of special offer?
- It was convenient?
- You loved the way you felt dealing with their customer rep?
- There were no alternatives?
- They were the quickest?
- They offered the best quality overall?

If you were that provider, wouldn't you want to know which of these factors was why your customers chose you? These are not the only questions you can ask, of course, but they represent a good start and they are the beginning, if not the end, of why you need measurement.

What to measure

The "what to measure" part is really the answer to the "why" part. It can change over time, and you really need to think creatively about what a given piece of data is telling you, as well as choosing the right mix of data sources to generate actionable insights versus a deluge of information that is so undifferentiated and complicated you don't know what to do with what you learn.

Many, but not all, of the insights you gather about your customers will come from how they behave online, interacting with one or more of the digital properties you run (website/blog, social media personae, etc.). But some extremely valuable data will come from your own observations of what clients say vs. what they do, the feedback they give you directly in answer to your questions or after-market feedback forms you use to solicit their input, and tracking over time who comes back, how frequently and whether any send you referral business.

Take price, for example. If your customers choose you because of price, then what price did they choose? Have you experimented with pricing, changing your offer with different clients over time sufficiently to understand what you can charge without pricing yourself out of the market, or (much, much worse) pricing too little so that you're leaving too much profit on the table? Gathering price data by asking for budgets, playing with offers that blend fixed and hourly rates, learning what competitors charge for the same service(s) and sometimes just outright asking your prospective clients what they are expecting to pay over time allows you to build up confidence in the price you decide to charge. If you've collected enough data on your price point, you'll soon start seeing better uptake on your offer. Ultimately, that will convert more prospects to buyers. You still won't win every bid you put in, but over time you should see an upward trend in your hit-to-miss ratio, which tells you that you're doing something right.

Though that's important, it's just one small piece of the puzzle, of course. Once you get started, you begin to get a sense for what else matters. The kinds of data you can collect using technology splinters into literally hundreds if not thousands of micro-slivers of information, depending on your level of technical sophistication. Your website analytics (e.g. Google Analytics, which is free), will tell you how many visitors are coming to your site, where they are coming from, what keywords they are using that lead them to you, what pages they land on most often and how long they stay there.

Without having an advanced degree in analytics, you can learn a lot about the functionality and effectiveness of your web presence by paying attention to just a few data points:

- Top keywords used to search for your specific service or offering: Keywords that are delivering lots of traffic should be reworked and used in new content to strengthen the connection and drawing power.

- Bounce rate (how many people land on your site and leave immediately): You want this number to be low and/or get lower over time.

- Sources of traffic (organic vs. paid, social media sites, etc.): Organic is good because it's free and means your marketing is working; strong referral traffic from a given social media site (Facebook vs. LinkedIn, for example) can also tell you where you need to put more time into content creation and which platforms are working best for you.

- Length of time on site (total, and per page visited): It's good to see more than a few seconds, but what matters most is what actions visitors take. Sometimes a long time on your site can mean it takes them a long time to find what they're looking for, so look carefully at the pages with the longest times to try to understand what is driving the length of stay.

- Pages visited (the actual posts or sections of your site): This tells you which of your content marketing is stickiest. Do more of what gets the most visits.

- And of course, any actions taken by visitors: Having CTAs (Call to Actions) on every page is important. A call to action can be a button for visitors to learn more, or a link out to an email that automatically generates that they can they use to reach you directly with. The CTA, ultimately, is what drives business directly to you, so pay a lot of attention to the ones that work and drop or tweak any that aren't getting a lot of action.

- What devices visitors are using to view your site (hint: over 70% likely use handheld mobile devices of some kind): This matters only so far as to prove that mobile is really where most of your customers are experiencing you and your brand for the first time, and therefore you want to be certain your digital presence is optimized for mobile devices.

The idea is to recognize that your market is like a puzzle you will never have all the pieces for. But if you're looking in the right direction, you can find a few of the edge pieces and enough of the image to understand what you're doing. You will be able to fill in the blanks using your own reason, logic and common sense.

Networking and business development

Think of yourself as constantly connected, in a networked web of people, ideas, technologies and tools that you can pull on or leverage when the time is right.

Being constantly aware of your connections and inherent connectability teaches you to become a more engaged listener and a more active thinker.

Whenever I meet anyone, I try to figure out two things: what that person is good at, and who I know that it might be interesting for that person to meet. I do this instinctively now because it's paid off over and over again, and I know that it helps strengthen my network. You can't just hit up your network when you need something – the best networks work when all members contribute. Being a person who helps connect other people adds value to your network, and enhances your own reputation when you are looking for referrals.

Always being on the lookout for connections drives you to ask more questions, and feeds your curiosity to listen and understand the answers you receive. Just by asking, you often uncover ways you can connect someone working on a project over here, with someone else you know who is working on something similar, over there. The two projects might be complementary. Thinking of yourself as the hub, the connector, allows you to treat other people's problems, challenges or projects as puzzles you can help solve by connecting them up with someone – or something – that can help them. The solution could be an introduction to someone you know, a recommendation for a product or software application that solves what they are struggling with. The more often you do it, the better you become at it. By constantly thinking in terms of connection, you begin to see connections everywhere.

Not only is this a highly satisfying activity in its own right, but it helps you immeasurably by turning you into the person people think of when they have a situation they need help with. When you see other people's problems as opportunities, the more problems people bring to you, the more opportunities you have to find solutions.

And sometimes the solution turns out to be you.

What is "biz dev" or business development?

Business development or "biz dev" sounds kind of sexy. But what does it really mean?

In very simple terms, it means creating the conditions for making business possible, if not probable. And in a networked world, it means making connections where you serve as the connecting node in a mutually advantageous relationship that wouldn't have materialized without your intervention.

Here are a few things I would categorize as business development activities:

- Connecting one person to another where you see a potentially mutually advantageous relationship developing;

- Connecting one company to a supplier you can recommend who can solve a problem they are currently experiencing or may soon be about to experience;

- Connecting or sharing one person's idea or concept with another person or group of people who will benefit from the new knowledge;

- Recommending a new technology or software to a person or group of people who will benefit from learning about it and/ or using it to improve what they do or how they work;

- Connecting yourself with other departments or teams within your current client's company (and tapping into their often separate budgets).

Networking and being a person who looks for and makes connections has had the single most influential impact on my freelancing business. By developing the simple habit of paying a lot of attention to making and maintaining my connections, I've been able to grow my practice from being a sole photographer covering one-off events to having a team of other photographers, videographers, web designers, digital marketers and others that, in turn, enables me to take on bigger and more diverse contracts.

Ask questions and listen to the answers

For example, when I'm talking to a client, I always ask a lot of questions about their business and their role in it. I've found that most of the time when a client is hiring for one project, they're working on other projects that require other resources. When they're looking for some photos to populate their website, they may also be looking for someone to generate blog content, or maybe even a web designer who can help them upgrade or redo their current website. And wouldn't you know it, I happen to know just the person who can help with that.

If you consider making connections as a spectrum of activities that includes talking to strangers, attending networking events, networking online, making real friends and Facebook friends, interacting with followers and commentators and direct sales, business development falls somewhere towards the end, closer to sales. It isn't selling, but it is often part of the dance that precedes selling, because its main purpose is to consolidate another person's trust in you as a reliable partner.

While business development is often conflated with prospecting, something you do with people who are not yet your clients, it isn't the same thing. Business development does happen with prospective clients — but it's an important thing to keep in mind with your existing clients as well.

Watch for changes

One of the main goals of business development with existing clients is to make sure you are paying attention to your existing relationships. You want to always be making sure your client is happy. You also need to know what's going in your client's company. Companies large and small are always undergoing changes. Sometimes these internal changes are big, sometimes small, but no matter what, they can affect you. Your client may get moved into a different department, or be planning to switch jobs altogether. Having a good relationship with your client encourages them to keep you informed of changes likely to affect your business relationship with their company. It also gives you an opportunity to be prepared and not get caught off guard if someone new comes in and wants to change all the suppliers, as sometimes happens when people switch jobs.

One of my long-time clients suddenly cancelled a standing contract I'd had with them for years, full of apologies. On probing, I discovered that there had been a lot of internal changes going on, and my client was no longer responsible for the events I'd been regularly hired for. There was a new person in the role who had her own team of suppliers. Having the relationship I had with my client didn't guarantee my contract, but it gave me insight into what was happening and allowed me to prepare a new marketing strategy to maintain the business I had with them.

Remember the concept of lifetime value of a customer? It's the idea that a single client over a lifetime can be worth a lot more than just the one gig you initially get hired for. Unlocking that value is partly the result of ongoing business development activities you undertake to deepen and strengthen that relationship. It assumes, of course, that you do great work, but it goes well beyond that.

It is not, despite what it looks like on early episodes of the hit series Mad Men, just about wining and dining your clients and new prospects. These kinds of showy and pleasurable extensions of your largesse can help, but they are not normally within the reach of a freelancer, especially when you are just building your book. Just because you can't afford to take your client and the team out for a big expensive meal at a fancy restaurant, however, doesn't mean you can't do business development.

Be known, be liked, be trusted

To put business development in the context of Gigonomics: the goal is to get booked.

To get the gig — to be chosen — you need three things to happen: You need to be known, be liked and be trusted. Of these, trust is the essential piece but it can't be accessed without having the first two in place. You can be known, and not liked or trusted, but you can't be liked without being known. And you can't be trusted without being both known and liked.

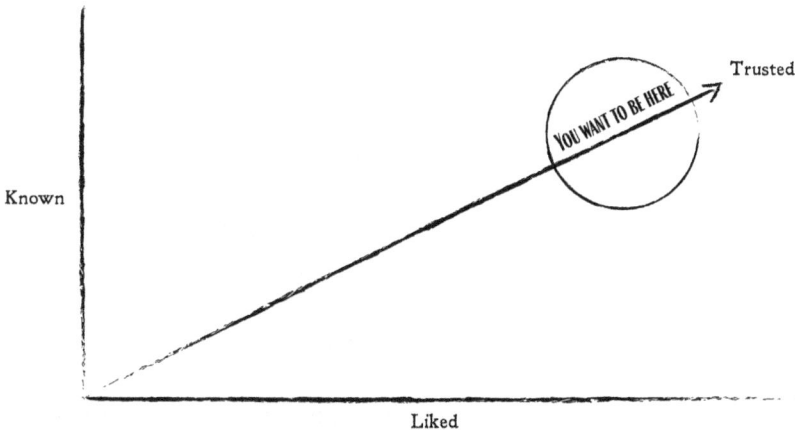

If you've done your networking well and consistently, you will be known. If you are genuine and helpful and actually care about other people, you will be liked. To be trusted, however, requires proof. That is where the rubber hits the road.

Your reputation precedes you

Your reputation matters. Trust is hard won and easily lost. Earning it requires delivering on what you say you will do over and over again. It requires consistency, integrity, authenticity and commitment to the long term — everything, in short, that you need to succeed as a freelancer. All of which you need to bring to play to do business development well.

Trust-building measures, done consistently, are as important as the big splashy spend. In most organizations these days, clients are prevented by their code of ethics from accepting gifts over a very low threshold anyway (usually around $25), so in fact, the small, consistent actions you can take are more likely to have an impact in the long run.

Building trust that deepens a relationship can take the form of many small actions. Consider just these few to get your mind going:

• Sharing an article you come across that you think your client or prospect would find interesting or helpful.

• Recommending a new tool or application that will help your client or prospect work more effectively or make their work less onerous.

• Showing up with something extra for a gig — perhaps a box of donuts for the office or some fresh bagels.

• Doing a little bit more than you're asked to do.

• Sharing ideas or offering to help out beyond your normal scope of work when you see the client could use the extra help.

These actions and many others you can come up with on your own can be classified as simple acts of generosity and kindness, which they are. But in the context of a business relationship, they serve another purpose. They tell the person for whom they are intended that you value the relationship and that you want it to continue and to grow, you don't take it for granted, and you're there to help.

For a freelancer, getting trusted is the hardest part, but once you're there, it immediately begins to pay off. (Unfortunately, one of the reasons it pays off so well is because so many other freelancers are either unreliable or flaky, or both). Having a person's trust is reinforced when you do things like refer them to another supplier (whom you may or may not also be subcontracting out through your practice), who does as good a job as you do on the work you do for your clients. In my case, for example, when helping a client with a big event, I may bring in one or more other photographers to provide complete coverage, as well as videographers. I am only as good as any freelancer I refer or subcontract to a client, but if they all deliver as I expect them to, my stock rises with my client because I was able to solve not just one of their problems, but several.

When you're approaching a new prospective client with whom you have yet to transact any business, your scope of biz dev activities will vary a bit from what you can do when you've already got a viable working relationship. At its core, however, the focus and intention is the same. Be helpful and earn trust.

If you're a web designer, for example, give a free assessment of your prospect's website, showing your expertise, and also value-add by giving them some free advice. If you're a business coach or consultant, offer a few tips on improving a prospect's LinkedIn profile, or make introductions where you see potential synergies between two people who don't know each other yet. By placing yourself in the middle of value-creating relationships, you earn the trust and respect of both parties, and through the basic psychological phenomenon of reciprocity, they will feel inclined (if not subtly obliged) to do some good to you in return. Call it karma if you prefer, but the notion of "what goes around comes around" is fundamentally what drives successful business development.

Providing solutions, solving people's problems, making connections where you can, are all components of business development. Being there and showing your support for fundraisers or charities your client or prospects support is another. If you're trying to win new business or maintain a good relationship with a client, show up for their charity events. If you can't be there in person, make a contribution. It will be noticed, and it will reinforce the trust they have in you as someone who is on the same team they're on.

Ultimately, business development is about bringing yourself into contact with people from whom you expect a business relationship and maintaining those relationships. Having and strengthening their trust in you is the key to unlocking the continuing and future value these relationships hold. It's how you get the next gig, and the one after that. Earn and keep their trust, and "yes" is just a few short letters away.

Being connectable

Humans are like the middle pieces in a puzzle. Not the easily defined edge pieces — those are what we spend much of our lives trying to find — but those pieces right in the middle, the ones with abstract splashes of colour that don't tell you anything until you find matching pieces to understand what you are looking at.

We are all built of connectable bits. The very essence of life, the double helix structure of DNA is made of base pairs (A with T, C with G) that need to be joined. A self is not a self, a human not a human, a life not a life without connectable parts fitting into each other.

This inherent connectability explains our seemingly inexhaustible drive to join online networks and build a web of connections by sharing the pieces of content and other sticky bits of intellectual unguent that bind us and hold us in place in a chaotic world.

Although there is no real definable end shape to a network of living things, we want to see the edges to it. We crave knowledge of the shape and extent of our world.

So we look to numbers to draw a thick black contour line around the inherently abstract shape of a life. We pay attention to the number of friends, followers, tweets, posts and connections we create, maintain and develop. The higher the number, the bigger our presumed impact. The social media networked world makes us conflate a high number of connections with our sense of self-worth and identity. We are what we count.

Unfortunately, what we are counting is mostly how many, instead of how important. We are focussed on quantity vs. quality. And that, in my opinion, is a mistake.

When it comes to connections, it's not how many, but how meaningful they are that matters. Better to have one real connection with someone at a networking event than speed through 20 flittery conversations where you hardly make eye contact and can't remember the name of the person you are talking to.

All connections count, of course, but some count far more than others.

How to network online and offline

Networking matters, and no matter where you fall on the extrovert/introvert continuum, if you want to thrive as a freelancer you need to master networking. It's a truism to say it's not what you know, but who you know. But how do you get to know the people you need to know will matter for you if you don't have any connections to start with?

Begin with an understanding of what networking is and what it isn't.

Networking is essentially...

- purposeful
- omnidirectional — you can network up, down and laterally
- about who you are and who you know
- about what you can do to help someone
- about contributing value as measured by connections — to people, ideas, technology
- about sharing
- curiosity-driven
- something you do everywhere
- an ongoing activity...

Networking isn't....

- about making small talk
- only about shaking hands and handing out business cards
- a job interview
- a series of personal advertisements
- just something you do when you need something

Four-way traffic

Of these, perhaps the most important point to remember as a free-lancer is the omni-directional quality of networking. A truly valuable network has members who all contribute something to increasing the value of the network by bringing new high-value connections to it, sharing ideas, making business referrals, and paying attention to the work you do.

Some networking does indeed happen in the context of a gated garden where only the elite gather and help each other out (think Da-
vos). But a freelancer operates in a much flatter world. The subcon-
tractor you've hired to help you out on a project one time may be
the person hiring you for the next project. A client today may be a
collaborator tomorrow. The stranger in line behind you may be your
next client. Sometimes you can help someone find their next gig,
sometimes they help you.

Being a good networker means accepting responsibility for your network. When you meet someone — anyone — your first thought
should be, "how can I help this person? Who do I know or what can I
share that will help him or her do what they are trying to do?" If you
adopt that mentality, and actually live it, you will find that people
respond in kind.

I helped launched a second career for a friend of mine who became
a masterful freelancer, simply by making a connection for him. I was
on a volunteer board for a charity and happened to be chatting with a
fellow board member who'd recently invested in a company and was
looking for someone to help with marketing. I knew my friend was
looking to make a career change, and though he'd not been a freelancer before, I knew he had exactly the skills my board colleague was
seeking. As it turned out, they were even old college buddies who'd
fallen out of touch. A quick email intro led to a conversation, which
ultimately led to a very profitable relationship for both sides, and put
my friend on an upward trajectory that's still rising.

Pay attention

What do you do when you don't really have that network built out? How do you get started? No matter how far you think you are from meeting the people you think can help you, you have something of value to offer in return. That may only be the gift of your attention, but don't underestimate its value. In a world of busy people rushing through life, slowing things down and truly listening to someone else leaves a genuine impression.

Even if your goal is as transaction-based as "connect with X person to access Y organization to sell widgets," treating people like parts of an equation is a guaranteed path to failure. Consider the person you wish to speak with as someone from another country with a fascinating culture you want to learn more about, even if you are both working parallel jobs in the same industry. Everyone is truly unique, and we each cling to our own uniqueness as integral to our core of what makes life meaningful to each of us. When you seek out and recognize the uniqueness of another person and genuinely commit yourself to empathizing with them, it is impossible not to connect. Real attention is like water on parched soil for most people. People crave it — they want to be heard, appreciated, understood. Give someone the real gift of your attention and they will open up to you.

MIND THE GAP

Meeting strangers is hard. It's awkward and uncomfortable, even for people who do it all the time. When you find yourself in a room full of strangers, none of whom really know each other very well, the first thing you'll notice is the spacing between people. There will be small pods of people here and there, pairs standing together near doorways or walls, and a lot of singletons looking around and at their phones or sidling up to the bar. If you're going to begin your upward trajectory in freelancing life, you need to brave the "no man's land," the spaces between people, pairs and pods, in any networking event. And all you have to do is shuffle your feet a few paces to the nearest clump of humans.

Somebody's got to do it. Why not you? It's easy to hide at networking events. You can sip your drink, check your phone, pretend you're waiting for someone, keep walking around, stuff your face with hors d'oeuvres — or you can do what you went there for. Be open, be receptive, smile and say hello to the person next to you.

I make a habit of saying hello to strangers, and not just at networking events; I do it everywhere I go: on the street, waiting in lines, at bars, on planes, wherever. Despite what you've been told as a child (which is still good advice for a child), you should talk to strangers. Strangers, as a thousand fridge magnets will attest, are just friends you haven't met yet. I've met people at conferences who've later hired me to shoot their weddings, or come to visit me when their travels bring them to my part of the world. I practice meeting people all the time, so when I do meet someone who turns into a client (or refers me to other clients) it feels natural, because it is.

When you meet a stranger, always keep in mind that you're connecting. You may never see the person again or you may end up working for them. Regardless, if you treat everyone you meet like someone with whom you may be forming a professional or friendship relationship at the very first point of contact, you've already broken through one self-limiting belief. No matter how brief or skittish it is, think and act as if the person you are with is someone with whom you may end up having a long-term, meaningful business relationship. By placing your focus on this outcome, you remove the myopic astigmatism that can short out a connection on contact due to nervousness or inexperience.

Practice with the pros

At every networking event, there's a core group of people who are professional networkers. I don't mean to say that's their actual job title, but rather, they've been to so many conferences and trade shows and client meetings that they have no trouble at all working the room. Odds are they already know half the people there, too, simply by virtue of their skill at networking. If you're the newbie or get an unpleasant feeling in the pit of your stomach when you face the chore of talking to strangers, latch onto one of these people and use them as your entry point to a pod of people. Invariably, they will be the ones doing the talking. You can just approach, listen on the edge and then pipe up with a quip or comment when you see the opportunity. But more importantly, watch what they do. Watch how they stand, the kinds of questions they ask, how they respond to questions. Just by studying someone in action you'll pick up a few cues and tips that you can then copy and make your own.

Online vs. real world networking

Everything that applies to face-to-face networking applies online as well, but there are some important differences. What you publish, comment on, react to, share, tweet, retweet, like, follow, love, and post online never goes away. It's ironic, actually, that such an apparently ephemeral medium as social media platforms is actually the most permanent record of our lives today. Never has there been a more ubiquitous and undeletable record following us around as there is today. Because of that, how you behave online is actually far more important than how you behave offline.

Obviously, posting hateful, hurtful, childish or embarrassingly crude things is plain dumb. As most people are on more than one network, don't assume that you can be more open on Facebook than you would be on LinkedIn, for example. While Facebook is inherently more personal and LinkedIn more professional, the boundaries are easily blurred, and the reality is that your data is out there and easily cross-referenced. Which is exactly what prospective clients, collaborators and new acquaintances will do. They will Google you, check out your photos, read through a few of the things you post and form an opinion about you based on your online presence. So pay attention to what's out there and keep it clean, civil, friendly and relevant to who you are and what you're about.

When making connections online, use the same rules you'd apply to approaching someone in person. It's okay to show that you've done your research on the person, but don't be creepy and comment on their vacation photos. And it's okay to reach out to someone you don't know if you think there could be something mutually advantageous about connecting, but don't be spammy.

And don't immediately follow up on the connections you make with a sales pitch. The most valuable connections are ones where you both benefit from being connected. Think about what you have to offer and contribute whenever you are reaching out to someone you don't know.

If you see mutual connections, ask for an introduction. If you have none, make it obvious in a brief text included with your request to connect what value you see in connecting. And don't be insulted or upset if not everyone accepts your request. Some people spend less time online than others, some have very specific criteria for accepting requests, and some just don't pay that much attention to people they don't know. Don't take it personally.

Here's a handy networking listicle you can use:

1. Be generous — give the gift of your time and attention.

2. Be authentic — be who you are.

3. Be bold — push a little tiny bit out of your comfort zone.

4. Smile often.

5. Ask questions.

6. Wait for and listen to the answers.

7. Be interested.

8. Be friendly.

9. Don't be in a hurry to blurt out stuff about yourself.

10. Try to find out why the other person is in the room.

11. If you can help, offer to help.

12. If you can't help, say you will keep them in mind in case you meet someone who can, and follow through.

13. Tell the truth.

14. Don't overstate, don't understate.

15. Ask for a card and ask if it is okay to follow up, and if so, when would be the best time and how.

16. Be sure to have several of your own cards on you to give out.

17. Be polite, but not obsequious.

18. It's not about what you can do for me now, it's about who are you and what you are about.

19. Recognize the person you are talking to as a person first.

20. Don't be purely utilitarian.

21. Keep in touch — being in a network implies others can network with you. Don't just network when you need something or are looking for a new gig.

22. You're always on — the network never sleeps.

How to make meaningful small talk (or how to talk to strangers)

Myth #1: Networking only allows for shallow small talk

Myth #2: Meaningful connections take a long time to build

Making small talk is what you do when you're with people you don't know well, or at all. It usually feels a bit awkward, because it is. However, no matter what your personality type, there are a few strategies you can deploy to not only make small talk less awkward, but actually turn it into a powerful networking device.

When done well, your conversation, like the hors d'oeuvres swirling around the room at a networking event, should be broken down into bite-sized chunks. Your goal is to move fluidly through the room, tarrying long enough to ensure that your prospects have had a taste and their appetite has been whetted for more. You're not serving up a four-course meal, but rather delivering a small selection of conversational tapas. You don't need to share your full bio, explain in minute detail what you do and what your company does. You just need to leave a firm, positive impression.

Easier said than done, particularly if you are shy, introverted, feeling insecure, looking for your next gig or just feeling your way in the dark trying to learn more about a new company or industry. Luckily, there are simple ways to open people up and the opportunities that come with them that I believe anyone can learn. The key is to not treat small talk like small talk.

The human animal

While the content of the conversation you have in "small talk" settings may appear to be insignificant, the important chemistry that is happening while you do it is what really matters. The human animal is right there inside each and every one of us as we exchange pleasantries about the weather or comment on the latest headline. That animal is noticing things you may not even be aware of — your posture and body language, whether you're making eye contact, your pupils are dilating, you are perspiring, how fast you're talking, the timbre and pitch of your voice, the distance between you, all while filtering out the rest of the room. There's a lot going on.

Much of what we read in others' behaviour is how nervous or how calm they appear. Confident people put us at ease, nervous people make us feel tense. Emotional states are contagious and social situations are where the contagion spreads fastest and easiest. There's a reason why networking events often come with inhibition-lowering alcoholic beverages. But regardless of how nerve-wracking you find it, you can benefit from deliberately slowing things down.

Breathe deeply. Go slowly. Take your time. Let the room warm up. You don't have to speak with everyone there. If you can come away with a single good connection made at a networking event, you've scored. One and done. Of course, you can stay on, and if you're on a roll, rack up a few other great connections, but there's no reason to push too hard. Just focus on having real, genuine interactions with the people around you, one at a time, and over time you will become a skillful networker.

Work the angles — the power of the side banter

This may be the photographer in me speaking, but the angles are where all the action is. In networking, the angle is the side banter you have with someone while you're both sort of engaged with something else. Often that's drinking or waiting for a drink at the bar. But it can happen anywhere. It's the kind of conversation that can spring up when you find yourself somewhere with strangers nearby and you all have some time on your hands. You could be standing in line for a movie (if you still do that), or sitting next to someone on a plane. You may be on adjacent treadmills at the gym or waiting around with other parents to pick your kids up from school. These unplanned, unscripted, unexpected conversations are classic opportunities for casual side banter. Use them as places to practice diminishing your fear of strangers (if you have one) or to work on getting conversations started.

Take whatever's at hand as a starting point (there's a reason so many people talk about the weather — it's usually the first and most obvious thing you have in common with a stranger). Then just open things up. Ask the person a little about themselves, based on whatever they've disclosed. Tell them what you do or what you are about first and often they'll reciprocate.

And then just let things flow. Don't try to control things too much, and don't push for anything. Side banter can lead to longer, more engaged conversations if the setting lends itself to it (think golf courses, fishing boats), but the real value (and I would even say, pleasure) of side banter is that it is almost always short. The drinks get served, the line moves on, the plane lifts off...and that's the point. You both have a ready-made, easy out so there's no pressure for the conversation to continue. It can happen in fits and starts, with long silences in between, and that's okay. Learning to be comfortable with silence is another powerful technique for managing awkward social situations.

Let others do the work for you

Another strategy for transforming small talk into real talk is to just let the extroverts in the room do the work for you. Just smile pleasantly (practice in front of a mirror if smiling doesn't come naturally to you). You'll be amazed at how easily other people start conversations with you if you just smile and look approachable.

Small talk can lead to big deals

Let me give you a real-life example. I was hired once by an American conference events company that found me online and was hosting an event in my home town (Montreal, Canada). During the event, as I was going about my work as conference photographer, of course I had to interact with a lot of different people. The client team onsite was rather large, probably about 15 people, and though I didn't know who everyone was as I made my way through the different events of the conference, I chatted with various staff members in a series of small, brief conversations. I offered up little ideas about things to do in Montreal, where to eat, that kind of thing, but generally the conversations were light and non-specific — what most people would call "small talk." At one point after I'd submitted one day of images, one of the staff said in one of these impromptu conversations that they liked my work and wished it were so easy to work with other photographers in the different cities where they host events. I promptly replied, half-jokingly, I'd be happy to cover all their events for them. "Really? Good to know," my client said. Then I moved on back to work. Little did I know this small exchange would lead to the single biggest and best long-term contract in my professional career as a freelancer. I wound up covering over 20 of their international conferences, staying in five-star resorts and having a great time doing it. And it all happened because of a little off-the-cuff remark I made in the context of a small-talk conversation.

So remember:

1. Recognize the human animal in the room — in yourself and others.

2. Look and act approachable. Let others do the work and come to you.

3. Be prepared: Small talk topics always include the weather, current events, local or immediate issues. Think about them ahead of time and offer some kind of insight or commentary that's one step past the obvious.

4. Ask questions, and really pay attention to the answers. Ask follow-up questions. Find out about the person in front of you. Who are they, why are they there, what do they do, what are they looking to get out of the situation? What connections are they looking to make?

5. Make connections: Once you find out what someone cares about, think of ways you can respond. If you meet someone later on who fits the bill, make the intro. If you know of a product/software/person, then offer to make the connection and exchange business cards.

6. Don't be in a hurry. Don't press the card into someone's hand the second you meet them. Don't speak too hurriedly. Don't interrupt or cut people off.

7. Be present. Don't keep looking over the shoulder of the person you're with to see who else is in the room. Or keep staring at your phone.

8. Be genuine. A lot of people mask the discomfort they feel in social situations by adopting an alternate persona — someone louder, more obnoxious, arrogant or brasher than they really are. Be yourself. People can see through personas easily.

9. Don't be afraid of showing your vulnerability. Nothing opens people up more than letting them see that you have a weakness. If you are nervous, say so; if you don't know anyone or feel awkward or are just starting out, say so. Turn a stranger into an ally. You'd be surprised at how willing people are to help you.

10. Be time-sensitive: Don't monopolize someone, especially if you've started to feel more comfortable with them.

11. Leave spaces in your conversation and physically between you, for other people to join, for one or more to walk away.

12. Don't take things personally.

13. Let things happen at their own pace. Conversations start and stop. People come and go. Entries and exits are awkward. Don't even think about it. Just let them happen.

14. Be okay with some silence. Let others do the talking if you don't have anything to contribute. It's okay to listen.

15. Keep smiling!

Understanding your prospects' needs before selling

Where do you draw the line between networking and selling? When is it appropriate to ask a contact for business? How do you do it without putting your contact off and making them feel that you only connected with them so you could sell them something?

As a freelancer, part of your work is getting people to say yes more often when you offer them your services. Hearing someone say yes to the price you submitted or the proposal you sent in is exhilarating and satisfying. But just as you can't expect a garden to yield a harvest without preparing the soil, before you ask for a "yes," you need to set up the conditions that are most favourable to getting one. Too often people who are trying to get to "yes" underestimate how important it is to create the conditions for that "yes" to be possible.

In effect, it all boils down to this: you need to build up trust first before you try to make a withdrawal. Wherever you go, whomever you are with, opportunities for growing your business will present themselves. Without tripping over yourself trying to advertise what you do, be aware of the people you're with and learn as much as you can about them. Just let conversations flow naturally and develop relationships first, then pitch your wares. If you can share something of value with someone you meet who later becomes a client, all the better.

When I meet someone I think may be a prospect for my photography business, I don't immediately start selling. Often, for example, I'll meet people at events I'm covering for another client. In many cases, these people may be interested in using some of the photos I am taking for their own purposes. What I do is get the person's contact information, let them know that if my client is okay with sharing the photos, then send them a link to where they can download the photos. Depending on the situation, sometimes I will even put together a small specific gallery for them. Or sometimes someone at an event asks for a headshot to update their LinkedIn profile, and I take one for them on the spot and email it to them afterward. I do all of this for free and with no strings attached. Nonetheless, these friendly encounters frequently turn into future business down the road when a person I have helped needs to hire a photographer. People remember me. And since I sent them an email in my earlier exchange, they already have my contact info and a link to my website.

Accepting a connection doesn't mean you can start selling right away

You don't always have the luxury of meeting your prospects face-to-face or the time to develop the relationship as much as you would like. Using online networking tools can help but even here — perhaps especially here — it's important to understand your prospect's needs before trying to convince them to buy something from you. Just because you've made a connection doesn't mean you have the right to start selling. If you assume you have that right, you risk alienating your potential client and damaging your own reputation.

For example, I was recently invited to join yet another business networking platform. An acquaintance of mine had sent me the invite and though I ignored it at first, I later decided to take a look and click through.

Signing up was relatively easy and quick, as you would expect from any business today. The concept of the platform is to connect people with sales leads. So I expected the behaviour on the site to be more direct and salesy than on LinkedIn. Even so, I wasn't ready for what happened once I completed the brief set of questions that asked about the kinds of leads I was looking for.

Within minutes, I received an email from a telemarketing company asking if I wanted to set up a call to talk about using their services to generate leads for my business. The next email was an offer from a search-engine-optimization (SEO) specialist, promising to get me on the first page of Google (already there), and the last — before I unsub-scribed – was from a developer in India offering to build me an app.

Now, I understand that the context of this platform is selling, but these kinds of immediate solicitations just turned me off. They felt spammy. I'm a photographer and writer in Montreal, so the interests I ticked off in terms of leads I was looking for related to photography and digital marketing. But rather than get people who might reason-ably be interested in my services, I felt that I'd just opened myself up to unsolicited overtures from businesses offering things I had no interest in, didn't want and didn't need. Had any of them even taken a cursory look at who I was, they could have saved themselves time and spared me a lot of irritation. Instead, I didn't even consider using the platform and immediately turned off notifications and deleted the account.

In this digital age, where reaching out and touching someone is easier than ever, it's even more important to qualify your leads and actually make an effort to develop some kind of relationship before you hit someone up for a sale. There's even a meme on LinkedIn that mem-bers post about people who connect and immediately follow up with a sales pitch.

It's like expecting someone to take you home with them after they've been nice enough to smile back at you at the bar. It's just sleazy.

Thanks for connecting with me on linkedin

and then messaging me 5 minutes later with a sales pitch

Selling is a tough racket. But you don't make it easier on yourself by talking to people who aren't interested in what you are selling. Sometimes you just don't know and you have to canvas the market to assess demand, but even that can be done in a way that doesn't make people feel like they're being targeted for something they don't want.

There's a way to talk to people and a way to approach people that doesn't make them feel like they're just one side of a transaction they didn't ask for. The art of selling, ultimately, is about connecting with other humans, as a human.

People are always people first, and nobody likes to feel like they're just a shot in the dark.

Selling (yourself)

Every freelancer has two jobs, whether he/she knows it or not. There is the work. And then there is the work to get the work.

You cannot ever hope to succeed as a freelancer if you cannot in some fashion reconcile yourself to accepting both roles.

The first part is actually the easier part, and most freelancers already know this. It's why you are here reading this in the first place. You have probably already started doing it and have been doing it for a while. Or you are thinking about doing (which is also why you are reading this book) because you know how to do something that people value and will pay you for.

The second part, doing the work it takes to get work, to find and win new clients, to convert someone's interest in you and your business into a sale -- that's the part a lot more freelancers are uncomfortable with. But without the sales, you won't have a business. You may have a hobby or a great way for you to fill your spare time, but you won't be able to fill your plate or make rent.

Given its essential nature, it is surprising how little time in a day the average freelancer spends actively working on the work of getting work vs. everything else. It should take up at least 20% of your time, and preferably more. In the beginning, it is likely to take up to 50% of your time, as you begin to create and fill your pipeline. So that's at least one full day a week, up to two and half days exclusively focusing on doing what you need to do to get the work you want to do.

This next section explores what that kind of activity looks like and how to work it into your regular routines.

Overcoming your fear of sales

Learning how to gig = Learning how to sell

Before you can learn to gig, you need to get one big thing out of the way: your fear of selling.

If you're not the one selling your own services or product, someone else is doing it (or you're not making any money, period).

Even if you think you'd prefer having someone else do the work of booking gigs for you and getting you work, you still have to overcome your fear of sales to reach that person.

The good news is, selling isn't hard to do if you stop thinking of it as sales and start thinking of it as offering something of value to the right person who needs what you have to offer.

So instead of thinking "sell, sell, sell," think, "how can I communicate the value of what I have to offer to the people who might care about it?"

Start smart

Let's get a few things clear right from the beginning. Nobody buys anything they don't want, and nobody can afford not to buy something they really need. Understanding where what you're offering lies on that spectrum will immediately make you a better salesperson.

Are you selling something someone wants or needs? If it's both, then your job is easy. Unfortunately, most people don't really need a new logo design the way they need food in the fridge, and even if they really want a good headshot, they don't really need one that costs as much as the one you're trying to sell. If that's the case, they'll pass you over.

So how do you break through that wall of indifference and break down the defences of price-conscious buyers?

You have to identify what your prospect values, and pitch your offer in those terms. If your prospective customer doesn't value what you have to offer, then it's not a prospect. It's a wrong number.

What do you say when someone calls and asks for a price?

Talking value is a nice idea, you say, but what do you do with the caller who just wants to know how much it's going to cost?

This will happen. It may already have happened to you. Your blogging and marketing efforts have yielded some tangible results. One day you get an email, text or phone call asking how much it costs for such and such a service or item on your site.

(Now, you may not have this problem if you're running an online store of some kind, but if you are, like most giggers, moving from one short-term gig to the next, you'll get this question a lot.)

The first thing to do is immediately push back with your own question. Your goal, remember, is to understand what your client really values in terms of your offering and zone in on that before setting any kind of anchor point in terms of pricing.

That is, unless you intend on being the cheapie cheap offerer with a big plan to raise your prices once you've established yourself (not likely going to happen).

Never present your price as a cost. Reframe the dialogue. You are providing something of value that has a tangible worth.

Does what you have to offer:

- Save your clients money in any way? Time or allocation on scarce in-house resources? Cost of re-work if they contract the cheapest supplier and he or she screws up?
- Make your client's life or job easier?
- Can they easily justify you – have you provided them with enough of a business case to run by their boss (or bosses) if they have to?

Your ideal price should be just at the cusp or even a little beyond what your client feels comfortable paying. You never want them to feel like they got a great deal, unless you are deliberately and strategically offering them one.

Turn all sales calls into conversations whose sole purpose is to better understand your customer's pain points, what they value (because it relieves them of their pain points) and how they buy. Sales conversations should be 99% you asking your prospect questions, listening to the answers and framing your offer in terms of what you learn.

If you're not afraid to have a conversation, then you're not afraid of sales.

Developing a sales mentality

This is a story about an accidental entrepreneur.

I have a good friend who spent 20 years of his career working for other people. He is a very intelligent person who works hard and likes to get deep into problems to solve them. He is not afraid of rolling up his sleeves and learning a brand new skill if it will help him do his job better, and while he's highly educated (he was a Ph.D. scholar on a full scholarship at an Ivy League school), he's also skilled at teaching himself new things. He devours books, stays up late reading and has taught himself how to code as well as speak Mandarin. In other words, he's no slouch.

But he hates dealing with clients, and he hates doing sales even more. In his last job, while his boss was largely ruling in absentia, he more or less ran the shop, but when I first talked to him about going freelance and doing his own thing — which in my eyes he was virtually doing anyway, and more than qualified to do — he balked.

He had never thought of himself as an entrepreneur. One of the main obstacles he saw on that path was having to do lots of what he likes doing least of, which is dealing face to face with customers. An introvert by nature, he shuddered at the idea of picking up the phone and cold-calling people to find out about their business needs and offer his services.

And yet, he's now a successful entrepreneur running his own digital marketing practice, with more business than he can handle.

How did he do it?

With a little help, of course, but the main thing was that he changed his mind. He changed his mind about how he thought of himself. He started telling himself what people close to him could see and had been telling him for years — that he was more than good enough, he had the right skillset, and he could, in fact, be successful working for himself. But most importantly, he stopped looking at sales as some kind of onerous, pushy, aggressive thing that made his skin crawl. Instead, he let his own introverted personality breathe and he treated his sales calls like conversations.

He realized that the hard part (to him) about sales — asking for money, pricing his work, etc. — was something he could do in a proposal. And he was already very good and confident at putting those together. The talking part — the part he most feared initially — was what he changed his views on. Rather than treat the sales pitch like, well, a sales pitch, he treated it like he would any other problem that needed a solution. He turned his natural intellectual curiosity into a sales strength.

He asked questions. And he was genuinely interested in the answers. He paid attention. He connected the dots for his prospect by showing him how his problem could be solved in a few different ways. And when he finished and was invited to submit a proposal with details, he took a walk-before-you-run approach and gave them something that solved their immediate issues and left the door open to more business down the road, once that had been done.

In other words, he made a sale. And a great one too, as it turns out, because the original client he was working for has him on year two of his monthly retainer mandate and has referred him to other clients too, helping him grow his business more.

All that because he realized something important about selling: it's mostly about understanding the problem your client has and offering them a solution. It's not pushy. It's not aggressive. It's not intrusive. It's a conversation.

Developing a sales mentality is mainly about looking for problems you can solve and getting paid for solving them. It's about knowing what you can do and understanding the ideal kind of client for you, and then meeting as many of them as you can and having those conversations.

This same friend often refers to me as a wild beast, having fended for myself so long in the freelance world, and to himself as a tame zoo animal, used to being fed at regular hours and living inside a cage.

It took him a long time to realize he could walk right out of his cage. The door was never locked. And he wouldn't starve.

And neither will you. You just may have to change your diet a little bit and get used to hunting for your own food instead of having it served up to you in regular doses.

Building your hustle muscle

Not everybody develops theirs, but everybody's got one. It's also called chutzpah, mojo, making s&*t happen, rain-making or being proactive.

To explain it best, I'll start by describing what it's for: hustle muscle is what you use to create opportunities. A freelancer requires hustle muscle to move from a state of dreaming and inaction to one where she convinces clients that the money they hand over is worth the value being created.

Hustling is not only necessary for freelancers, of course. Anyone who's ever wanted more responsibility/recognition/money/resources requires a deliberate hustle muscle training regime. You need to stand up, go out there and ask for what you want from the people who have the power to give it to you. Whether your job is sales, copywriting, lawyering, accounting, cooking, tour leading or programming. You don't need to use it every day or all the time, but if you've never exercised it, you probably already know you need to start.

All businesses need to keep a steady stream of clients coming in the door to stay alive. Finding them and bringing them in takes hustle muscle. Otherwise, you've got a pipeline without any prospects in it, which is, well, just a pipe. Not very useful.

A business feeds on new clients. New clients bring fresh perspectives, varied and sometimes helpful feedback, and best of all, revenues.

People with money like to keep it. People only give you money if you're giving them something in return that they perceive as more valuable to them than the money in their bank account or stuffed into their pocket. In simple, straightforward businesses like mine (photography), I create images for my clients who can use the pictures to feel good and remember their great event, or market and sell access to their next one. They can use them to bring in new customers to their business, thereby bringing them more money. So they're not really buying something from me so much as investing in the tools and materials they need to help grow their own businesses.

Of course, it's not always easy get your hustle muscle activated, especially if you haven't used it in a long time, or ever. The only way to do it is to do it. Just start. In my case, that sometimes means finding a new list of clients to cold-call and email, or sometimes it means walking out into the world and literally knocking on doors.

I've sold a lot of things in my life, both tangible and intangible. I've sold email by the millions, coconut water by the hectolitre, wedding photography, real estate photography, conference photography and portraits. I've sold online ads, spaces for rent for artists, fine art, lawn cutting services, and stuff on eBay and Craigslist. I've sold to CEOs and strangers. I've sold out of my car, online, in the back alleys of grocery stores, in the office towers of commerce, to bankers, to homeowners, mothers and fathers. It doesn't matter what you have to offer or who you need to sell it to. Whatever it is, you need hustle to get it from you to them.

Selling on the phone and by email is comfortable for some people. Others dread the thought of calling a stranger and interrupting them to try to get them to notice you. But for those who really get a high out of hustling, as I do, nothing beats door-to-door and face-to-face. It's the boot camp of sales training, and worth trying if your business has some retail aspect to it or involves making direct personal sales pitches and doing product demos. Some kinds of businesses really can only be reached this way.

When I was selling coconut water to grocery chains, going through the front door was pointless. Try selling any food or grocery store item to any one of the large chains in Canada and you'll see. As a small, unknown supplier, if you're lucky enough to even find the name of the person to contact and actually connect with them by phone or email after months of trying, you might one day hope to get a meeting with a category manager.

If that day ever comes, and it will take far longer than you think, you'll go out to their office with your products in tow and give your pitch. If they seem at all interested, they'll table their terms to you, which will include a long and deep range of fees that you'll have to pay them in order to sell your product on their shelves. That's right, you'll have to pay to sell. Of course, if you sell a lot of your product and get onto a lot of shelves, your volume in sales will more than cover your costs and you'll make money. But there's no guarantee that's going to happen, and you're going to have to be ready to put money into promotions and in-store marketing, taste tests, etc., for as long as it takes to find and then hopefully build a market for your product. Needless to say, it is a long, expensive and highly risky endeavour, with no guarantee of success at the end.

The other way to do it is to go in through the back door. Literally. Go around back, or walk through the store to the back, where there will be a guy (or sometimes a woman), in a little office crammed between pallets of products. This is the manager, the person you work your hustle on. You show him what you've got. You explain your pricing, show him the best deal, tell him what extra stuff you'll throw his way, and sometimes you make a sale right there. Sometimes they'll pay you out of the till in cash. That's fun. It's not going to get you rich, but the practice of learning who your prospect is and how to reach them directly is well worth the effort it takes to get up off your butt and hit the road.

If you can't hustle, you're going to be beholden to someone who can.

BURN THE BOATS

There's a famous story about the Spanish Conquistador Hernan Cortés, who travelled from the shores of Cuba to the Yucatan peninsula of Mexico in 1519. He had 500 soldiers, 100 sailors and 16 horses on 11 ships sailing to the New World with the sole purpose of conquering the Aztecs and stealing their gold. Several months after his arrival, however, he was facing mutiny by his troops. Their morale was flagging and they wanted to go home. So he did what any rational, ruthless leader would do. He burnt the ships, which gave his men one choice: fight to win and maybe stay alive, or lose and surely die.

Guess what they chose?

My brother and I did the same thing, though in much less dramatic circumstances, when we were selling coconut water in Montreal. On days when we really wanted to push ourselves and not take no for an answer, we'd fill up one of our cars with as many cases of coconut water we could cram in and hit the road on one condition: not to return home until the car was empty.

Sometimes we'd drive for a long time and go far out of our way to sell those cases. Sometimes we'd hit it big and get an order for 20 cases or more with one stop. It was hit and miss, but we never failed. If we came back with even one case left, we were disappointed with ourselves. To reach our self-enforced quota, we had to get creative. We'd try out venues we wouldn't have thought of without the pressure we had put ourselves under. We hit up offices, hair salons, dépanneurs (the word for general corner stores in Quebec) and gyms. I even sold a case once to a bank teller while I was depositing a cheque.

These days weren't about building great clients; they were about moving product, no matter what it took. Many of the clients were one-offs, but that didn't matter. What mattered was that we did it, and always sold out.

How to do a cold-calling sales blitz

Selling is an intrinsic part of freelancing, as you've probably learned by now. Leveraging digital marketing tools, networking and powerful word of mouth generated by doing good work will deliver clients. But sometimes that's not enough. It may be that you want to target a new kind of client or are in a low period of work and things just aren't coming your way fast enough to keep pace with bills and ongoing costs. That's when you have to step it up a level and go after new business. One often overlooked tool for doing that is cold calling.

Dialling for dollars, or reaching out to people you don't know on their phones, can be intimidating and awkward, and it makes a lot of people uncomfortable at first. It's often associated with very negative perceptions of telemarketers. But the difference in your case is, you're not a telemarketer. You're not going to be calling a completely random list of people scraped from the Internet. You're not taking a shot in the dark. You're a freelancer and you're going to be calling prospective customers who you know could use your services if they only knew more about them and if you manage to get to them at the right time. That kind of planned, well-researched, targeted campaign of creating opportunities for conversations with prospective new clients is an activity that you may even learn to love doing once you see the results.

Here's what you'll need to do to give it a shot:

1. **Make a targeted list:** Group clients by type and work the same vein, just like a gold miner. By staying within a similar group of clients who share similar traits — job title or function, geographic market, company size, industry, events like conferences, or any other means by which you can strategically group your client types — you can leverage what you learn from each one of them as you go down your list to get more information to work with on your next call, and so on and so on.

2. **Prepare an email template:** Have an email already written and ready to send if/when your prospect invites you to send them one. They'll usually ask for samples of your work, links, etc., as well as your rates. Use that email to tell them who you are, but keep it tight. Write it assuming that it will be forwarded to others, but always make sure it is personalized to the person you are sending it to. In my case, I include a brief paragraph up front, saying what I do and why I think I could be of help to the organization, offering a range of pricing, and then include links to my work in the bottom of the email. Get the important stuff out and up front because nobody reads long emails and many people don't even open them up. And even if they don't ask you, you should ask them if you can follow up with an email just so they have your contact info should something come up.

3. **Prepare your pitch:** Having written the email first, you already have some practice in what you are going to say. Now

say it out loud. Imagine picking up the phone and calling. Who are you asking for? What do you want to learn? I always start my cold calls by making a statement that proves I've done some research on the prospect. In my case, I'm usually calling conference organizers or event planners, whom I've researched and can see have an upcoming event. I then immediately follow with a question, asking if they've chosen a photographer yet. Knowing as I do that a photographer is often one of the last people to get hired, and that the task is generally assigned to a junior staffer, if I have my timing right I can be fairly certain that they haven't hired anyone yet, or if they have, it's because there's someone they regularly work with whom they plan on calling at the last minute. (In this case, I switch gears and ask if they'd be interested in getting a proposal just to have a few options, because "it never hurts to have options." Often, they'll agree to let me quote.)

4. **Set a daily and weekly quota for yourself:** A sales "blitz" by definition is a focussed attack. You are setting aside other work to concentrate exclusively on selling yourself. It's a different kind of work than you're probably used to, has big ups and lows, and takes more time than you may think. When I do a blitz, I actually spread it out over a few days to give myself the best chance of success. I use one day to build up the list and search out opportunities, then try to make between five and 10 calls on the blitz days, and do it every day for a week. If I'm feeling strong, I push on, and if it's a grinding day, I stop when I hit my fifth call. Doing that every month for just a few days each month will bring in additional clients and keep you focussed on building and growing your freelancing business.

5. **Hit the phones:** I am a believer in the effectiveness of doing direct sales for yourself when you're properly prepared and have done your research. No one can sell you better than you. Cold calling, as archaic as it sounds to the elite digerati, does actually work. Because when it's done right, it's not entirely cold. Technically, calling up a stranger and pitching them on your

business is a "cold call," but if that person is someone you've looked into, and if you have a good understanding of what their business is and how your service or product can actually help them, the call is an opportunity. Not everyone has time to take one and not everyone likes to talk to sellers, but you may be surprised at how many calls do actually get answered, and how many of them can lead to business that can turn into long-term clients. Some of my current regular clients today are the result of cold calls from years past. If you've never done one, it can be nerve-wracking. It takes practice, so don't give up or despair. Understand that you will have people reject you, but very few people are actually rude or mean about it. Even rejected overtures can lead to some new kernel of information that can help you. Ask questions: who else they are working with, how much they are paying, etc. Not everyone will answer all your questions but as you work a market, you can put pieces together and accumulate real knowledge about the space you operate in.

6. **Don't leave voicemails:** Very few people answer voicemails, fewer still if they don't know you. Better to note the time and day you made the call and try back again at a different time or on a different day. If, after repeated efforts, you don't get through, then you can consider leaving a very brief voicemail with your name, number and reason for your call. But the odds you'll ever get a call back are slim.

7. **Be nice to gatekeepers:** Sometimes when you feel you're getting the run-around or are feeling frustrated trying to figure out who to talk to, try being nice. The person answering the phone is usually someone who has to field a lot of flak for his/her boss, and that someone may be stuck at a desk all day. Be nice to them. Treat them like a real person. Be open and honest and say that you are not trying to make a hard sales pitch, just trying to understand who would be the best person to talk to and ask for their advice. Often the person on the other end of the line will help by giving you the name of someone you

hadn't thought of or confirm that the person you are trying to reach is the right one.

8. **Take notes:** Using whatever system comes easiest and naturally to you (an online CRM system or a notepad and pen), write down everything you hear on the call, even things that might not make sense or don't seem immediately relevant. You'd be surprised at how quickly you can learn about a company and an industry by talking to people on cold calls. Don't waste the opportunity. As you work through your target list, be sure you take notes: names, numbers, best times to call back, who's doing what, if there's anyone else on the team you should try, etc. If someone who talks to you realizes that you're pleasant and offering something that is relevant (if not immediately pertinent) to their business, they will yield some information. Use whatever you learn in your other calls. Mention that you've spoken with so-and-so at such-and-such a company. Any level of familiarity you establish can shift their perception of you from outsider to someone who knows the industry, someone they can see themselves working with. As you grow in experience, you'll be able to reference similar customers you've worked for and gain more trust.

9. **Follow-up:** Once you've done this a few times, you'll build up a list. Some of the names on your list will be people who weren't ready to buy or didn't need anything from you right away, but they weren't an outright no. Follow up with them. Check them out online and see if anything has changed in their organization or if there's any new hook you can use to restart the conversation. Follow-ups open doors when done right. Don't call too soon after the first call, and don't call too often. You can also do the same by email.

10. **Pace yourself:** Don't be too ambitious when you start out (even one or two calls a day is better than none), and give yourself a chance to recover after the first few really awkward calls. It's not an easy thing to do, even for people who are used to doing it. You'll have good days and bad days. But whatever

your personal quota is, hit it.

Working the phones can be a bit of grind, no question. Some days may yield nothing but a hot ear and a lot of names struck from your list. But then, every now and then, you'll hit a home-run. You'll find someone who is looking for exactly what you have to offer, and right now, too. They are actually grateful you called because you've saved them the effort of having to go out and find someone on their own. That's when you hit pay dirt. And if you do it regularly, it happens more often. Some of those clients will tell their friends about you. And you've turned a cold call into a revenue stream.

NAME-DROPPING, OR HOW TO BECOME AN INSIDER

I learned about the power of name-dropping when I started a side business with my brother distributing coconut water. At the time, it was a big and growing trend and we were hell-bent on making a go of it. But with zero contacts in the food industry and no experience at all in food distribution, we were really starting from scratch and had to claw our way in. We were the ultimate outsiders.

We grew the business from zero to over 300 regular clients by doing sales the old-fashioned way. We went out and "took doors," walking up to stores, restaurants, yoga studios, gyms, health clubs, golf resorts and hotels and pitching directly to the onsite manager. We knocked on over a thousand doors in the two years we ran the business, and one of the best tricks we learned was leveraging the names of people we met when talking to other prospects.

We quickly learned that the food industry is a racket, like everything else, and there are really only three or four major distributors that bring in the bulk of the foods on grocery store shelves, along with an array of micro-producers/distributors like us trying to edge our way in. As we went from store to store, we'd focus on a specific chain of grocery stores, for example, and refer to our meeting with a store manager in a different neighbourhood. When we were making a pitch to a new store owner in the same chain, we'd refer to a conversation we'd had with someone at the head office. By dropping names like that, we'd win trust. Somehow, just saying the names gave us a little extra credibility — enough to give us time to make our actual pitch, which would often result in an order.

As with any hierarchical structure, the higher up the person whose name you are dropping is, the more effective the impact of dropping it. To get the higher-up names, we'd go online, look up the head office of a given chain or management structure, and then call them. Even if the conversations never led to much of anything, we could always reuse that name in a conversation with a store manager lower down on the food chain. Simply knowing and saying the name was enough to win us time and opportunity, again leading to more sales.

It worked just as well on cold call blitzes as well, and once we had a base of clients we were able to use names to mention new prospects' competitors that were already buying. It made prospective clients feel they'd be out of the game if they passed us over. In other words, using names of people we gathered gave us "insider" status in a world we'd entered not long before as complete outsiders.

Alas, all the hustle in the world couldn't save Cocobros (the name we'd give to our coconut water distribution business because we were selling coconut water and we were brothers, obviously). Although we'd been profitable from day one, we ultimately decided our time and effort was better spent elsewhere. When you have more than one source of revenue, sometimes you have to choose to shut one down to focus more concentrated efforts on another. That is both the joy and pain of freelancing, and it's part of the game.

Although we had built a large client list, the economics of buying and selling on small orders stopped making sense as the U.S. dollar rose against the Canadian dollar and increased our costs. Pricing wars from new competitors were also cutting into our selling price. We'd hoped to leverage our client base to introduce more product lines, but it became apparent to us that we weren't able to grow fast enough to keep pace with our much larger competitors, and so we folded the business. Sometimes even a strong client list can't keep a business alive when all the macroeconomic factors are working against it.

Speed matters

There are many different names we could use to describe the time we're living through now, but one of them is most certainly the age of acceleration. American writer, futurist and businessman Alvin Toffler famously examined the dangers and potential of rapidly accelerating change in his 1970 bestseller *Future Shock*. Toffler mused about the difficulties we as a species would have in adapting to continuous and massive change – like giving people a sense of "future shock" similar to the concept of culture shock that inspired it. As it turns out, we have proven ourselves adept at incorporating change, especially the technology-driven change that operates like a horizontal force across all industries and all cultures with remarkable ease.

All freelancers need to develop speed as a core competency.

Start with technology, which is the engine driving this rapidly evolving world we inhabit. As a freelancer, you have a responsibility to learn about the latest and newest technological tools available that are relevant to your trade. This goes beyond simply working with productivity-enhancing apps and software to better manage your life and your business. If you are a photographer like me, that means you have to actually try out the latest camera technology. You need to learn how to use it before it goes mainstream. You need to stay ahead of the curve so that you can actually bring value to your clients, who will be curious about the latest new thing but may not have heard much about it.

Answer your phone

Speed is especially important when it comes to responding to your clients' needs – both current and prospective clients. For freelancers more than anyone, being the first responder can mean the difference between getting the gig and not getting it. Clients don't think on your time; they think on theirs. And never discount the power of the last minute. When that call or email comes in, the last thing the sender or caller wants to do is wait for an answer. They are literally running out of time. If you're quick to respond, you are already more than 50% of the way towards getting the gig. And clients always appreciate prompt replies to their queries and other sundry requests that may arise. Training yourself to be able to respond quickly and comprehensively to a new client request has a direct impact on your bottom line.

I answered a call from an unknown number once that turned into the biggest contract of my life to date: a huge conference for a major blue-chip company, where I ended up running a team of 12 photographers and two videographers covering over 50 events in a span of four very busy days. When the call came in, I didn't feel like answering. I remember it distinctly: I was in a lineup at Costco with a hungry child begging for a hot dog. I was fumbling for my card and feeling a little hypoglycemic myself, but since I've trained myself to always answer the phone no matter what (despite the fact that I get calls at least once a day with offers to "put me on the front page of Google," which I know is not something that can be bought), I couldn't let the call go to voice mail, and I answered.

That initial conversation led to several more, with twists and turns along the way, until I eventually wound up taking on the role of the lead photographer. Hitting the little green phone icon to accept that call turned out to be one of the best business decisions I ever made. Except I didn't have to make it, because it was already a habit.

Patience and attention are scarce commodities today, and even scarcer if you are on the service side of a relationship. Clients don't like to wait. Making them wait is a good way to encourage them to look for other suppliers. It may be that we live in a highly technological era, but the early bird still gets the worm.

Selling

This is it. The hard part. The thought of having to sell something fills a lot of would-be freelancers with dread. If the something you're selling is you, it can be even worse. If you've never had to do any kind of selling in your life, then it may loom before you like a giant, insurmountable hurdle. Depending on your personality type, it may feel completely unnatural, awkward and embarrassing trying to sell yourself to someone, especially a stranger. Introverted and shy people tend not to like sales, though I believe that introverts make the best salespeople because they are well practiced in listening and paying attention. All they need to do is overcome their fear of being themselves in public.

Avoiding sales is a logical result of having two related core beliefs:

1. Selling is a negatively perceived behaviour, like being pushy, aggressive, self-centred or self-aggrandizing, crass or even obnoxious.

2. Asking for money is embarrassing, awkward and unpleasant.

Weeding out and neutralizing these two core beliefs and replacing them with positive alternatives can unlock your inner salesperson.

Sales avoidance tactics include:

- Not being able to concisely tell a stranger what it is you do, the problem you solve and how you help people.
- Not having business cards at all — or never having any on you.
- Never answering your phone.
- Not putting your contact information in your email signature.
- Not having an updated LinkedIn profile.
- Not keeping track of leads.
- Not having a list of target businesses that need your services or product.
- Not returning messages promptly.

How can I help you?

Let's start with the first mistaken belief about selling: it is basically a socially awkward behaviour that requires you to interrupt people and push them into buying from you. Selling well is never anything like that, but the perception is based on observing some people who haven't learned or don't care to learn how to do sales right. What selling is, at its core, is providing a solution to a problem.

Take fishing, for example. Say you're a first-time fisherman, invited out with some friends for a weekend at the cottage and wanting to join them for a day of fishing. You go to the nearest outdoor supplies store and what do you do? After finding your way to the fishing department, you may spend a bit of time looking through the variety of rods available, but you'll want to speak with a salesperson to ask for their advice and guidance on which fishing rod to buy. You will actively seek them out if one isn't around. The salesperson is viewed as a resource, and a good one, who will ask specific questions about where you'll be fishing, what kind of fish you'll be trying to catch, how frequently you plan to fish, what your budget is, etc. He or she will be able to direct you to the best solution for you. If you need the rod and trust the salesperson, you will probably take their advice and buy the rod they recommend.

At no time is the salesperson acting in any of the negatively perceived ways described above. But now imagine you went to that same store not because you wanted to buy a fishing rod, but because your husband dragged you along. You couldn't care less about fishing. If that salesperson acted the same way with you, you'd leave the store as soon as possible, feeling wholly justified in thinking all salespeople are just out to harass you into spending money.

The difference, of course, is not in how the salesperson acts, but in you. If the person you're interacting with is selling — and has the knowledge of, interest in and passion for – something that you're interested in, then that person is a helpful resource. Most importantly, when that salesperson makes the effort to understand your specific needs by asking a series of questions and presents you with a solution, it's not just a one-size-fits-all offer, but actually a solution tailored just for you. It solves your problem.

If, on the other hand, the person trying to sell you something doesn't bother to ask you questions about your intentions, assumes that because you're in the fishing department you're fair game (no pun intended), and is only thinking about selling you something because it adds to their monthly quota, then of course that salesperson will confirm your negative core belief about sales.

Money, money, money

Now let's dismantle that other hugely unhelpful core belief about asking for money, or just generally having a negative view of associating money with what you do or make.

People who view asking for money as somehow déclassé or are embarrassed to ask have either too much or too little of it. If you see yourself in the first category, you probably don't need to continue reading this book, as you obviously have a way of making money that sustains you and keeps you in the style of life you've grown accustomed to. However, if you find yourself more uncomfortably situated in the second category — that is, needing more money — you need to learn how to talk about it without feeling shame or embarrassment. It may mean the difference between being about to do the work you've chosen to do and not being in that position.

So let's just take a quick look at what money is. The money we use today is a currency. It is fiat money, meaning it represents value, but in and of itself, is valueless. The thousand-dollar bill and the one-dollar bill are printed on the same kind of paper and take up the same amount of ink, but one is worth a lot more than the other.

The point of this very short economics lesson is that money is a representation of value. When you sell something to someone, you're asking them to agree to the value of what you have to offer, in exchange for which they will give you money equivalent to the value that agreement represents. When you sell a painting for $10 or $1,000,000, it's not because the latter used 100,000 times more paint; it's because, of course, the buyer agrees that your painting is worth at least that much (and probably thinks it will be worth a lot more down the road). Asking someone to pay you for what you do or make isn't asking for anything more than an agreement.

Of course it involves a discussion at first. However, this is not about you personally, but about the value you are generating for your prospective client. If you can come to an agreement or, if you've been able to learn over time and through research and observing other vendors in your market selling the same or similar thing to you, then you'll have a sense of what that value should be. Failing to ask for value in return for value would be senseless, unless you are in the business of altruism and are not in imminent need of food or other necessities of life that money provides for.

For the rest of us, learning to trust that money is only and always a representation of value is fundamental to being able to ask for it. You are doing the work you are doing because you believe it has value. There would be no point to it otherwise. Therefore, when your work is done on behalf of, or for, someone else, that value you generate is transferred to that person. In return, value is transferred back to you. The medium used is money.

What to include in a proposal — and what to do once you've sent it

Writing a proposal can appear daunting if you've never done it before. In fact, you can break it down into really quite simple components that are much easier to handle than you might expect.

A proposal needs to include the following:

1. A cover sheet containing the name and contact details for the person you're sending the proposal to, as well as your own name, title and contact details.

2. Your understanding of your client's problem (which you will solve), and the context within which your client is operating.

3. Your proposed solution.

4. Your methodology or approach: how you will address your client's needs and solve their problem.

5. Deliverables: what you will do and deliver that solves your client's problem.

6. Out-of-scope: anything your solution excludes or does not cover that would be a complete part of your client's solution (if applicable).

7. A timeline: how long it will take you and when you will deliver (in its entirety or by milestones).

8. A quote: how much it will cost your client, as well as how and on what terms and timelines you are asking them to pay.

9. A summary of the proposed agreement and a place for signatures or text stating that acceptance by email is acceptable.

If relevant and requested, you may also include some samples of your work, or links to your portfolio or past projects. You may also include references (former clients and/or partners) if requested, or if you think it will help you win the business.

In its most basic form, that's it. As in most writing to do with business transactions, keep it short and to the point, without leaving any holes.

Before you write a proposal, try to gather as much information about the client and the mandate as possible. If you have the option to ask questions or have a quick call with the client, do so. Ask what the criteria are for choosing one supplier over another (price? speed? quality of solution?) and what their budgeted range is (if they have not already indicated this information). Ask who will be evaluating the proposal, and if there is anything not explicitly mentioned in the initial request for proposal that you should be aware of. More questions mean more chances for you to write a proposal that tightly fits their real requirements.

Depending on the nature of your business, you need to balance how much detail you include to protect yourself from the possibility of having your ideas ripped off (if your proposed solution includes a strategy or plan of action), without leaving the details so sparse as to make it impossible for your client to assess your submission.

It's good practice to include the word CONFIDENTIAL on every page in the footer, and add in a preamble text that the contents of the proposal are meant for a specific audience (your client) and are not to be shared or distributed or copies kept after a decision has been made.

Also include a time frame during which the proposal is valid, and an expiry date. I try to keep this window as tight as possible – usually three days max. If a client is interested and needs more time to evaluate, they will reach out to you. This in turn creates another contact point that you can use to try to influence their decision or gather more information. While clients rarely abide by these deadlines, having an expiration date on your submission gives you an excuse to follow up directly if you haven't heard anything back from a client, and provides you with a blackout clause should you find yourself unable to take on the work, say, because you've been booked by another client.

There are many templates available either built into word processing programs or found online. Find one or two that suit your particular business or industry and customize them for your use.

Once you've submitted your proposal, be sure to send both a quick follow-up email (if you've sent the proposal as a linked attachment, storing a copy online in Google Docs or Dropbox), as well as a quick call to make sure the client received the document. Then wait until your expiration date and do a follow-up call.

Don't be too disappointed if your proposal misses the mark. There are many reasons why companies request proposals and sometimes it's simply to show that they canvassed the market when they already had chosen some insider for the job. But if you are rejected, ask for the reason and keep track of your hits and misses so you can see over time if you are getting better or worse at submitting proposals. You can make changes in your approach as necessary.

ACCEPT MULTIPLE CURRENCIES

Freelancers based in Canada have a lot going for them. In my opinion, they should be much more aggressive pitching their services to American clients. If you keep your pricing in U.S. dollars (USD), landing just a few U.S.-based clients can make a big difference to your bottom line.

At first, you may be tempted to adjust your rate to reflect the USD equivalent of your Canadian rate. Resist the temptation. Here's why. Most U.S.-based clients don't pay attention to our little Canadian dollar. It's not an obsession for them the way it is for Canadians, who get updates on the exchange rate with their local news. Americans by and large don't think in terms of anything but their own currency and are used to seeing quotes in USD. They will just be comparing your fee with what they're used to, so there's no need to give them an instant 30% discount by adjusting your rate.

The upside, of course, is that you actually earn 30% more for your work.

I learned this lesson by sheer luck. I was approached by an American company that was coming to Montreal for an event they were hosting. I landed the gig after the normal back-and-forth regarding contract requirements. As an afterthought, I suggested we just draw up the contract in USD as it would be easier for them to pay me. I told them it was all the same to me. So we did. At the time the Canadian dollar (CAD) was close to the U.S. dollar, so the value difference wasn't a consideration for either of us. Little did I know, however, how much extra revenue this one detail would earn me over the next four years, as that one contract for one gig grew into a renewable contract for six gigs annually, each one based on the pricing in the last. Over those four years, the Canadian dollar tanked with the drop in oil prices and suddenly I found myself getting a 30% raise.

While you're at it, consider accepting payment in one of the main cryptocurrencies as well. It may still seem confusing to use and hard to access, but cryptocurrencies like Bitcoin, Ethereum, Ripple (to name some of the more well-known variants in a crowded space with new currencies coming online every day) offer advantages to freelancers that no other currency does to date: you don't need a bank account, you get paid instantly and there are no foreign or wire transfer fees that can eat into your profit.

Using cryptocurrency isn't as easy as getting paid via other methods, but there are new and emerging startups addressing this accessibility issue, trying to simplify the buying and selling process, and make the whole process more transparent. Do your own research but take a look at CoinField, CoinSmart, Coinsquare, QuadrigaCX and Kraken to start getting a feel for how to use crypto currency. There are even platforms aimed specifically at freelancers who want to get paid in cryptocurrency, like XBT Freelancer.

(Conversely, if you are a freelancer based in the U.S., don't overlook your northern brothers and sisters if you have mandates that can be outsourced in whole or in part, and take advantage of your stronger currency to get a 30% discount on the sub-suppliers you hire.)

Leverage your T and Cs (using your Terms and Conditions to do passive selling for you)

Whenever you're sending an estimate, quote, proposal or invoice to a client, you have an opportunity to do some silent selling by including additional information about your services in the Terms and Conditions portion of your document.

If the trick to selling is "offer, offer, offer," (as Todd Herman notes in Amy Porterfield's podcast *Online Marketing Made Easy*) then you need to exploit every space you have available to drop offers into.

The terms section of a standard estimate or invoice document is usually filled with boring language about asking for payment (normally net 30 days, even though there's no real way for a freelancer to enforce that). Why not use this section to include info about your blog and any additional or complementary services you have to sell? You'd be surprised to learn how little your first-time clients actually know about your business. While you may think they've researched you and checked your site out and decided to hire you based on what they found, the truth may be that you happened to be the first to respond.

Don't assume that your client — new or existing — has figured out everything you do. For example, while I am known primarily as a photographer, I also have contracts in writing and creating content for corporate clients, manage a team of videographers, do live social media reporting for clients during events, and more. Even within photography, if I am being hired to cover a conference, clients may not realize that I could also offer photo booth services or headshots on site. So I tell them, by making a clear list of everything I offer (with pricing!) right at the end of every estimate and invoice document I send to clients. They may gloss right over it, but I know it works because every now and then I get an email from a client saying, "Oh, I didn't know you did X!" and even better, I am often asked to add services drawn from the same list, which gives me additional revenue on contracts I'd already won.

Think about the main thing you do and then think of all the ancillary services (or digital products) that go along with it. Even if you don't provide these services very often, spell them out. Can you write an e-book on what you do? Do you have additional supplementary services that complement what you do that you can sell alongside your main contract? Do you deliver goods online? Can you offer your clients hosting of online materials?

The extra services don't have to be something you do yourself. They can be complementary services that you offer by hooking up with other suppliers, and then sell at a price that includes your finder's or management fee. Say you offer hip-hop classes to kids for their birthday parties. Can you also include photo and video to go with your product, then strike a side deal with sub-suppliers to sell through you with you taking a cut?

This is how one client can, over time, turn into a long-term revenue stream for you. I've had clients from whom I've made over $100K over a few years, who had initially hired me for a small contract after finding me online. This lifetime value of a customer (LCV) — also known as the customer lifetime value (CLV), or (CLTV) or life-time value (LTV) — is how much the relationship with your client is worth to you. Hint: it's usually far more than that first contract and part of the way of tapping into it is by offering your client more value (i.e. more services or products).

Contract negotiations

Contract negotiations begin long before you've put anything down on paper. On the very first contact with a prospective client, no matter how far removed you think you are from getting a gig, you've begun a negotiation. You, and your potential new client, have begun evaluating each other and gathering information about each other.

And anything you say or do may subtly influence the kind of contract you finally agree on, so be aware of what you say, do and leave unsaid, as well as what you learn from speaking with your prospect.

I learned this in the early stages of my life as an event photographer. When I started out, I worked at a much lower hourly rate than I charge today. Like many newbie freelancers, I was uncertain what I should charge, and scared of being perceived as too expensive. I didn't want to lose any gigs I was contacted for. While working one of these gigs, which was a recruitment event for a large firm, I happened to get into conversation with a woman who was involved in organizing several other events for the company. During our exchange, she let me know how much the other photographer she used regularly charged. When I heard the fee their other photographer was charging, I tried hard to hide my surprise. It was more than double what I was charging. But I took that information to heart. When I was asked back for another event a few months later, I raised my rates, and my bid was accepted without any question. My rate was still (just) under what at least one of their other photographers was charging.

Price is just one of the kinds of things you want to be thinking about when you draw up a contract with a client (or another freelancer). The goal of a contract is to help you maximize your earning potential and protect yourself against the remote (but possible) downside risk.

First off, actually have a contract. It's amazing how often freelancers just set off working without a contract. This doesn't always happen because a client is trying to take advantage of your enthusiasm or leverage a tight deadline (though that is sometimes the case). Contracts usually get overlooked because conversations move rapidly from the proposal to working on the solution, skipping the critical middle step, which is agreeing to the terms, getting the condition on paper and signing.

I can't stress how important it is to make sure you have a real contract that is relevant to the mandate you are undertaking. Signing an NDA (non-disclosure agreement), for example, is not the same as signing a contract for services. While an NDA is often used to ensure that both parties in any kind of working relationship respect the confidentiality of the information they are sharing while working together, it does not spell out the terms of your agreement, the mandate you will be taking on, what your responsibilities are, what the client's responsibilities are, when you will deliver by, the rates you will charge, and so on. For that, you need a proper service contract or independent consulting contract. You can make this yourself based on a template, or use one provided by the company (just be sure to read it over in its entirety).

You don't need a lawyer to create a contract — you can do it yourself, just using plain language. The key thing is to clearly define your role and deliverables, your client's role and your terms. (If you don't trust your own ability to do this, you can always check out an online legal technology company like LegalZoom for templates and access to — you guessed it — on-demand freelancing lawyers.)

The important things to include in a contract are:

- **Project mandate or scope of work:** What are you being hired to do specifically. This can be very important to protect against what's known as "scope creep" — you're hired to do one job (say, make a video for client), then asked for a series of edits to cut the video into different formats for different social media channels, free of charge. The point of this section is to clarify expectations and ensure that you and your client agree on exactly what you are being contracted to do.

- **Timeline:** Some projects have hard-stop deadlines ("we need this live in 24 hours!"), and some allow a bit more slack. In most cases where a freelancer is being hired, the deadlines are likely to be shorter and more definite. Put them into your contract and be careful to note if any of your deliverables are contingent on receiving client approvals or materials. You can protect your deadlines with a +X days buffer triggered by receipt of whatever you are waiting for from your client. Importantly, if your timeline includes estimates of how long it will take you to perform a given task, think very carefully about how much time it really will take and make sure the deadline you are committing to is realistic. If it's going to take three days, then say so. If the timeline is really far too short for you to handle on your own and you need to bring in sub-contractors, then add that line item to your budget (below) and include a margin for you to manage them and integrate their contribution(s) with yours. Don't be caught out. (Having once accepted a mandate to edit 800 photos in less than three days, I learned the hard way that accepting work you can't actually deliver on within the specified time frame can hurt you. In this case, I was unable to deliver the quality of work required in the time allotted, and had to forego my fee.)

- **Budget:** Be clear about how much you are working for and specify any and all factors that could trigger a new contract (e.g. extension of mandate, excessive delay or extension of timeline). Any significant change to the original terms you've agreed to should necessarily trigger a new contract or amendment to your existing one to ensure you are properly compensated. A lot of freelancers allow their clients to shoehorn extras into their contract, then feel awkward about asking for more money to cover the additional work. Don't be one of those freelancers. Expect changes. Have a plan clearly spelled out in your Ts and Cs. If, for example, you are contracted on an hourly basis and you've agreed to a four-hour shift, make it crystal clear in the contract that if your client asks you to stay longer (because they are off schedule, or were not able to stick to their agenda), they will be billed for the additional time at your applicable hourly rate.

- **Define deliverables:** Who delivers what and when? What does your finished product look like and who is it to be sent to? How is it to be sent? If you're submitting a digital product (like photos or video), what sending service are you using? How long will you keep it up there for? If a physical send on hard media is required (or subsequently requested), what is the charge for the materials and mailing cost? Think through every possible scenario so you don't wind up eating into your profit by paying for unexpected bandwidth usage or shipping costs.

- **Add a competition clause:** This one is a bit tricky because it can be difficult to enforce, but it never hurts to err on the side of what is favourable to you. If you hire sub-contractors or if your team is larger than just you, and your client works with them as part of your service, put a clause in place that prohibits either party from working directly with each other for a period of 12 to 24 months. This can easily be challenged, but having it there at least makes it clear that you expect everyone to play fair and respect the value-add you've brought to the equation by bringing all parties together in the first place. (Another way to handle this is to simply charge your subs a finder's fee, but I don't recommend it because it's hard to get after the first contract, and you lose the direct contact with your client, which you never want to do.)

- **Terms and Conditions:** Include all the logistics here. What are your terms payable (I ask for on receipt, but acknowledge that up to 30 days net is the norm)? Spell out the payment modalities (cheque, bank transfer, online or credit card), and include language specifying that copyright or ownership of anything you've created for the client only transfers upon complete payment in full. I also include information here about my other services and add-ons, because "offer, offer, offer," right?

Contracts are nothing more than formalized agreements between two or more parties. They can range from a set of bullet points in an email to something carefully composed in a PDF. Unfortunately, if someone sets out to deliberately screw you, no contract will completely protect you, but having one in place acts kind of like a "Beware of the Dog" sign. It gives everyone pause to think twice. A contract is also just a convenient way to define your project, clarifying a beginning, middle and end. Putting one in place before you begin is a little extra work, but not doing so is a mistake. If you wait to define the conditions of a job until you run into problems, it's not a good time to negotiate. Trust me.

Short vs. long-term contracts

People often think of freelancing as a series of one-night stands or a string of short-term contracts. In fact, many freelancers wind up working with one or two main long-term clients from whom they derive the bulk of their revenues.

Sometimes it's your former employer who hires you back to work as a consultant. Sometimes it's just one or two major clients for whom you do a lot of work. In casino parlance, these kinds of clients are known as whales — high rollers who spend a lot of money and for whom the casino will offer comped rooms, all-expense-paid trips and any other perk they can think of to keep that whale at the tables spending money. You can survive for a long time off a whale if you play your cards right. One way to do this is to have yourself placed on a retainer.

Rather than working at an hourly rate, breaking everything you do down into pieces, working on a retainer is an option that can be mutually advantageous to you and your clients. A retainer contract is just what it says it is: a client retains your services for a fixed rate. You get peace of mind knowing you have a fixed amount of revenue coming in for the predetermined length of time your retainer contract is drawn up for, and your client gets a set predictable cost that makes budgeting easier to manage.

In many companies, teams or departments begin each year with a budget, and by the end of each year, they're stressed out trying to either justify why they went over-budget or using up the surplus so it's not cut the next year. Pitching clients on retainers or fixed monthly contracts is sometimes easier for a client because they can put your numbers right into their budgets, effectively making your fee a part of their spending plan for the year.

The advantage to you as a freelancer is predictable revenue — you'll be able to bank on having a set number of dollars coming in over a fixed period of time (usually three months up to a year). Your client, meanwhile, can relax a little and use you more as a resource on call.

There are a few different ways to structure your retainer contract, each with their advantages and disadvantages.

- **Monthly, no rollover:** You can offer a fixed bundle of hours or service availability per month, much the way your phone company sells you a monthly allocation of bandwidth for data and talk time with no rollover, so the allocation resets each month.

- **Monthly, with limited rollover:** You can offer a monthly set of hours that are available to the client over the duration of the contract, allowing one month's rollover. This gives your client a bit of leeway on how they choose to use your hours, but still sets some limits.

- **Bank of hours:** A fixed number of hours available for use by the client at their discretion.

- **Mandate-driven:** A results-oriented contract based on a prescribed set of actions or deliverables that you guarantee.

This can mean a service that delivers a finite amount of results monthly or quarterly (could be a fixed number of posts on social media, a certain number of meetings, consultations, impact on public opinion, published articles etc.).

Use it or lose it

Having a guaranteed fee that doesn't depend on your client sending you work on a recurring monthly basis seems ideal to a freelancer. However, the big risk is that your client doesn't use up all of your time in more than a month or two running (depending on how tight a ship they run). In that case, they may determine that your cost is not justifiable and kill the contract. While you may have squeezed out a month or two worth of retainer fees without having done any work, in the long term this model only really works if your client keeps you busy. If you find after the first month that your client isn't using up their allocation, you will usually be better off developing an arrangement for your client that allows them to make better use of you and your availability.

Roll with it

The second method, providing a bank of hours or service availability for a fixed amount and period of time, is often more advantageous to both you and your client. This allows the client to better match your work with the ebb and flow of their own business and keep you in their roster. Offer a bank of hours over a limited but fixed period of time. So rather than 25 hours a month, offer 75 hours over three months, with a maximum of 50 hours in any one month. This gives the client some incentive to take advantage of your availability, but also gives you some protection should the client suddenly try to hit you with a big ask all at once.

YouBank

This gives the client the greatest amount of flexibility and is their lowest-risk option. Unfortunately, it is the freelancer's highest-risk option, as it means your client can suddenly hit you with a whack of work during a time when you're busy with other clients. (In my early days as a freelancer, I used to provide a bank of hours without specifying exactly when they needed to be used up and had clients come back to me literally two years after the initial mandate wanting to "use up the balance." This either creates a very awkward conversation or puts you in the position of having to work effectively for free, so I'd recommend against the YouBank option unless you include an expiration date.)

Show me the money

This is the highest-value type of contract for both you and your client, and usually commands a premium because it is also the hardest to achieve. From a freelancer's perspective, it's an all-or-nothing type deal where your fee is linked directly to a desired outcome, for which you negotiate a predetermined amount of time needed to achieve it, at a fixed rate. Typically, you are paid monthly and may have to provide progress reports, but the ultimate objective is the determining factor in your success. If you can do this well, you can get rich on this type of contract. Failure, however, can result in a total write-down, fee renegotiations or in the worst case, legal proceedings against you.

Not all clients have the potential to turn into long-term customers, but it's not always easy to tell which ones will and which won't. A good approach is to treat all clients as potentially long-term partners, and judge when it is worth making a pitch for a retainer contract or some form of longer-term commitment. Sometimes just proposing the idea is enough to get a client to sign you up. By being proactive and attentive, you may turn a few of your minnows into whales of your own.

Follow-up

Everything you do in terms of marketing and networking, business development and outreach is about opening loops. Starting conversations, piquing interest, driving people to change. The follow-up is when you close the loop.

Following up is really the simplest thing to get right. Not doing it is also the easiest way to leave money on the table. All it requires is putting basic interpersonal social skills into action: reply to emails, answer voice mails and follow up with anyone you don't hear back from.

If you meet someone at a networking event, a conference or waiting in line for a coffee and you've exchanged contact info — follow up!

If you told someone you'd send them something you think they'd like — a book referral or the contact info for someone who can help them with their problem — follow up!

If you've submitted your proposal and not heard back within the specified time frame you indicated in your proposal — follow up!

If you've received comments on any of your social media channels — follow up!

If you've been given the name or contact info of a company or person that someone who knows you and your work thinks would be a potential lead for you — follow up! You get the picture.

Regardless of what kind of freelancing you do, you are in the business of client service. Clients never like to be kept waiting. You have to recognize that despite being amazing at what you do, you are not their top priority. Keep after prospects, and follow up with people who have given every indication that they care but may just be too busy to close the loop with you themselves.

Asking for the business (closing)

There's a famous scene in one of the greatest sales movies of all time, *Glengarry Glen Ross*, where Alec Baldwin's character is sent down from Mitch and Murray to give a little pep talk to the salesmen on the floor. It's called "Put that coffee down!" The office is dimly lit, it's raining, it's late at night and nobody is happy. It may be the bleakest portrayal of the life of a salesperson you'll ever see, and for a lot of people who've never done sales, that's what they fear.

It's fiction, of course, and completely unlike real sales, but it does make one strong and truthful point, illustrated on the chalkboard Alec Baldwin swings during his soliloquy: "ABC: Always. Be. Closing."

Closing, or asking for the business, is what sales is all about. If you don't learn how to do it, you will waste a lot of your time and energy chasing your own tail instead of earning money and focusing on the work you've chosen to do.

Okay, easy to say. But how do you close a deal it if you've never done it before?

Prepare

First, be prepared. Have your website up, your portfolio ready to send, and know who you're speaking to. If you've done your work and understand your client's real needs and pain points, your "ask" (that is, what you are asking the client to agree to) is really a presentation of a solution. You don't want to be scrambling around assembling your marketing materials if the person you're connecting with asks you to send over a proposal. Being prepared will also help reduce the anxiety of selling.

Listen

The next thing and the next thing after that and the next thing after that is listen. Listen when your client talks. Listen for what's really bothering him or her. Listen for what's really going on within the organization and where hidden problems lie. Listen for what's coming up and what's changing. And at every juncture, identify what you see is missing and what you know you can help with.

Ask

Then ask. Not for the business right away, but to figure out what they are doing to address the issues they've shared with you. Who are they working with, how's it going, what's holding them back, where do they want to be with "x" project by when? How are they going to get there?

Suggest

Finally, suggest. Suggest that you can solve or know someone else who can solve their problem. Ask if they'd be interested in receiving a proposal. Then send one in, give them a few options to choose from and ask them to choose.

The worst thing that can happen is they say no, which is where you were before you asked, so you've lost nothing. But the upside is huge. You may get the work outright, or be given a chance to come back with something tweaked to fit a more specific problem statement or within a specified budget. Or you may be referred onwards to someone else within the organization or within your client's network.

Whatever happens, you can't lose.

Asking for referrals

The best and cheapest sales force you will ever have for your business are your existing customers. Once you've completed a mandate and delivered work that you're proud of and they're happy with it, ask for a referral. Failing to do so is tantamount to leaving money on the table. Your very best clients may actually be disinclined to share you with others as they won't want to lose you as a resource, but it's still worth asking for a referral.

Target your requests

You can also reach out to your network — online and offline — and ask for a referral. It's best to be as specific and targeted as possible. Rather than put out a status update on Facebook asking if anyone knows anyone who needs a copywriter, send out a link to some recently completed work that showcases your talent and ask if anyone can connect you to people working in a similar company/organization grappling with a website redesign project or new product launch. Or target your referral requests to time-triggered events, like companies on a hiring spree, or those that are restructuring, referencing a recent project you completed for X company that's just gone through a similar restructuring. A referral is basically a form of advertising, and the most effective ads are ones that speak directly to your prospect.

By aiming your referral request at a targeted client type and linking it to related and relevant work, you make it much easier for one of your contacts to just forward the request to someone they may know. You basically bypass all the filters and gates that are set up to keep out unsolicited pitches like yours.

Make it painfully easy for other people to help you

Never underestimate how tired, overworked, busy and possibly indifferent most people are when it comes to helping you out. Even those who really care and want to help can get sidetracked by a million different intervening responsibilities. An undifferentiated, general and generic request just doesn't have enough of a point to reach the over-solicited minds of most people getting through their working day. You need to make your request for a referral seamless, painless and easy to execute.

People actually like to refer people they feel confident about. It makes them look good. It enhances their reputation if they pass along a good contact to someone they know who goes on to do an equally stellar job for them.

People will also be more inclined to refer you if they believe you have a real passion for your work. Showing enthusiasm and being glad to talk about and share success stories from past projects gives people ideas. They start thinking about who else they know who's doing something similar or could use a person with your creativity, talent and energy.

In the best-case scenario, your clients are so inspired by the work you've done for them that you are top of mind. Your name is the only one that comes up when they are asked, and they effectively give you exclusive access into their networks.

You can incentivize people to give you referrals as well by offering to pay finder's fees or a percentage of the value of a contract you get through the referral. This works better for lateral relationships (between suppliers or from other freelancers) than it would in a client relationship. However, you can consider building a referral system into your client relationships, offering a discounted price on their work if they refer you to a given number of new contacts within a specified time period, a bit like earning a free cup of coffee after buying 10 cups.

Give and you shall receive

Referrals are also big in the online world. They can actually be a way for you to earn money, both by being a referrer and by paying to have others refer you. Known as affiliate marketing or affiliate referrals, they apply when someone clicks through a specific uniquely identified link from one site to a destination site. For example, if you sell hand-drawn icons, you might offer to pay a percentage of tracked sales to web design sites or ad agencies that refer work to you through links on their sites. Conversely, if you are a copywriter, you may earn referral revenues from book recommendations you include in your blog that link directly back to Amazon (known as the Amazon Associate program) if someone clicks through and purchases the book.

Being a referrer helps you get referrals in turn. Sometimes by referring someone else, you benefit from the boomerang effect of that person also reaching back and bringing you in on a project they are working on.

When you do good work, people are happy to share your name and contact info. Make it easy for them to do, and tag it with a piece of specific content from your portfolio that's related and relevant to the kind of work you are going after. Keep the request short, targeted and open-ended and let them know it's fine if they pass you around.

Pricing

"How much does it cost?"

The first time you hear that question from a prospective buyer who's come to you directly as a result of your marketing efforts, you will feel an initial surge of pride and excitement, like the first tug on the line when you go fishing. And just like in fishing, if you react too quickly or too strongly (or not), you risk losing the catch.

Having heard this question (or some variant like, "What do you charge? What's the price?) hundreds of times, I've learned that how you answer has a direct impact on whether or not your get the work. And more importantly, how you answer will help you figure out if it's even worth trying to win the contract.

That's because this relatively straightforward question carries a lot of built-in biases and preconceptions that you need to be aware of before you answer.

The first few times you potential clients ask your price, you will want to answer immediately. Your primary concern will be whether your price is low enough to appeal to the buyer. When you are just starting out as a freelancer, just attracting attention feels like a victory (and it is!). You are so grateful you're ready to do the job for free just to get the work. Don't. Or if you do, make sure it's for the right reasons (i.e., a genuine marketing opportunity, a cause you care about, or where it is necessary to build your portfolio in an area where you are lacking experience).

Talk value, not price

What you are forgetting in your enthusiasm is that while the person on the other end of the line is asking you about cost, what you need to seal the deal is a conversation about value. It's not a trivial distinction. One question is framed from the perspective of someone thinking about their budget and how much of it your particular offering is going to eat into it (or not — and believe me, they are looking for the "not" part). If budget cutting is their only concern, they will always give the same answer: you are too expensive. That's because they are thinking only in terms of the value they lose (i.e., their money) for the thing they are looking to buy (i.e., your service, your product — you!).

Your challenge is to make the discussion about value, about how much what you have to offer will improve their lives, their business-es, and their ability to meet their clients' needs.

As tempting as it is to give a low price to win the business, you need to develop, right from the start, the habit of pricing yourself in terms of the value you have to offer.

How do you determine that value? Now that's a more interesting question.

What is your value when you are just starting out? You may, un-derstandably, feel insecure and possibly doubt yourself. Many free-lancers find pricing their work the hardest part of what they have to do. Putting a price on something feels so definitive. It's especially hard when you don't have a track record, don't have any clients and need the money. The problem is, thinking that way drives your price down. Your buyer doesn't even have to say a word.

What you have to do is think about how what you are offering solves a problem. Presumably you have launched into a freelancing career because you believe you have something — a product, a skill, some expertise — worth sharing. You are good at what you do. You care about what you do. You have a passion for what you do. You want to do it for people who recognize that, and who want to work with people like you.

You want people to stop seeing you as cost and see you as value. Your clients need to realize that while they might be able to find someone who does what you do for less money, no one will do it with the same gusto and passion.

You need to make people understand the advantages of working with a real professional. Professionals will exceed expectations. A profes-sional cares about their work enough to make sure that it is done right. If a mistake ever happens, they fix it. A professional values the client relationship, and genuinely wants to deliver something that will make the client happy. A professional will do what it takes to make sure that happens. That's valuable.

Don't enter a race to the bottom — you might win

Someone who sells at the lowest cost doesn't care about any of that. They only care about selling as much and as quickly as possible. The lowest-cost bidder doesn't stick around and check back after delivery to make sure things went well. The lowest-cost bidder doesn't try to maximize their client's value. The lowest-cost bidder does, however, look for ways to tack on hidden fees, and sell "extras" that should really be part of the full service. The lowest-cost bidder is playing a zero-sum game. Buyers shopping for low-cost providers are doing the same. The less I spend, the more I keep; the more I get, the less you have. It is a reductive scenario and there is no happy medium.

You, on the other hand, the professional freelancer, know better. You aren't trying to gain at your clients' expense. You are making something, doing something, enabling something that makes your client stronger, smarter, better, faster, and yes, ultimately, richer. Your gains are your client's gains. Your client pays you, you gain in wealth and experience, and you deliver something of such value that they gain the same.

That's the only kind of client relationship that matters, and the only kind that freelancers want.

So when you get the question, "What does it cost?" you should respond with another question. Dig into the prospect and find out what they are looking to do. Why did they think of you? What do they need help with? Show that you care, and understand — or want to understand — the specific challenge that brought a potential client to you in the first place. By doing that you are already proving your value. Potential clients who stick around to hear more have already tacitly accepted that.

And what about the ones that don't? Well, you let those little fish go. Even if you won them, you would lose. Clients who are only interested in getting the lowest price won't provide you with a rewarding experience. They will prevent from doing your best work, and instead, make you do the least work possible to justify their low price. They will drive you away from excellence. And in the process, they are likely to complain about something or another, and try to get even more for less. That is just how they think.

Remember the fable of the frog and scorpion? The scorpion comes to the river's edge and asks a frog sitting there to carry him across. The frog is reluctant and tells the scorpion, "If I do, you will sting me." The scorpion promises he won't and begs and pleads with the frog until finally the frog relents and lets the scorpion on its back. When they are halfway across the river, far from either shore, the scorpion suddenly plunges its stinger into the frog's fleshy back. As the dying frog sinks into the raging river, he asks, "Why did you sting me even when it means you'll die?" Just before the waves seal its fate, the scorpion answers, "It's in my nature."

If you take on a client looking for the lowest price, you're the frog, and look what happened to it. A client who thinks price (meaning, the lowest possible) is the only factor in hiring you, is the scorpion. You can't build a thriving freelance practice with that kind of client. At best, they'll drain your energy. At worst, and if you take on too many of them, they will compromise your future success. Don't do it.

On discounting and using deal services

You may be tempted to kick-start your sales by offering a steep discount or using a daily deal service like Groupon or Living Social.

I know because I tried both. While it works in the short term, in the long run it will work against you.

Let's look at the pros of offering a 50% off deal:

- It brings in new clients.
- It brings in revenue, fast.
- It makes you busy.
- It makes you feel popular.

But here's what's really going on when you sell yourself at half price, or more.

- The clients it attracts are the wrong kind of clients. They are the bargain hunters, the tire kickers, the people who use the Internet to chase down the lowest price and don't care about you, your quality or your brand. All they care about is paying the lowest price.

- Yes, you get fast revenue, but how much does that revenue cost you? The bargain hunter client is also one who has no qualms about asking for more or trying to squeeze an even better deal out of the good one they already have. They'll offer to pay you less to take it out of the deal platform network to avoid paying the platform commission or try to get you to throw in extras. And they'll eat up your time — time you could be spending building up your content and attracting higher quality clients who will pay you what you are really worth.

- Yes, you'll be busy. Too busy. You'll have people who buy up your deal and want to book you for work a year later. Or you'll be busy doing non-productive things like responding to multiple emails and phone calls from client who are paying you half price but eating up all of your time. Then you'll waste time dealing with unhappy clients who expect everything for nothing and are never happy with anything.

- You'll get a lot of action in your inbox and your phone will light up. You'll feel like you're in demand. But you're not in demand. You're just today's special. Ground beef a day before its expiry date. Tomorrow you'll be in the bin and no one will remember your name or ever call you back.

People who shop for heavily discounted products or services are not your clients. They never will be. Offering big savings to these kinds of people will never grow your business.

You'll make some fast cash, but you'll never build wealth relying on them.

What RFP really stands for

RFPs or Requests for Proposals make sense when the government is issuing a tender for a mega construction project. In that case, the money is coming from the public purse, and the government wants to get the best possible price for the highest quality. In theory, RFPs provide a transparent judging process that awards the project to the best bidder and wards off corruption and bid rigging.

Of course, corruption and bid rigging happen anyway. So you have to wonder, if RFPs rarely work for big public works, why would they work any better for small contracts fielded to independent workers or freelancers?

The answer is: they don't. Ninety-nine out of a hundred RFPs are not really a Request for Proposal, despite what you're led to believe by the lofty sounding title and subject line. In most cases, RFP stands for Request for Price, as in: we're looking for the lowest and we're going to make you feel like you're in stiff competition to scare you into knocking your price down and then we're going to play you off your competition like a pinball paddle does a shiny silver ball.

How to respond to an RFP

The question is whether you should bother. It's almost never worth the trouble. However, it may be tempting, especially when you're starting out. You may feel flattered at being approached in the first place, or feel like you actually have a chance at winning. So, even though you probably shouldn't, if you do make the effort to reply, keep the following in mind:

- Unless the selection criteria are crystal clear and you knock it out of the park for each one, you shouldn't bother responding. Ambiguous criteria, terms that aren't clear and issuers you can't reach are big red flags that you should not waste your time with an RFP. If it's not clear how your proposal is being judged, by whom, on what timeline and when you can expect to get a response, you will be wasting your time and energy. The deciding factor is very likely just price, so think about that and then decide if it's still worth going for.

- If the RFP is issued on behalf of some other entity, you probably shouldn't bother responding. They're just looking for a bargain and will only pass your name along if you leave enough margin for them to profit on.

- Be very careful how much you give away in your proposal, especially if you are being asked to present your ideas and lay out any kind of plan or strategy. People get their ideas stolen all the time. There are all kinds of sleazy companies out there willing to put you through the wringer just to see what kind of creative thought they can squeeze out of you for free. As with any proposal, make sure you label every page with a big CONFIDENTIAL and be as light on detail as you can without leaving so much out as to be without substance.

- Don't waste an inordinate amount of time on it. Design your response as a template and re-use as much material as possible on all RFPs. They always follow a similar format, asking for your experience, a description of your company, samples of your work. All you really need to do is write a cover letter about how you'll address their particular problem. This is the only part you really need to change or focus on, but keep it to a bare minimum. Look at the total value of the contract, assume your hourly rate and allocate a reasonable percentage of time to completing the task that is justified by the value of the project.

- If there is no budget allocated to the RFP, walk away. If the issuer is asking for, say, a video project or series of short videos, but either lacks market knowledge (which is one reason they've gone to RFP) or doesn't know what a video actually costs or worse, knows what it can cost but is looking for a better price, they should still be able to provide a budgeted range for the project. If they don't, then you are dealing with a lowest-bidder situation and even if you win, you will ultimately lose working with a client like this.

When people want to work with you because of what you do and how well you do it, they won't pit you against your nearest competitors (some of whom will likely be your friends and sometime collaborators) and they won't ask you to give them all kinds of information up front while providing as little as possible about themselves in return. If you're doing good work, making yourself known through your clients and your continuous marketing efforts, you shouldn't need to respond to an RFP. A simple quote should do for most jobs, and even when you do that (as I discuss in the next chapter), the pitch should be about value, not cost.

Don't use round numbers in your pricing

One of the most useful things I find about being a conference and event photographer is having the chance to be a fly on the wall in all kinds of seminars and presentations from world-renowned experts. Not every conference has subject matter that I find immediately useful (annual meetings for radiologists, though they're wonderful people, are not really helpful to my line of work), but some presentations are so interesting I spend as much time jotting down my own notes as I do taking pictures.

In one of these sessions I learned a little trick about pricing from a professional negotiator, Michael Sloopka. His advice has had a significant impact on my earning power ever since. He proposed a seemingly simple technique, but one that can make a big difference in how much money you earn per job.

Here it is: Don't use even numbers.

That's it. When you price your time, your product, your service, or any combination thereof, make sure it ends in an odd number. So instead of pricing yourself at $75/hour, try $77.37. It's just $2.37 difference. Trust me, no one will notice. But if you work 10 hours a week for 50 working weeks of the year, that's worth $1,185 more to you for doing nothing more than changing your invoice items. Imagine if you went to $79.97 instead of $75. Now you're earning $2,485 additional revenue this year. That'll cover a nice all-inclusive week in the sun somewhere, or buy you a new Mac. All for doing nothing but altering your pricing.

Here's why it works. First of all, most clients don't look too closely at how the line items are broken down in an invoice. They look at the total price and then compare that with the other totals they've gathered from other bidders on the job. If everyone else is using round numbers, yours will stand out. If someone else quotes $80/hour and you quote $79.97, the job you've estimated will take you 20 hours will show up as $1,599.40 vs. $1,600.00. What's the difference? Well, what's the difference between something that costs $9.99 and $10? Not much, but the $9.99 sells out a lot faster.

Furthermore, your odd-numbered pricing implies that you've thought through your rates. You're not just saying, "$100/hour" and hoping it sticks. You say $107.55/hour because, hey, there's no way you could have pulled that out of the air. It must be calculated, right? That's what a client is going to think anyway. And if you're worried that one day you'll be asked to justify it (which you won't be), then go back to a base number like $50 or $80 or $100 or whatever makes sense to you and then run a compound interest equation on it to account for inflation for a number of years.

For example: Assume your hourly rate is $50/hour. You now start charging $55.20. If ever you are challenged on it (and you almost never will be), you simply say that your rate is adjusted to account for regular inflation, at 2% a year since you started out. Even if you only just started this year, no one needs to know that. The price of everything goes up. People expect it to. Keeping your rates the same as they were when you started out is just leaving money on the table.

Assumed inflation	2%	Year 1	Year 2	Year 3	Year 4	Year 5
Starting hourly rate	$50	$51	$52.02	$53.06	$54.12	$55.20

Want to give yourself a bigger raise? Play the economist and fiddle with the inflation rate. If you want to be really inscrutable, use an odd number for the inflation rate as well.

Assumed inflation	2.43%	Year 1	Year 2	Year 3	Year 4	Year 5
Starting hourly rate	$50	$51.22	$52.46	$53.76	$55.04	$56.36

There you have it. And you thought you weren't good at math.

Minimum orders and volume deals

Another good habit to get into when pricing yourself or your work is to establish a minimum order for your product or services. Almost all contractors do it, so why don't you? Think about the last time you hired an electrician or a plumber. Did they come to your house for free? What about the time you had to have an appliance fixed at your house? Or every single time you step into a cab? Everyone has a base price they use to begin any contract. Not having one actually is the mark of an amateur and works against you both financially and professionally.

Your minimum can be a number of hours (two or three, or even a half-day rate for some fields), or a minimum order size if you sell products. Once you've established a minimum, you can then go around the bend and offer a discount or rebate on any contract that meets your target volume.

How low can you go?

In my case, I charge a base hourly rate for photography and have a minimum of three hours. This saves me from wasting time on contracts that are less time working than they are transit time, and gives me some leverage if a client really only needs a short shift. They understand they will need to pay a minimum regardless. On the other hand, if I can get a full day or multi-day contract, like covering a conference or a festival, I'm willing to make a concession on my hourly rate because the volume of work justifies it. So I offer a day rate that's cheaper than what my hourly rate would work out to.

You can do the same thing with product sales. When I was schlepping coconut water around town, our minimum order was five cases, as it really wasn't worth loading up our cars for anything smaller than that. On the volume side, we'd throw in a free case if a client took 20 or more. Both techniques act as incentives for clients to spend more with you, which is what you want.

Both minimum orders and volume discounts also give you something to talk about and negotiate when you are in discussions with your client. They create up-sell opportunities (a chance to sell a client something else that you offer for a higher price that your client wasn't initially considering), as everyone always seeks to optimize their position. If I have a client who wants me come into the office twice to do some work — in my case, take a portrait of one person, then come back a few days later to do another — I use a minimum charge to encourage the client to combine the two into one day. This also often results in the client putting a few more people in front of my lens than they would have otherwise. They reason that since I'm already there and set up, they are "saving money" by taking advantage of my presence on site.

Think about ways you can implement both minimums and volume discounts in your pricing. It's helpful to clients, as it sets expectations in terms of how to work with you, and it's better for you and your bank account.

Getting paid, chasing after unpaid invoices and all that other fun stuff

You did it! You launched a blog, got yourself some attention, marketed, networked and shook the bushes hard enough to get noticed, and you landed a paying customer who is not related to you. Success!

You do the work, and like a smart freelancer, you promptly submit your invoice, which includes all the relevant information your client requires to pay you. It's better yet if you're set up to receive online payment so they can pay you sooner rather than go through a lengthy internal process that requires layers of approvals managed by an outsourced accounts payable team in India.

But then you wait.

And wait.

And wait.

A month later, still no payment. You send a gentle reminder email to your client, as things like first-time supplier invoices, sadly, sometimes get "misplaced."

And then you wait some more.

In the meantime, your quarterly sales taxes are due and you're paying the portion allocated to this account even though you haven't yet been paid.

Welcome to freelancing.

The cheque is in the mail

The vast majority of clients really do want you to get paid. However, depending on the size of your client, the one who hires you may not be the same person or department that pays you. This is a particular problem with larger corporations, where it is almost certain that you will be paid by a centrally managed (sometimes outsourced) Accounts Payable department. But this can even be the case with small- to mid-sized businesses. It's a good idea to query your client about their normal payment terms in advance to know when to expect to receive payment (and ask for a PO (purchase order)).

If the process looks like it will take a long time (it is not unusual for the largest, most cash-rich entities to impose onerous payment terms such as 45, 60 or even 90 days), you may want to consider offering a credit card payment option, which has a 3% charge, but is quicker.

Adding charges like automatic late fees of 10% after an account has been outstanding for more than a fixed period of time (45 days+) can help speed up payments. Make sure your estimate indicates that this fee is chargeable and agreed to when the quote or estimate is accepted. Most clients will balk at paying any late fees, but it can provide you with an excuse to contact Accounts Payable directly. You can sometimes speed things up by just agreeing to waive the late fee.

Ultimately, small, sole-proprietorship businesses like those of most freelancers have little to no leverage over their clients. In the very worst cases, clients can simply refuse to pay and leave you high and dry. Fortunately, this rarely happens. In 20-plus years of freelancing, only one small client has failed to pay me, and that was because they went out of business. The waiting game, however, happens often.

Ask for a deposit

Another tactic you can use to close the gap between doing the work and getting paid is requiring a deposit up front. You can ask for any-thing between 10% and 50%, or even higher. A deposit is easily jus-tified if your business model includes subcontracting other workers to help you deliver. You want to be sure that you have their costs covered in advance of delivery. Your subcontractors may even require a deposit from you.

Don't forget the Terms and Conditions section of your invoice, ei-ther. As mentioned earlier, you can use it to do all kinds of things that are advantageous to your business. I've used mine to mention a raft of additional services and some clients have jumped on them. You can also include any provisions for reasonable additional charges. For example, you're being paid at an hourly rate, but for reasons that are entirely the client's responsibility, you end up working longer hours than agreed to. Your Terms and Conditions can include a line stating that your applicable hourly rate applies for all work extensions requested by the client.

I recommend that your first line should be something like "Payment due upon receipt" or "Net 15 days" to start the clock ticking right away. Here, too, is where you notify the client of any applicable late fees and the relevant payment schedule. Also indicate how you prefer to be paid, with the understanding that while cheques are cheapest for you, they will take the longest time to process. Be ready to accept online payment (e.g. PayPal, which handles most major credit cards) and factor in the 2.9% fee you will pay as a result. Few clients want to pay a higher rate for what is ultimately a convenience to you, but it doesn't hurt to ask or also include a note that a 3% surcharge applies to online or credit card payment. However, to do this properly you should include the revised total somewhere so that you avoid having to re-invoice for the additional surcharge.

Always follow up, politely

While it's almost impossible to actually make someone pay you, making it easier helps make it happen. Use a professional invoicing template or, better yet, a software like Freshbooks.com or something similar that you can access via an app on your phone. These allow you to immediately create and send invoices (when necessary) and show how long you've been waiting to get paid. You can see when your client viewed the invoice and keep track of other important things automatically instead of manually. Maybe you are one of the lucky ones who can thrive with just one or two major clients, although putting all your eggs in one basket is never a good idea. But the vast majority of freelancers will have a lot of smaller contracts that ideally add up to something sizeable by the end of the year. Don't waste time trying to stay on top of all them; let automated software handle that problem for you.

Getting paid is the most important part of your business. It's what allows you to keep doing what you do and get better at it. While you may not like handling the administrative side of your business, as a freelancer you don't have the luxury of neglecting it. You need to understand it and own it. At some point, if your growth merits it, you might be able to outsource the whole process to someone else. But in the beginning, your client relationships are gold and every touch point you have with them is an opportunity for you to learn and grow. Putting in estimates or quotes, delivering on the service and understanding how your client pays will inform your growth as a freelancer and help you do more.

Clients: customer relations

Client relationships are at the very heart of your freelancing business. Understanding and managing the dynamics of your relationships with clients is your most challenging — and also most important — job.

Get the relationship right and treat it with respect and care, as you would any other kind of relationship, and you will be rewarded. Take it for granted, ignore it — or worse, actively abuse it — and you'll soon be out of business. What clients need, how they want to communicate, what they care about — these are issues of vital concern to you and your business. If you don't take the time to learn enough about your customers, one of your competitors will.

Your clients are people first. It doesn't matter how big the firm is behind them, whether it's a major multinational corporation or a small mom-and-pop shop down the road, you are always dealing with a person first. And people like it when you remember their name, look them in the eye, smile when you talk to them and listen to what they have to say. Even if all your communications are by email (which I don't recommend), you have to make the effort to understand the person in the customer.

That being said, clients can also be difficult, demanding, rude, inconsistent, disorganized and downright hostile. They can interfere or obstruct, help or hinder. They may resent you because they wanted the job to go to their cousin or love you because you make them look so good.

In this section, we'll look at the different types of clients you may encounter and various situations that may arise, with some ideas on how to handle both.

Client care for former clients

Every client is your number one client. Or that's how you need to make them feel.

If you're coming from a corporate background where you may well have been on the client side of the business for a long time, you will need to take some time to recalibrate your working style. Your experience being a client can help you understand what a client expects, but that same experience can handicap you when it comes to interacting with clients from the supplier side.

As a client, you got used to speaking and being heard. You may have thought you were just having a conversation with your consultant. In reality, he or she was busy taking notes, interpreting what you were asking for, and making sure the conversation kept going. Your consultants — at least the good ones — were listening to you. Asking questions for precision and listening for more insights.

As a freelancer, you will do a lot more listening than you ever did as a client. A client can afford to say one thing and do something else. A freelancer can't.

This might hurt a little

Of the many client conversations you had as the one paying the bill, you'll never forget the first one you have when you're the one charging it. The dynamic is completely different ,and you may wonder how little you noticed (cared) when you had the might of your corporation behind you and just needed to get done whatever needed getting done.

Being in the gig economy means, above all else, learning how to make each of your clients feel like they're the most important customer you have, regardless of whether they actually are. In the beginning, of course, you may only have one client so you won't be doing anything other than what you would be doing otherwise. But before long, you may be stretching yourself between two, three or even more clients. All of them are going to expect the same kind of service they would get if they were your only client.

My point is: if you don't learn to manage these expectations, you will burn out. Many freelancers do for precisely this reason.

Stay in your lane

One method to keep control of your life while still providing excellent service to your clients is to schedule blocks of time in your calendar for each client file. Stay within your own prescribed time limits (as discussed in the "Leverage constraints" section of this book) as much as possible. Expect to be interrupted by client emergencies. Build flexibility into your schedule. Leave at least one floater day or half-day per week – some slack in the schedule – to allow you to expand any time a client calls or contacts you with something that needs immediate attention.

A client you ignore won't stay a client for long

While you can choose to work whenever and wherever you want to, don't think for a second that means you can also choose to ignore a client who contacts you when it's important (to them). Clients expect you to answer the phone when they call, or reply quickly to any email they send. Ignore them once and you may not get a second chance. Train yourself to be a quick responder. While you can't be expected to solve every problem or deal with every crisis that erupts instantaneously, you can respond immediately with a note saying you have received the message and you are looking into it. Then provide the nearest possible time to connect with them.

Responding to clients this way gives you a method for triaging their concerns while still displaying attentive care. If the problem is not urgent, but just something the client wants you to look at and take off their plate, the quick follow-up call or email lets the client know you're on the case. When you've created that breathing space, your client, in turn, has the opportunity to give you a clearer sense of their priorities. You often end up establishing deadlines that work for both of you.

While everything usually seems urgent at first, most things don't turn out to be. Responding quickly to client concerns lets both you and your client identify true emergencies, and then decide what issues can be shunted back into the schedule you've already created for them.

Understanding client types

One of the joys — and challenges — of being a freelancer is the opportunity to work with a wide range of different client types. Having many clients is a good idea for many reasons. The broader your client network, the more widely dispersed are your proverbial eggs in your proverbial baskets. In financial terms, you're diversified, and theoretically insured against any major disruptions should one or more of your clients be affected by something in their company or industry.

Having a few or even one major client seems like a dream come true for many freelancers. In fact, it can turn out to be a nightmare. If you only have a single client for whom you work the majority of your time, you may just be working like an employee without benefits. And tax authorities do not always consider you eligible to claim the tax benefits that are available to self-employed people (tax write-offs). Furthermore, you're at great risk of being put out of business if that client disappears for any reason. In short, you aren't really getting the real value and benefit of being a freelancer.

Having a lot of clients is a good idea, but of course, it comes with many challenges. The first is learning how to deal with the different personality types.

Here is a list of some of the more common client types you will likely encounter as a freelancer. There are many more, but these cover most of the behaviour they will exhibit. There are distinct ways to work with and handle these "personalities" so you can keep getting your work done and stay true to yourself. Here are some tips on how to identify different client types and what to watch out for when dealing with each of them.

The over-planning client

- **Warning signs:** Sends lots of emails and requests for planning meetings. Is not a risk-taker; doesn't want to be "caught out"; doesn't like surprises; likes being prepared for all eventualities. Wants to know and understand things "just in case." Likely a person with limited or restricted power within the organization and someone who will also require lots of approvals from higher-ups.

- **Impact/risk:** Causes a lot of additional work and eats up time with email queries, meetings and phone calls. Will ask for lots of (potentially unpaid) pre-work and additional materials like idea or vision boards, summaries and reports.

- **Recommended strategy:** Be careful to build in extra budgeted time to handle the additional work that this client type will create. Include planning sessions and meeting time as part of your initial forecast budget (with pricing attached) to make client aware of the cost of any time they spend with you.

The hands-off client

- **Warning signs:** Wears Hawaiian shirts to work, pays no attention to requests for input or comments and rarely replies directly to emails. A big forwarder and delegator; doesn't want to know how something is done; just wants the expected result. Doesn't give much feedback. Doesn't want to learn or understand details.

- **Impact/risk:** Can cause a lot of wasted time and effort if, on finally seeing results, decides on the spot that the work is not what they wanted or was expecting; puts undue pressure on suppliers without bothering to consider constraints they may be operating under that could have an impact on the work. Can be difficult to convince or persuade to change from a set opinion.

- **Recommended strategy:** Include milestone meeting points that require the client's feedback and involve disbursement of funds and/or approvals without which the project cannot move forward; in parallel, treat the delegated contact as the principal client unless you hear otherwise, then make it clear you were doing only what was requested.

The micromanaging/interfering client

- **Warning signs:** Just like a micromanaging boss, the micromanaging client will be more involved in your work than necessary; if you perform work onsite or in the presence of this client type, he or she may actually physically invade your space and direct you on the specific details of tasks you normally perform with no supervision.

- **Impact/risk:** Causes stress and raises irritation levels; can negatively affect the quality of your work, either through counter-productive direct interventions or by just rattling you and throwing you off your game.

- **Recommended strategy:** Tie them down in details that exceed their comprehension. Copy them on every email, no matter how inane, including two-word emails like "thank you." Provide them with complete and total transparency until they become so used to seeing you working that they stop looking (and factor this into your budget!).

The non-responder/late-responder client

- **Warning signs:** "Bueller...Bueller...Bueller..." You send an email, leave a voicemail, then another voicemail, and another email...and get nothing back until bam! you get an email with answers to all the questions you asked and more. The email usually comes after you've already begun working. This client type spends a lot of time away from his or her desk, directs all calls to voicemail, and may have one of those annoying ("I'm more efficient than thou" type auto-responders on their email that tells you they only check email twice a day). They are also the type to avoid taking a decision, and will not hesitate to use excuses like "I'm waiting for approvals" if you do manage to get hold of them. Most of the time, they will just leave you in the limbo waiting to hear back from them. Also known as "bottleneck."

- **Impact/risk:** Unless this person is directly involved in the project, you can work around their stalling obfuscations. The real danger lies when this is your point of entry to the client (or is the only client), and you are reliant on him or her for sign-offs or materials in order to proceed.

- **Recommended strategy:** Build more slack into your schedule and work on parallel tracks wherever and whenever possible to gain some of the ground lost to delays. Establish a protocol according to which work is approved unless you hear otherwise.

The needy client

- **Warning signs:** Asks you for your input on everything from emails they have to send to colleagues to what kind of font to use in a text. May let you know they're new to the job. Has a worn, slightly anxious look around the eyes; never seems to get a lot of sleep; is slightly ruffled in appearance and is unable to make decisions independently. Constantly asks you what you think they should do.

- **Impact/risk:** Requires sensitivity to their anxiety-driven behaviours. Wastes a lot of time on non-productive questions and queries aimed mainly at placating their insecurities.

- **Recommended strategy:** Set your boundaries and make them clear; be friendly and understanding but don't be an enabler.

The hostile client

- **Warning signs:** They let you know within the first five seconds of meeting them that you were not their first choice, or that they inherited this project and they make it clear they don't believe in it. Probably has a friend or preferred vendor they would have preferred for the work, but were overruled by higher-ups in the organization. Is generally unhelpful, unresponsive (except when cc'd on emails with superiors), and very hierarchical. Deferential (even obsequious) to authority; denigrating and condescending to inferiors (which includes you).

- **Impact/risk:** Aside from creating a toxic work environment, they can have a negative impact on your self-esteem and confidence and make work unpleasant and tedious. If they are your direct point of contact, can cause delays and may actively seek to sabotage you.

- **Recommended strategy:** Avoid altogether if at all possible. If the contract is absolutely critical, adopt a courteous and professional attitude, minimize contact and don't take anything personally. Deliver the project as you would for any other client, ignoring any comments or queries not directly related to what you have to deliver.

The disorganized client

- **Warning signs:** Sends you the same email in draft form multiple times; asks for work on projects you've already completed and submitted, or assigns tasks on extremely short deadlines. Forgets whether he or she has responded to you on anything and generally seems distracted.

- **Impact/risk:** Wastes a lot of your time and is almost guaranteed to forget to process your invoice on time; will likely lose it.

- **Recommended strategy:** Provide structure for your client; be the one who sends meeting requests and hosts calls, sets deadlines and reminders, and stays in regular contact and communication.

The bully/demanding client

- **Warning signs:** In many ways similar to the hostile client, but differs mainly in that he or she deliberately tries to "push you out of your comfort zone," as if this were somehow doing you a favour; repeatedly disrespects boundaries (e.g. calls late at night, on weekends, emails at 4 a.m.). May mistakenly believe that his/her pushing results in squeezing better work out of you, but ultimately shows egotistical/narcissistic tendencies and is never satisfied. May appear overly friendly and ingratiating in the company of authority figures or superiors within the organization (which is why he/she is sometimes confused with the wolf in sheep's clothing client). Is not respected (though is feared); plays favourites and has a divide-and-conquer mentality. Makes people feel intimidated deliberately.

- **Impact/risk:** Negatively affects self-esteem, impairs the quality of the work and morale of everyone with whom he/she works.

- **Recommended strategy:** Stand your ground, make your boundaries clear and defend them, ignore taunts, focus on the work and avoid interactions. If at all possible, ignore late-night calls and excessive emails.

The wolf in sheep's clothing client

- **Warning signs:** Appears wonderful at first, then turns into a version of the hostile client and/or bully/demanding client.

- **Impact/risk:** Can trick you into accepting or doing work you might otherwise have declined.

- **Recommended strategy:** Look before you leap; pay attention to how colleagues and others react and interact with him/her.

The unhappy employee client who wishes they were a freelancer too

- **Warning signs:** Looks at you intensely and asks about all your other gigs; wants to know where and when your last trip was; overshares personal information and asks you to do the same. Has read too much Tim Ferriss and believes that when you are not working with them, you are drinking margaritas on a beach making money online all the time. Is passive/aggressive and deep down, kind of resents you for your "freedom." Pretends you'll be friends outside the office and is always talking about that drink you're going to have together, but never do.

- **Impact/risk:** Is envious of you and so is very heavy-handed with comments and critiques of your work, challenges you to do better "because I know you can," but really just needs to overwrite and mark up anything you submit to justify his/her role in the organization, causing unnecessary rework and delays.

- **Recommended strategy:** Overlook the passive-aggression and sympathize with his/her position; underplay the positives of your freelancing career and highlight all commonalities to help close the gap between his/her idealization of your life and their own.

The go-between client/client-who's-not-really-your-client-client

- **Warning signs:** Is on a temporary or short-term contract. You likely know more people in the client's company than he or she does; is required to take every decision back to a manager and circulate among several others for consensus gathering.

- **Impact/risk:** Everything will take longer than you think it will; there will be a lot of "hurry up and wait" deadlines.

- **Recommended strategy:** Find out who the real decision-maker(s) is/are and assume you are working for them; show understanding and patience with your go-between client who is likely feel stressed and pulled in too many directions at once.

The indecisive client

- **Warning signs:** Never makes a decision; long silences between emails or calls; sits on proposals until long past their expiration; likely has limited or no real decision-making authority within the organization.

- **Impact/risk:** A major time waster and destructive influence on longer, multi-step projects; can tie you down on a slow-moving project, potentially risking losing out on more productive contracts elsewhere.

- **Recommended strategy:** Encourage/force decisions by using hard stops and no-flex deadlines.

The nightmare client

- **Warning signs:** Overly critical and impossible to please; you wake up at 4 a.m. thinking about him or her with a sinking feeling of dread and anxiety; you jump every time your phone rings and are afraid to open your email; you find yourself drinking more than usual and fantasizing about a simple little job in a cubicle where no one knows your name.

- **Impact/risk:** Can drive you back to looking for a 9-to-5 job or burn you out so completely you need to stop working altogether.

- **Recommended strategy:** Avoid at all costs; refer to a competitor and feign illness.

The dream client

- **Warning signs:** Friendly; responsive; clear in expectations and quick to provide positive feedback. You feel happy, even joyful working for and with them; you would do the work for free; are sad to see the project end and with a bit of luck, wind up becoming friends.

- **Impact/risk:** Becomes the elusive standard against which all other clients are judged.

- **Recommended strategy:** Always prioritize their project over all others and do whatever it takes to do more work with them; add to your offer and deliver new unexpected bonus work that makes your client appreciate you even more until you become indispensable.

The better you understand your client's personality type and working style, the better you will be able to adapt and modulate your own in response to ensure an productive relationship. It is always incumbent on you, the freelancer, to make the accommodations, no matter what the client says. You can choose who to work with and who to avoid, but once you've committed to a project, eyes wide open, it becomes your responsibility to make the relationship work. So choose well and figure out the client type you are dealing with quickly.

Situations

"We got a situation over here."
—The Situation, Jersey Shore

There are a lot of "situations" you can expect to arise over the course of your freelancing career. Here are just a few of the more common ones:

- Scope creep
- Extensions/delays
- Rate break (also known as "Can you give me a discount?")

How you choose to handle situations that occur depends both on your own personality type as well as your insight into the kind of client you are dealing with.

Scope creep

A common problem freelancers have to watch out for is scope creep. This happens when your client slowly starts introducing changes to the work you've been asked to do. Little by little, that adds to your workload. The mandate is stretched to include a bunch of extras you hadn't planned or budgeted for. When this happens, you must immediately call it to your client's attention. You must make it clear that the changes or additions to your mandate are beyond the scope of work you've agreed to. If you are willing to take on the extra work, renegotiate a new contract with an increase in fees. Most good clients will recognize that out-of-scope work should be compensated. If they don't, you can either complete the initial work as mandated, or choose to stop work altogether until a new agreement has been reached. (More on this in the next chapter.)

Extensions/delays

It's not always easy to stick to a predetermined schedule, especially if there are a lot of moving parts in a project. It's good practice to always include a bit of slack/buffer in your project proposal to account for predictable delays. However, if you are forced to deal with unpredictable delays due to something within the client's control, that's different. For example, you have a deadline for the delivery of a final, edited video but your client missed his or her deadline to submit their comments or change requests, putting everything on hold. This could delay other work you are doing for other clients, so it will cost you money. Make it clear to your client — through the text included in your contract as well as direct, verbal and written communication during the process — that delays extending beyond X number of days will not only result in a new final delivery date, but could incur additional "rush" fees if you are forced into a situation where you have to scramble to complete one project in order to take on a new one from another client.

Rate break

In some cases, a really good client who has given you a lot of work may go through a rough patch and need a bit of break on the rate you agreed to. You may decide to cut him or her some slack because you value the client relationship and expect the client's business to improve in the future. The same request from a new client who has no apparent need for a reduction in fees, other than an explicit desire to get a better deal doesn't warrant the same treatment. Dropping your rates, for whatever reason, is never a good idea unless you are getting something of equal or greater value in return (e.g. real valuable exposure to a relevant audience, a tax credit, or good karma because you are doing it for a charity or cause that you believe in and want to show support for). In cases where you do give a discount, always show your full rate on the invoice and then add the discounted percentage so that your actual real rate does not disappear. Treat all rate breaks as temporary, one-time offers and make that clear on the invoice so the client doesn't expect the same treatment on any renewals or future contracts.

As with many aspects of freelancing in this new gig economy, the onus is on you to stand up for yourself and always be looking out for your own best interests. Clients come in all shapes and sizes, and sometimes situations arise that are beyond everyone's control. But no matter how strong the relationship when a situation does occur, don't leave it up to the client to determine how it will be resolved. Be proactive, professional and communicative. A lot can be accomplished with communication and transparency. Working out a new arrangement usually entails compromises on both sides, and there is usually no benefit to being completely intransigent. If you believe your client is acting in good faith and feel that the relationship matters, coming to an agreement when these kinds of situations pop up will ensure a successful completion of the contract that leaves both parties satisfied.

How to deal with unplanned change requests

You won the contract, you got the gig and you're thrilled. You really want to do a great job and impress your client and they seem really happy with you — so happy that they ask you to take on even more than they originally discussed. They have such confidence in you they are giving you even more work...but wait, it's for the same price? Wha...???

It will happen. You'll be working on a project that's been properly scoped out, planned, scheduled and budgeted for, and then midway through, your client will ask for a bunch of changes or add something new to the mandate or shortens the deadline. What do you do?

Things change

Most clients will understand, if they don't bring it up themselves, that significant changes to scope result in additional charges. Problems only arise when you don't agree on what a "significant change" is. Video projects, copywriting and design projects are particularly susceptible to this kind of challenge because, regardless of how much you talk about the project, and how well-planned out it is, with mock-ups and template examples to work from, some clients just don't know what they like (or dislike) until they see it in front of them. They may tell you they want one thing, but when you give it to them, exactly as they've asked for it, they realize that's not what they want after all. (Someone once told me something worth sharing here: "Most clients ask for options, but when you present them with sexy, spicy and mild, they always choose mild.") These kinds of clients are the most likely to ask for lots of changes and they need to be managed right from the start.

As a precaution, when you are designing a contract, take into account that there will be some client input and requests for revisions. Rare indeed is the creator who nails it completely, blows the client off his or her feet and gets approval immediately with no need to tweak anything. Change requests and comments are a natural part of any creative process, particularly ones involving a creative producer on the one side and a paying client on the other. Great clients enhance the final output by filling in information gaps or providing context or industry awareness that helps the creator achieve the desired outcome. Not-so-great clients are the ones who actually take your good work and make it worse by running it through a blender of approval processes and gathering feedback and input from so many other people in a vain attempt at "getting consensus" that your work becomes unrecognizable from your original intention.

Be very specific about how you handle change requests

Most clients fall somewhere in between those two phenotypes. That's why it's so important to design a contract properly. Build in a change process, allowing for a reasonable number of revisions, and define as explicitly as possible what the scope of change requests can look like. For example, in a text, a reasonable change request would be to reduce the word count or provide more substantial backup for a specific statement or idea in the work. An unreasonable change request would be to have to rewrite the entire piece because the assigned topic is no longer what the client wants to communicate and there is a different story to tell. In video work, a reasonable initial change might be a request to change a clip for another, extend a certain scene, or cut another. Clients should be able to comment on textual and graphical elements and request additions or deletions. But it would be unreasonable to request, say, major script changes to the work after the video is near completion, or a completely new element that affects the timing, music sync and full editing of the entire video after the initial change request windows have closed.

When you determine that a request for changes is effectively a new work order, the first thing to do before implementing the change or proceeding with any work is to get your client to agree that this change will entail additional charges. Be ready to show how these changes affect the budget. If additional funds are not available, you must discuss what can be cut in order to maintain the amount of work you originally agreed on.

Don't work for free

Many freelancers balk at the idea of asking for more money midway through a contract, but sometimes it's unavoidable. Not asking for money that you are rightfully owed will ultimately have a negative effect on your relationship with your clients, and sometimes the work itself. If you don't feel you're being properly compensated for the work you are doing, you're likely to feel less motivated and more likely to begin fielding other work that has a better payout for you. You may also develop resentful feelings towards your client, which they likely will pick up on, and the relationship will sour.

It's far more efficient and effective in the long run to simply be transparent and communicate clearly about being compensated for extra work so that your client fully understands and appreciates where you stand. This gives the client the opportunity to either retract the change request or bolster the budget to compensate you for the extra work. As with many client situations, a conversation, ideally face to face or at least over a video or phone call, can resolve things much sooner and more effectively than a long thread of terse emails.

Asking for reviews

Asking for reviews is just like asking for the business or asking for referrals: it's all about timing and convenience. But before getting into tactics, let's briefly explore why reviews are an important, if not critical, part of your marketing arsenal.

Pause for just an insta-second and think about the last time you bought anything. Anything at all. A toothbrush, a trip to Italy, a pizza, a car, a can of paint... Did you make a single one of those purchases without first looking up the item in question online? Didn't you then almost immediately look to the reviews and read a few before deciding to proceed or not? Did the reviews or recommendations you read influence your decision to buy? Very likely they did.

And what happened after you bought? Within a brief interval of time, you received an email or a text asking you to rate the service/product you received. Now whether you did or did not depended on a few variables, such as the timing of the request, the method required to make the review and the intensity of your feeling about the product or service you acquired. For freelancers, understanding these variables (timing, convenience and emotional resonance) is key to getting the golden five-star review you're after.

Timing

There is a moment in every completed contract, just after you've submitted your final delivery and received your client's acceptance but before you send your invoice, that I believe is the optimal moment to solicit a review. Assuming you've done an excellent job, delivered outstanding work and know your client is happy, there is no better moment than this to ask for the review. Your client is still focussed on you and your work, the project is fresh and top of mind, and they have not yet felt even a pinprick of pain at having to pay the bill.

Convenience

How you ask for the review and what you ask to have included will have the greatest impact on your ability to collect reviews at all. For most people, the idea of filling in a form of any size or length for no reward is about as appealing as waiting in line for someone else's dentist's appointment. There's nothing in it for you, and no matter how much you may care about the company or product you are being asked to review, your time is likely more valuable than your feedback, so you probably won't do it. (The one exception to this rule is if the review sites themselves become a kind of platform for you to display your curatorial acumen and verbal virtuosity. Sites like Rotten Tomatoes, Goodreads, Yelp reviews, LinkedIn recommendations, and Amazon fall into this category. In fact, there is a breed of freelancers who act as professional reviewers, and while it would be unethical to give a product review for cash or in kind, many earn payment in some form from companies that trust and value an objective review. Be careful, however, about offering to pay for reviews online. Most of the sites where reviews matter don't like purchased reviews, and may even block publishing the review you receive.) But when the motivation is merely to express your opinion with no real expectation of gain, what you're being asked to do is give something for nothing in return.

As the review requester, you need to make this process as painless as possible without compromising the integrity of the review system you are using. I've discovered that Google+ reviews work very well. (You can leave one for me if you're liking this book so far.) There are a lot of reasons why I've chosen Google+ as my review platform of choice, not the least of which is simply that Google, as the world's primary search engine, favours its own content and products. So having reviews on its platform enhances your ranking in searches. But another important reason is the ease with which a review can be solicited. You simply click, and up pops a window with the stars already filled in for you and a blinking cursor where you can write as much or as little text as you want, and boom! you're done. You've collected a highly visible review from a real person that other people — hopefully, prospective customers — will see and use to base their decision on when thinking of hiring you.

Now to make it work for you, you first need to be sure that you have your own Google+ profile for your business and if you don't have one, create one. Once you have one, create and copy your shortened

URL and stick it on the end of every email communication you send out in your signature. But most importantly, use it in your email when you are specifically asking for the review.

Keep the text short and sweet, something like:

"Thank you for choosing me as your partner on the _____ project. It's been great working with you and I would like to ask one small favour: can you please write a brief review for me on my Google+ site here ___LINK___? It can be as long or brief as you have time for. Reviews are a very important part of marketing for me and positive ones have a big impact on attracting new business. Thank you!"

Use whatever wording you feel comfortable with, but the key is including the short link and making it clear that you are looking for a POSITIVE review. As icky as that may make some people feel, there is no point in actively seeking out a low-star review. So obviously, only send this request when you've really nailed the contract and you know your client loves you.

It's how you make them feel that counts

Finally, when asking for a review, use your emotional IQ and make sure that the person you are asking has a good impression of you and your work, and cares enough to leave some kind of thoughtful comment. It's always better if your reviews sound genuine and refer to something specific about your project and your working manner. People writing reviews will only provide those elements that if they actually liked working with you and care about you as a person, so keep that in mind throughout your working relationship.

Strong and positive online reviews will act like a lead magnet for your business. It takes time to gather and collect them but they don't happen on their own. You need to go out of your comfort zone and ask, but if you do it right, it will pay dividends with a stream of new customers.

Dealing with unhappy customers, or what to do when something goes wrong

Your customers are the most important part of your business because without them, you don't have a business. But just because they are the lifeblood of your freelancing practice doesn't mean you will always value and appreciate them like you want to. And it doesn't mean that every customer will always respect you and your work.

Some will probably annoy and irritate you, waste your time, take advantage of you, pay you long after their invoice was due and otherwise leave you feeling resentful. Some will be downright rude, obnoxious and belligerent. But before you walk away, take a deep breath and decide how you want to handle the situation.

When you are singlehandedly delivering a service and dealing with the customer directly before, during and after the contract, lots of thing can go wrong. Here are a few sticky situations you may find yourself in:

- Your client may not pay you right away, or seek to renegotiate the deal after you've completed the work, claiming they are dissatisfied or that your work is somehow sub-par.

- Your client may change the mandate on you midway through the job, or try to shoe-horn in a bunch of extras not explicitly agreed to when you made the deal.

- Your client may turn out not to be the client at all and you end up having to deal with someone else who has a different understanding of what you agreed to do for them.

- Your client may turn out to be a difficult person — rude, incommunicative, unfriendly, disrespectful.

- Your client may be unprepared and disorganized, but blame you for any issues that result from his/her shortcomings, not yours.

- Your client may have highly unrealistic expectations with an equally unrealistic budget.

These are but a few scenarios that may arise that you have to learn how to deal with.

Ideally, of course, you do not do business with a client who falls into any of the scenarios described above or whose behaviour would lead you to believe that something like one of these scenarios is likely to occur. But that is not always possible, or predictable. Sometimes we give clients the benefit of the doubt (and they disappoint us) or sometimes we simply overestimate our own abilities to deal with a situation if it occurs. Don't beat yourself up (or your client!) if this happens. Deal with it, forgive yourself and move on.

But in case it does happen, here are a few pointers:

- **If your client changes the mandate midstream:** Always work from a contract in which you summarize exactly and explicitly what you've agreed to do and deliver on, in what time frame, for what price and what your client is to do in return. Leave nothing to chance or open to interpretation. Be explicit. If your client then asks for what essentially amounts to a scope change, pause before proceeding and refer to your agreement, indicating that either they must agree to compensate you for the additional work or you will not be able to complete it as it falls beyond the scope of your agreement.

- **If you have a disagreement or altercation on site:** Always remember that whether this is your first contract or your 7000th, you are a professional and must act like one. This means that regardless of what your client does or doesn't do you have to stay on the high road. Keep your cool, never use profanity and make it clear through communication what the basis for disagreement is. You don't have to accept being pushed around or bullied, but you can handle a situation with aplomb even if your client is acting like a turd. Once the heat of the disagreement passes and if/when you negotiate an end to the contract that is favourable to you, you can fall back on your more civilized conduct.

- **If, after the job, your client expresses dissatisfaction with your work:** Examine the details of your contract (in which you've captured the full scope of work) and verify that you did indeed do what was asked of you. Sometimes clients' dissatisfactions have nothing to do with you. Sometimes a client just doesn't know what they want until they see it and then tries to pin the blame on you. If you had a contract that spelled out your obligations and you fulfilled them, then stick to your guns and insist on payment within a specified period of time. If, however, there is some room for interpretation or subjective disagreement, then use your judgement and come to an agreement. Offer a rebate on the final price, or a rework option if the relationship is not too contentious.

- **If your client is a class A A-hole:** Don't agree to work for them again. No matter what the money looks like, walk away. Don't lower your standards or work for people who lack basic respect and courtesy. It is never worth it.

- **To put it bluntly:** dealing with customers even though you need them (or perhaps because you need them) can sometimes be a real pain in the butt. And once in a while, you may get one who is difficult to deal with. But treat these like the learning experiences they are. Handling a situation where things didn't go as planned with a client can be illuminating and teach you more than having nothing ever go wrong in the first place.

How to Keep on Keeping on

part five

How to Keep on Keeping on

....

Keep on Keeping on
(or why you need the hard part)

KNOWING WHEN TO push harder and when not to is an important life skill, but for freelancers, it's essential to crafting and guiding your life.

You've opened up your sails and set out into the great blue sea of free-lance life. You will encounter new islands and obstacles very soon. What may look like smooth waters at first will turn out to be rapids and channels that are difficult to navigate. At times you will feel ill-equipped, or worse, demotivated, and you will long for the safe harbour you left behind. You knew it wasn't going to be easy, but you may not have expected it to be so hard. And at some point you may — in fact, you will — feel like quitting.

I came close to quitting freelancing many times, but the worst was several years ago in the middle of a cold month of March, after a particularly slow start of the year. I was depressed, and really doubting whether I'd made the right choice in going all in as a freelancer. Should I have gone back to school and become a lawyer like I'd once thought of doing? Should I have buckled down and just taken a regular job like everyone else I knew at the time? I was putting out blog posts and doing some online marketing through social media but nothing seemed to be sticking. Nothing seemed to be working, least of all me. It was tough.

And then I got an email from a woman in California who'd found me online and was organizing a conference and looking for a photographer. I called her back. We talked about what she was looking for. She sent me a long detailed list of the kinds of shots she wanted. She asked for links to similar work. I really wasn't sure even after talking with her and responding to her several email queries that I'd get the gig. Then all of a sudden, I was booked.

That one contract grew into 20 more with the same client. The work gave me international experience and marked a turning point in my career. Maybe it was just coincidence, but right away after that first gig, I started booking more work with more international clients, and really started getting busy. Looking back I can honestly say that I went from the lowest point in my career to some of my highest. But had I given up at my lowest point, I never would have experienced the better times that followed.

You will always feel like quitting when you are at the hardest part. I could fill this page with reasons why you should keep on pushing. Instead, I'm going to talk about one. Because there is only one reason to "keep on keeping on": It's simple: the hardest part is the most valuable part of all.

You can change your mind, and decide freelancing is not for you. That's completely fine and understandable. You may find that you weave in and out of freelancing throughout your career, with some gigs turning into jobs, and some jobs becoming gigs. But quitting at the hard part puts a full stop on something that is meant to both ebb and flow. And that something is you.

When it gets harder, it means it's working

When you get to the hard part, that's when your energy, your talent, your drive and your focus are all tested to the limit. Sticking it out when things get hard is the equivalent of those last ten reps you do in a workout, the ones that actually make the muscle grow. Everything beforehand is just warm up. Rather than run from the hard part or try to avoid it, you should actually try to engineer your work so you get to a hard part as soon as possible. Because only then will you get the satisfaction, the learning and the sense of real accomplishment from working through it.

After you stick it out, look back at the hard part and realize it wasn't that hard at all. But you will feel stronger and more confident, and more capable of tackling the next tough period.

No one ever got better at anything by sticking to their comfort zone. The reason you have a comfort zone is not to live there, but to recognize where its edges are. When you are comfortable you are not learning, not growing, not adapting. Comfort is a reward for hard work, but if you stay there too long, you lose touch. Like the antennae on a snail, what you feel on the edge of your comfort zone teaches you about the world far more than what you can learn curled up inside your shell. Sure, you'll need to take refuge sometime, you'll retreat, you'll pull back if you feel something too hot. But that's just a midway point. The knowledge you gain from feeling at the edge guides your next steps, gives you the information you need to course correct and then keep going.

When the hard part — the breaking part — is the middle of a project that's got you so turned around you don't know what to do, you can always just quit, walk away. Eventually you'll find another gig. But if you can stick with it and struggle through it, not only will you finish that project, but you'll have gained insight and knowledge into a problem as well as how to deal with it that you never would have otherwise. And that is future fuel you'll never run out of.

You're just not that big a deal — yet

One of my favourite songs from the '90s is a lesser-known song by The Smiths called "You just haven't earned it yet, baby." It comes to mind when, after I've spent hours crafting what I consider an absolutely amazing post for my photo blog, I hit send and then...nothing. Weeks later, two likes. Or none at all. WTF? Why isn't this on the cover of the Huffington Post by now? And then I hear... the song. "You just haven't earned it yet, baby."

In one of his posts, Seth Godin, who has written about every iota of any idea in marketing, calls it credibility. It can be your follower count, market reach, dollars in your bank account or the number of people on your email marketing list. But whatever it is, when you start you'll be at zero.

If that thought fills you with hopelessness and despair, go take a walk, pour yourself a glass of something cool or warm, meditate and then come back here.

Guess what, you're still at zero.

But that's okay. Because starting from zero is exactly what you can do today and still (eventually) make a good, even hugely successful living. You just have to get started, do the work, focus on your daily habits and stick with it. For as long as it takes. One piece of content at a time. One customer at a time. One day at a time.

You may get lucky, of course. You may end up writing a post that goes wildly viral, get invited to be a guest on Oprah, have your life story turned into a Hollywood blockbuster or sell the little app-thingy you made in your spare time with a friend in a basement apartment and make billions of dollars.

But that's probably not going to happen. And looking for that to happen, or worse, feeling a vague sense of disappointment because it hasn't happened out of the gate, will only reap negative feelings and weigh you down with a false sense of failure. That might lead you to quit. in which case, it will be failure.

You just have to earn it, baby.

Complacency

Complacency is a hidden cost of success. Whether you are gainfully employed or a proudly independent entrepreneur, when you get good enough at what you do to get known for it, it tends to creep up on you.

It begins with a casual lowering of the guard. A loosening of the habits that put you there in the first place. Under the guise of living for the moment and "taking it easy," you let little things slide.

At first, nothing changes. You still get the job done. No one seems to notice any difference. You are paying the bills.

But soon you begin to feel soft in places that were once firm. Your energy levels begin to dip. You push yourself less.

The gentle slide may continue, unobserved, until something jolts you back to an awareness of the change. I've experienced this a few times in my career as a photographer. When things are going really well and my calendar is booked, I start taking it for granted that business will keep rolling in. I get a little lazier with my marketing and blogging. And then a major regular client suddenly drops me, or a big contract I was counting on gets cancelled. It often has nothing to do with me, but the net result is I'm suddenly feeling like a first-time freelancer all over again, worrying about my other contracts. Then it hits me that I've been too lax with myself. I've become complacent. I've been busy working IN my business and stopped working ON it.

One way I've learned to avoid the risk of becoming complacent and taking my clients and the work they are giving me for granted is to make sure I stay in touch with my reasons for doing what I am doing in the first place. I ask myself, am I still feeling purposeful and doing work that I want to do? I periodically check in and ask myself these questions:

- Is what I am doing right now related in any way to any of my goals?
- Do I have a true grasp of my assets and am I leveraging them to the best of my ability?
- Am I feeling energized and excited about possibilities in my life?
- Or do I feel uninspired, foggy, unfocussed?

I think when I am feeling the latter, it's usually because I've let myself go somehow. I've supplanted real action with false ones, like checking email or social media. I've skipped out on the routines I've learned are important to me (like working out, meditating, daily writing, etc.).

Rather than get hung up on the fact that it has happened (because it will), expect it and design your life with an awareness that complacency is more likely to set in when you are doing well than when you're not. The more "successful" you are (however you define that term), the more at risk you are for developing complacent attitudes and behaviours.

Watch out for these warning signs:

- Are you feeling bored with what you doing?
- Are you less motivated to connect with people?
- Do you find yourself not getting excited when a new client contacts you or someone sends you a referral?
- Are you spending more time on social media than usual?
- Do you feel envious of other people's successes or changes they are making in their lives?
- Are you skipping your workouts? Sleeping restlessly? Eating, drinking, going out too much?

Every professional, freelancer or not, will experience periods when their passion ebbs and they question what they are doing. It's this hidden doubtfulness that actually underlies complacency. Be aware that it can happen to anyone, including you.

Here are a few ideas you can try to turn yourself back on and reverse the decline that happens when complacency takes hold:

- **Start something new:** New starts bring with them an activation energy that can be leveraged to inject new energy into everything you do. It doesn't need to be related to your work. If you've grown tired of your regular workout, join a class or try a new regime that you've never done before. If you are creatively blocked, challenge yourself to do something creative in a completely different field. For example, if you're a writer, try to paint or draw something and vice versa. All forms of creativity create flow that helps all the others.
  - » At the start of every year, I take on one new creative project. This year it's taking one Fujifilm Instax photo a day. One year I wrote a poem a day. And for years I've kept a handwritten journal. If you make a space to be creative where there is really no purpose but to play and experiment with your ideas, you'll find it feeds into your work well.

- **Get involved:** If you are bored at work or in your business, look around you for projects to get involved with or a charitable organization or cause to put your effort into. There may be a local chapter of an international charity you can join or start, like Room to Read, or you can donate some of your time to a shelter for homeless men, or women, or both.

  » I worked with a homeless shelter a few years ago and started an art gallery in their cafeteria. We held monthly shows. It was a uniquely rewarding experience to bring local artists in to speak about their work and giving people an opportunity to visit a homeless shelter and learn a little bit more about the lives of the men there.

- **Meet someone new:** Whether it's a new colleague at the office or a stranger at an event, making the effort to meet new people is always invigorating. Networking isn't just something you should do when you are looking for a new job. In fact, it can be more effective when you already have one. Making new connections with new people forces you to make an effort, a bit like the idea behind dressing for success. When you set out to meet someone new, you ask questions about who they are, what they do and how they got to where they are in life, and you are likely to get asked the same kinds of questions. Listening and answering honestly can recharge you in unexpected ways.

  » Monthly Meetups are a great way to meet new people. Look up whatever you are interested in at meetup.org, and you'll probably discover a group that meets monthly somewhere nearby you can join. I regularly go to start-up events and meet-ups to look for new prospects, see what other people are doing and just to get out of my bubble. I always come back with a few new contacts and a headful of ideas.

- **Take a trip:** Sometimes, if you're in a deep funk or have been feeling uninspired for a very long time, everything just seems so hard. If you can manage it, take a trip. Even a short trip, a day or two, will give you energy and new ideas. Travelling always brings you into closer contact with the present moment, and that's an excellent cure for complacency. Reacquainting yourself with what it feels like to be really involved and engaged in the present helps you shake off the dull-headedness that follows a period of life where you may have been sleepwalking a bit.

» I'm a big fan of the mini-vacation. An epic three- or four-month journey is a powerful way to explore the world and really dive deeply into what travel can do for the soul. Unfortunately, it can be very difficult to organize, especially if you have responsibilities like children, rent or a mortgage. So instead, I take an extended weekend here and there, ducking out early on a Friday to go visit friends in another city or making a short visit to the countryside for a hike.

- **Go for a walk:** Walking is probably the easiest, safest, quickest and cheapest/free thing you can do to motivate yourself and recharge your body/mind/soul. All you need to do is get up and go. It's a wonderfully simple and effective cure-all that is often overlooked.

» One of my best friends and I have a decades-long tradition of taking long walks together, which we call Odyssey Walks. We set out in a direction and generally don't plan the route. The only purpose is to walk together. Invariably, we fall into a rhythm and have deep and enriching conversations. We'll walk for miles and not notice it, stopping wherever we feel like it for a pint (or two), and then carry on. We've walked in cities and in the countryside, and though we no longer live in the same city, we still plan for and do at least one Odyssey Walk a year. Many real projects have been the direct result of the ideas and inspirations that happened on these walks.

Making change happen in your life is ultimately what keeps life exciting. When things have been going well, it's easy to view change as a threat to our comfort and security. Nothing could be further from the truth. When change is the one constant you can count on, the best security you can have in life is to be the one behind it, rather than one waiting for it to happen.

When will I feel secure?

Like many freelancers, you will probably wonder this at some point.

As an employee, you may have grown so used to working inside a company that you took security for granted. Just having a job was security in and of itself. While you may have worried about losing it from time to time, you never worried that you might not have a cheque every two weeks or at the end of the month.

And then BOOM! You're out here on your own and you're acutely aware of not having that safety net. Suddenly you start asking yourself increasingly anxiety-driven "what-if" questions like:

"What if I lose my client?"

"What if I screw something up?"

"What if I get hit by a car and can't work!?"

When you realize that these doubts and worries are intrinsically part of the freelance lifestyle, the freedom in freelancing can seem a lot less appealing. It is destabilizing. You can never really be sure that the worst case won't happen, even though it rarely does. (Or if it does, it's almost never as bad as you thought it would be before it happened. "Fear has big eyes," as the saying goes.)

The more successful you get, ironically, the less secure you may feel.

You feel losses more than you feel gains, and you have more to lose.

So when can you stop worrying, put your feet up and just coast on your victories? When can you stop working it?

Never.

And you shouldn't think there's anything wrong with that. On the contrary, the fact that you can never grow so comfortable you stop thinking about how to improve is a great thing. You will always have to look for ways you can earn more or do more with what you have to offer. And that's good. You never stop learning or growing, because when you do, you're done. And that's not the kind of security you want.

Wanting to feel secure is completely normal. If you didn't ever feel the need to feel secure there would probably be something wrong with you It's a primal human need, right there at the base of Maslow's hierarchy, just above breathing, eating and sleeping.

Not having security is just as uncomfortable as it sounds. It's standing in the rain without a raincoat. It's wandering through the jungle at night, aware that all kinds of predators are out there. It's stepping out onto ice, not knowing if you're going to break through and plunge into the frigid waters.

That's why they call it "growing pains"

Something interesting happens when you recognize the inherent riskiness of being a freelancer, and you do it anyway. You start to develop muscles you didn't know you had. You start to see things with new eyes, and notice things you never did before. While you may still get caught in the rain without a raincoat, you will also get much better at finding shelter or knowing where to stand so you don't get wet. You develop night vision and start to recognize the richness the jungle has to offer. You learn how to avoid getting eaten by a jaguar. You learn to spot the thick ice that will bear your weight.

You can't get there without the uncertainty, so the best thing to do is acknowledge it, then ignore it.

Learning to live with the ambiguity, the not knowing, the uncertainty is a fundamental skill every successful freelancer must learn and develop. That feeling that success is temporary doesn't ever fully go away, but you will get better at dealing with it. Eventually you will hardly notice it at all.

While you won't know exactly who will be on your client list next year, you can reasonably expect someone to be there. Another word for this is faith. Not blind faith in some higher power but faith in yourself, faith that the work you do every day will pay dividends. You might not know when or how much, but keep doing the work, stay true to your purpose and it will happen.

Don't compare

In the play *No Exit*, Jean-Paul Sartre famously observed, "Hell is other people." (*L'enfer c'est les autres*). Comparing yourself to others is an excellent way to beat yourself down. In a world that is constantly reflected back to us through the filters of social media and five-star rating systems, it can be difficult to lift your head above the noise and learn how to focus on what matters. But in the words of another famous quote-meister, Yoda, "Focus, you must." If you don't, you risk losing the freelancer's most precious resource: self-confidence.

While it is important to know your market and understand who else is offering a service similar to yours, benchmarking, as this process is known, should only be used to gauge market requirements, not to compare yourself to the competition.

In every niche there are top performers who can deliver outstanding value and charge top dollar for it. You may well be or become one of these providers. Until you do, however, focus not on what your competitors are doing or charging, but on discovering and executing what your clients truly value.

All freelancers are not created equally. But assessing your own worth and value in comparison to other freelancers is invariably an apples-to-oranges game that yields little, if any beneficial information.

Drawing comparisons is also a waste of time and energy that could be better spent on the things you control and can improve. Your competitor may have a beautifully designed website that fills you with envy and dismay, but obsessively comparing yours to theirs does nothing to improve your site. It just drags you down.

Choose compassion (for yourself) over comparison

When we compare ourselves to others, we have a tendency to overestimate their value and underestimate our own, creating not one but two distorted perceptions, neither of which is helpful.

Researching the market, gathering intelligence, looking for new ideas... these are all useful activities if performed systematically, while focusing on delivering value to your clients.

You don't have to be a Zen master to experience the strength of having inner peace and contentment. You can get that feeling after a hard workout, when you really give it your all, or after completing a project and seeing your work out in the world, taking on a life of its own.

Your business will thrive if you are able to tune out the distractions, which include paying too much attention to what other people are doing. Don't worry about having competition. Healthy competition is often a sign of a strong market. If you are the only provider in town, your market is probably too small to sustain you. You need competition to keep yourself striving. Just remind yourself that the only measure of success that matters is whether you've done your best work, delivered on your promise and created value for your customers.

Do that enough times and you will have a thriving business. You don't get there by constantly looking over your shoulder, but rather by keeping your focus on what lies ahead.

The dangers of limited thinking

Limits have their uses. But limited thinking — consciously or unconsciously setting upper or lower limits on yourself — can do tremendous long-term damage to your freelance business.

Thinking small keeps you small. If you believe that you'll never earn more than $XK a year freelancing, or if even that number seems out of reach, then you're experiencing limited thinking. It becomes a self-fulfilling prophecy, subtly eroding your confidence and your drive like water washing away at a sandcastle on the beach.

Limited thinking can have deep roots. It could originate in your childhood, the product of unsupportive or overbearing parents. It may come from early experiences trying something and failing, or from a lack of self-worth. But wherever it comes from, it's in your mind, and therefore it is something you can change.

Real change takes time

Like getting fit, you can't expect change to happen immediately. What you can do is practice lifting the limit. Whatever yours is set at, lift it right now by an imaginary 10%. Just do it. You can justify that to yourself. What does it take to increase your revenues by 10%? One new client? An add-on service to your existing clients? An extension by one week of a current contract? Whatever it is, imagine that as not just possible but likely, because you will take action towards making it a reality. Don't be surprised when it works — it will. Then go back and try lifting your new limit by another 10%, or higher.

You can also, of course, try going all in and ditching the idea of limits altogether, But I don't recommend going cold turkey that way. It's really hard to do, because even if your limit is an irrational one, your mind will become churlish and demand proof if you try to change it too much, too quickly. You can't just say, "Okay, I'm getting rid of the artificial limits I've placed on myself," (though that helps) and expect it to happen. The mind is also ingenious; it has a way of putting the factors that control your limited thinking beyond your control. Like how much money you earn, for example. It presumes you can't control that, that it's up to your clients and your success and finding them is outside your control. So what do you do?

Aim for incremental gains

Take back control. Reset the limits. If it's money, then look at what you can do right now to add clients to your practice. If you've been doing this through blogging, ask yourself if you can raise your blog post frequency. If you've found new clients through word of mouth, ask yourself if you can reach out further to your network, or tap into your network's network. If cold calls have worked for you, can you make an additional five or 10 calls a week? Turn your attention towards things you can do, actions you can take, choices about your time and effort that you can make. Your limits aren't set and controlled by forces outside of yourself any more.

Limited thinking isn't just about money. It's about how much and how far you think you can go in life. Many people believe, for some reason, that their success (or lack of it) is predetermined or affected by external factors beyond their control. They've internalized this belief and it's solidified inside them. People say things like:

- I'd be more successful if I lived somewhere else.
- If only I had started sooner, I would have made it by now.
- If it weren't for having responsibilities (kids, a mortgage, car payments, bills), I would have done X instead of this job...
- I'll never write a book; I don't have the discipline.
- I'll never get good at sales; I'm too much of an introvert.
- I'll never be able to charge that much for my time.
- I can't raise my rates, my clients would all dump me for someone cheaper.

And on and on and on. I've heard this depressing litany of excuses and self-defeating statements from countless people who were smarter, more talented, more capable than they thought they were. It's a pernicious and insidious habit that afflicts many because it is easy to form and hard to break.

People acquire this bad habit because it's more comfortable to blame others for what we're not doing.

Ultimately, the limits we set on ourselves are there because, like having a bedtime at night, they make us feel safe, even if they are sabotaging our success. The trick, of course, is to realize that and have the courage to let go of them. To wake up, in other words.

Staying on top of your game

Freelancing is a skill. Which means it can be learned, improved upon, mastered and taught. There are beginners and masters. Where you are along the spectrum doesn't matter as long as you recognize that freelancing is something you can learn and get better at doing.

It doesn't require an innate ability or talent you either have or you don't. It's not like having blue eyes.

It's something that gets better with practice. Like writing, or playing an instrument, or doing heart surgery.

It's something you can start and keep working at every day of your life.

It's something anybody can do. Many are called. Few choose.

Choose yourself. Move forward. Learn and keep learning.

Learning is a lifelong habit

The workplace of the future will demand skills for which no courses are offered today. Your children will have careers in fields that haven't been invented yet. And you might too, perhaps sooner than you think. No matter what education you start with, in today's economy you need to be a lifelong learner. Nano courses and skill-upgrading classes offered online, in workshops and within your community need to be a part of your working life.

Technology changes, clients' needs change, and your skills get rusty. Keep sharpening them through training and learning. Knowing how to learn is a more important skill than what you learned in the past. It doesn't matter if you studied engineering but have decided to become a professional house flipper, or if you're an English major and want to be a fashion photographer. Take your ability to learn and apply it to what you want to learn.

And keep at it.

Become master of your domain

By this I don't just mean just buying up domain names. I mean become the expert in your field.

To begin with, know who the experts in your field already are. Know them by name and be familiar with their work and their influence. Every field has its gurus and voices that dominate the agenda. These are the ones who continuously produce, who are defining the industry and are at the leading edge of the newest thinking in your field. Follow them, think about what they do and say, and learn everything you can from them.

Then join them.

Sure, it's daunting, but that's why it's worth it. Learn. Everything you need to know about is out there, and most of it is free. It's in YouTube videos and blogs and online courses. Scavenge the Internet for information and ideas that inform and inspire you that you can relate to your area of focus and the work you do. Keep it all somewhere that you can access from anywhere.

Turn all that information gathering into usable content by writing blog posts on ideas or themes that explain your work and your industry. Add to ongoing conversations rather than simply rehashing already-written-about concepts or ideas. Personalize it, give your opinion as a practitioner and insider in the space. Never underestimate the value of your insights as someone who cares and is passionate about what you are doing compared to some paid staffer who is churning out content to support an ad-driven site. Believe in yourself, believe in your capabilities and observations, and put them out there. Do it as often as you can. In time, you will be an authority on your subject by dint of your hard work and commitment to becoming one.

Don't worry about being recognized for your input right away. Recognition will come. But however long it takes, what matters most is that you are committed to becoming a master craftsperson, a thought leader. You don't inherit a place in the world, you make it. Whether it takes one year or 10, you will make your mark by doing good work and being the one who cares so much about it that there is nothing you don't want to learn.

Freelancing is not a destination. It's a journey. There will always be more to learn, new technologies that change everything, and new challengers and influencers and talents to observe and be inspired by. That's the joy of it.

Those who can, teach

Becoming a teacher is easier than you think. Do an inventory of your skills and knowledge and break it down into teachable modules. If you know just 1% more about something than the average practitioner, you've got something to teach. Teaching opens up new opportunities, keeps you honest about honing your craft, and puts you in contact with new people, some of whom may become clients.

You never know where your next gig will come from, so treat every opportunity to meet and talk with someone about your work as a chance to show off what you know and how you do things.

Try to break down everything you know about your work into the most discrete steps possible. While you may not think you are qualified to teach anything because you don't have a teaching degree, or don't feel you know enough about your subject, remember that there are thousands of absolute beginners behind you who know less than you do and want to learn what you know.

As a teacher, you can create "teachables": lesson plans, guides, podcasts, infographics and other forms of content that break concepts and techniques down into bite-sized chunks. These can also easily be converted into lead magnets for your website and offered as free downloads in exchange for an email address, thereby serving more than one purpose. Produce a series, bundle them together and you've got a ready-made e-book or a series of blog posts or an email course offering you can set up with Convert Kit or some other email program that allows you to automate a series of sends based on timing or behavioural triggers from the recipients. In short, thinking like a teacher is a lot like what you are going to be doing anyway as you market yourself. It adds a new dimension to the content you are most likely already producing.

Teaching also consolidates your own knowledge and sparks your curiosity to fill gaps in your own understanding or know-how on a given topic within your field of expertise. By formulating your knowledge into a format that can be transferred and shared with another person, you build yourself up at the same time as helping someone else grow. The connections your teaching will bring to you then further expand your circle of influence and enhance your own learning.

You can start teaching without anything more than putting your thoughts in order and laying out a sequence of short lessons. However, if you want to step it up a level, there are more and more platforms for teaching online available. Coursera, Udacity, Udemy, Skillshare, Lynda.com and many others are set up for turning subject-matter experts like you into profitable teachers. They offer tutorials on getting started and allow you to scan the current offerings to get a feel for what is popular, how to price your course, and even take a course on how to create an online course. So all you need to really do is get started.

The personal development day

As hard as it is to switch from having a structure imposed on you to developing your own, once you've fully made the transition and are able to easily divvy up your day into workable chunks, you will face a new challenge: how to avoid becoming so obsessively focussed on productivity that you forget the major benefit of being a freelancer: autonomy.

Once you start rolling as a freelancer, you'll feel subtle pressure to make all your waking hours productive. When you're not actively working on a project, you're prospecting or researching and writing a blog post or engaged in some kind of goal-driven activity. There's a hidden cost to this kind of behaviour: over time, you may start to feel your passion (and energy) for the things you used to love to do waning. Your creativity may start to feel less creative and your ideas less fresh than they used to be. That's because you're forgetting to replenish the well.

Nothing is inexhaustible. Your creative energy, just like solar power, needs time to recharge the batteries of your brain. You need to recuperate regularly from the things in regular life that can wear you down, sometimes without you even realizing it is happening. That would include technology, food, work, entertainment, other people and your own mind. Everything you do and deal with most of the time has a saturation point. You need to regularly pull back, break routines, pause, and empty yourself out to make space for new energy to flow into you and for new ideas to bubble up.

Take a break

Taking a personal development day (or half-day) at least once a month — if not once a week — can help. Block off the time in your calendar and hold fast to your commitment to yourself. Don't treat the time as something you can raid if (when) a competing demand arises or some new "emergency" distracts you.

One of my favourite things to do with my free days is to take my little girl out on a Daddy Date. We go to the museum and take pictures of each other in front of works of art, drink hot chocolate and eat crêpes (well, she does), wander around the city and just hang out. I'm sure one day she'll be too old for this and not want to hang out with her dad, but for now I know I'm making memories with her.

When I can't do that, I go to the gym for a long sauna, then walk to a café to read. I might use an afternoon like this to start writing something new or flip through some of the ideas I've jotted down in my notes to see if anything resonates or piques my curiosity enough to pursue it. Or sometimes, in the warmer months, I just string up my hammock and take a lazy nap.

Your time belongs to you. Use it to do the things that make you feel free and open and at play in the world. Customize your experience according to what inspires and interests you. Go back to where you began and see it through new eyes. Use it to read novels or go through all the articles you've Instapapered/Pinterested away for a rainy day. Use it to delve into your Someday file (if you're a follower of the David Allen GTD method), or to learn a new skill on Lynda. com or just surf through YouTube. Go for a long walk. Take a tour of your hometown. Grab a novel and plunk yourself down in a comfy chair in a café and read all day. Visit a museum, look at art. Do anything you want to do that isn't for a client or a task on a project you're working on. This is a day exclusively designed by you, for you, for learning, appreciating and re-energizing yourself to keep yourself feeling curious, engaged and creative.

Know what you're good at, and do more of it

In the start-up world it's called your USP, or your unique selling proposition. In plain English, that means knowing what you're really good at and focussing all your energy on getting better at it. As Roy Spence's mom told Roy, back when he was a crappy speller in grade school, "Don't waste another minute trying to get better at what you're just average at. Put all your energy into getting great at what you're good at."

I learned this the hard way doing product shoots. To a photographer who specializes in live events, product shoots are about as different as you can get while still technically being in the same field. Both require camera equipment and a photographer, but that's about as far as the commonalities go.

Product shoots are technical, specific, extremely detail-oriented and usually require meticulous preparation and execution, a systemic methodology. The image usually has to meet a highly organized set of parameters.

Live events are first and foremost about emotions. Being there to witness them, anticipating reactions, recognizing moments and capturing fleeting expressions and feelings on a face, in a crowd, on stage, in a room. They are highly intuitive and require speed, agility, responsivity and high emotional EQ.

Product shoots are almost clinical in nature, requiring consistency and repetition. You are not creating an image so much as conforming (usually) to a set of requirements. They are highly repetitive, extremely time-consuming and deadly boring, at least if you are more interested in taking photos of people, as I am.

Product photographers deal with things, event photographers deal with people. Introvert vs. extrovert. Yin and yang.

So why would an event photographer take on product work in the first place? Alas, for the same reason a lot of freelancers start taking on work outside their specialty or area of expertise. Sometimes this is a way to grow and expand your services, so it fits well with a freelancer's business model. Sometimes it's because you want to try something new and challenge yourself. Sometimes, yes, it's for the money. But sometimes, as in my case, it turns out it's just not the right kind of work for you.

Roy Spence Jr. couldn't spell, and I'm not great at product shots. I take on the work when I have the opportunity to do something more creative than just a product against a white backdrop, but I've had more problems with product shoots than any other photo work I do.

But even knowing that, I have taken on jobs in my freelance career that caused me more trouble than they were worth. Like the time a client asked me to shoot 30- or 40-odd printers and other office products. At first glance, I thought it wouldn't been too much work (wrong!), and that the items, being all roughly the same size, wouldn't require too much adjusting (wrong!), and that they'd be new printers that were clean and ready to go (wrong, wrong, wrong!). It took two days. The guideline document (turns out they needed the same item shot from five different angles) was screwed up, and the products were either still in their boxes (which entailed a good deal of hefting and unpacking and repacking) or actually were used items that were lying around the office (scratched, dirty and effectively unpresentable). Oh, and the budget was fixed. And did we tell you we also need them cut out from the background and delivered Monday? (I started the job on Thursday.)

A lot of red flags were waving there, but I ploughed on through it, letting pride get in the way of both good business sense and plain common sense. It was a virtually impossible task under the kind of time pressure I had, but I foolishly took it on. I wanted to prove to myself that I could do product shoots. Yeah, I got this.

Except I didn't. The shots turned out okay but I wasn't remotely meticulous enough editing them. Ultimately, I ended up chucking most of the shots, and nearly 24 hours of my time.. I ate the bill to save the relationship, but no one was happy. And all I learned was what I already knew: that product shoots suck (at least for me).

I don't do product. I'm not a technical shooter. I'm not interested in repeatability. I want to capture moments that may only ever happen once in my lifetime. I don't care about products. And it shows.

Know what you're good at and get great at that. Don't waste another minute getting better at what you're just average at.

Just in case that didn't sink in:

KNOW WHAT YOU'RE GOOD AT AND GET GREAT AT THAT. DON'T WASTE ANOTHER MINUTE GETTING BETTER AT WHAT YOU'RE JUST AVERAGE AT.

I've finally learned the lesson here. Turn down or outsource work you're not passionate about and don't want to do — no matter how good the money looks , it won't be worth it.

You can't be more "average." But you can go from great to greater.

Choose to be great and your clients will love you for it. Choose average, and you'll both be disappointed. And the more you aim for "average," the farther you get from great.

SORE OR SOFT?

••••••••••••••••••••••••••

FREELANCING IS A bit like working out. When it's working well for someone, it shows. And just like your fitness level, or your art projects or your personal relationships... it's a work in progress.

When a freelancer is doing well, she seems happy and appears to have ample free time to do the things she loves doing. She's busy, but good-busy, and she can't imagine living any other way.

But just like someone on a fitness regime, there are workout days and rest days, and in between you feel energized but sometimes a little sore. You sleep better, eat more healthily and hate to miss a workout.

However, when you lay off the workouts for a few days, or even a week or two if you've gone on vacation, you start to feel soft. There may not be any visible change in your appearance, but inside you feel weaker. You feel flabbier, and your energy levels droop.

The same goes for freelancing. It's okay to rest a bit when you need it, but if you skip days between your routines or decide to give yourself an extended break from doing the daily or weekly things you have to keep on top of to keep the wheel turning, you start to feel it. It may not show up in your business right away, but if you take too much time away from the building blocks — the ongoing marketing, networking, blogging, producing, that you have to do to keep new clients coming in — eventually your business is going to start to sag.

It's a choice. You need time to refresh and recharge, and taking time off to reflect or do a deeper dive into yourself once in a while can contribute an overall boost to your creativity and output. But giving yourself too much of a slack schedule, only working here and there when you feel like it, waiting for optimal conditions before starting or only putting in an hour or two a day instead of really giving it your full attention ultimately is going to delay your lift-off, and may keep you grounded for much longer than you have the stamina for.

Showing up every day to do the work, just like a storekeeper who rises early to open up shop and stays at the cash until closing time, isn't always fun, easy or even rewarding. Sometimes it's slow, tedious, and unprofitable. But then there are those banner days when you nail it, when work sails in and your creativity and productivity are on a high. You blow past your goals for the day or even the week in a few hours and feel like the sun is shining just for you. The thing is, you can't always predict which days will be up days, and which will be slow. So your only choice really is to show up and be ready for anything.

It takes more effort and leaves you feeling a little sorer, but showing up for your freelance career is better than waiting around for your life to happen to you, or just hoping things will change. Being in charge means being responsible, and your first responsibility is to yourself.

That's where it starts, and where it — with this book – ends.

Bon voyage!